Global Monitoring Report 2010

The MDGs after the Crisis

The MDGs after the Crisis

1818 H Street NW
Washington DC 20433
Telephone: 202-473-1000
Internet: www.worldbank.org
E-mail: feedback@worldbank.org
All rights reserved

1 2 3 4 13 12 11 10

This volume is a product of the staffs of The World Bank and The International Monetary Fund. The findings, interpretations, and conclusions expressed in this volume do not necessarily reflect the views of the Board of Executive Directors of The World Bank, the Board of Executive Directors of The International Monetary Fund, or the governments they represent.

The World Bank and The International Monetary Fund do not guarantee the accuracy of the data included in this work. The boundaries, colors, denominations, and other information shown on any map in this work do not imply any judgement on the part of The World Bank or The International Monetary Fund concerning the legal status of any territory or the endorsement or acceptance of such boundaries.

ISBN: 978-0-8213-8316-2
eISBN: 978-0-8213-8424-4
DOI: 10.1596/978-0-8213-8316-2

Cover image: "Escape Route," by Iyke Okenyi, 2006, courtesy of the World Bank Art Program.
Cover design: Debra Naylor of Naylor Design.
Interior photographs: Yosef Hadar / World Bank (10), Curt Carnemark / World Bank (28), Ray Witlin / World Bank (68), Curt Carnemark / World Bank (96), Tran Thi Hoa / World Bank (120).

Contents

Boxes

Figures

Maps

Tables

Foreword

The world is five years from the target date for the Millennium Development Goals (MDGs). We are still recovering from a historic financial and economic crisis. The recovery is uncertain and likely to be uneven. We know from past crises that the harms to human development during bad times cut far deeper than the gains during upswings.

Under these conditions, it is especially important to consider actions to achieve the MDGs by the 2015 deadline. We need to learn lessons from MDG experiences to date. This 2010 *Global Monitoring Report* can contribute to that assessment, as part of an MDG review led by the United Nations.

How has the world performed in overcoming poverty and fostering human development since the onset of the crisis? This year's report, *The MDGs after the Crisis*, aims to answer this and other critical questions. It highlights lessons from the crisis and presents forecasts about poverty and other key indicators.

We learned from the 1990s crises that macroeconomic stabilization is not enough. If strong safety nets are not in place when crises hit, malnutrition and school dropouts increase, potentially leading to the loss of an entire generation.

A key lesson from this financial crisis is that the economic and social impact of the downturn would have been far worse if not for the effective—and often extraordinary—policy responses adopted by many advanced, emerging, and developing countries, as well as the swift and sizable assistance provided by international financial institutions and multilateral development banks. Policy responses and international cooperation have been better than in previous crises.

The postcrisis MDG scorecard is still being tallied. Numbers can only be gathered with time-lags and are often incomplete. It is therefore difficult to take a sharp snapshot of the developing world and to analyze the effectiveness of international aid in real time.

Despite these measurement challenges, we will certainly see significant harm to education, health, nutrition, and poverty indicators, especially in low-income countries. This is not a time for complacency. It is a time for exceptional efforts. For example, timely and well-designed conditional cash transfer programs not only increase household incomes, but also help children—boys and girls—stay in school and learn. To beat major diseases and reduce maternal mortality, we need to work on health systems in a holistic manner. This means addressing issues ranging from financing, service delivery systems, regulation, to governance of the systems. To mitigate the damaging effects of the crisis, we must ensure inclusive and sustainable global growth, maintain and expand an open international trade and financial system, deliver on aid commitments, and encourage the private sector.

To meet the MDGs, the developing world must revive its growth and reinforce its resilience to shocks. Countries that sowed in times of plenty were able to reap in times of loss. Fiscal policy buffers must therefore be rebuilt to allow for future countercyclical responses. Effective and efficient social safety nets—the first line of defense against adverse shocks to the poor—must be strengthened.

Progress on Goal 1—halving extreme poverty and hunger—is advancing in fits and starts. Poverty rates are forecast to continue falling in the wake of the crisis, but will do so more slowly. The global rate for extreme poverty is projected to be 15 percent in 2015, down significantly from 42 percent in 1990. Much of the progress in reducing extreme poverty has taken place in East Asia, where poverty dropped from 55 percent in 1990 to 17 percent in 2005. If this report's baseline projection for a recovery holds, the developing world will reach the poverty reduction goal by 2015.

However, the crisis has harmed many people. By the end of this year, we estimate that an additional 64 million people will fall into extreme poverty due to the crisis. And by 2015, 53 million fewer people will have escaped poverty. We estimate the poverty rate for Sub-Saharan Africa will be 38 percent by 2015, rather than the 36 percent it would have been without the crisis. The continent will therefore fall short of Goal 1.

Goal 1 also encompasses the aim of halving the proportion of people who suffer from hunger. The developing world is off track to meet this goal. Reducing malnutrition deserves more attention, because nutrition has a multiplier effect on the success of other MDGs, including infant mortality, maternal mortality, and education. Child malnutrition accounts for more than a third of the disease burden of children under five. And malnutrition during pregnancy accounts for more than 20 percent of maternal mortality.

We will likely meet the Goal 3 target of achieving gender parity in primary and secondary education by 2015. More girls than ever in history complete primary school. Almost two-thirds of developing countries reached gender parity at the primary school level by 2005. However, at higher levels of schooling, female enrollment lags seriously. And the quality of secondary and tertiary education needs significant improvement.

Progress in reducing maternal mortality is advancing more quickly than we had estimated earlier. This report includes the new findings just reported in *The Lancet* that the maternal death toll worldwide dropped from 526,300 in 1980 to around 342,900 in 2008, far below the latest UN estimates of some 500,000 for the same year. These signs of improvement are encouraging. But the progress is fragile and we are still far from reaching the global target of a 75-percent reduction in maternal deaths by 2015 from the ratio that prevailed in 1990. As we emerge from the crisis, we must also renew our efforts to achieve universal access to reproductive health.

The World Bank Group and the International Monetary Fund have stepped up to the challenge posed by the crisis. We have taken numerous initiatives to limit the slide in global economic growth and avert the collapse of the banking and private sectors in many countries. We have also provided financing to governments and the private sector, helping to soften the impact of the crisis on the poor. And we have scaled up our support for social safety nets.

With the deadline for the MDGs fast approaching, we must recognize and overcome obstacles in reaching the targets for tackling extreme poverty, hunger, and disease. Business as usual will not work. At a time of uncertainty, we need to extend our limited resources further. We must build upon the progress made in improving gender equality, education, and environmental sustainability. The actions we take today will shape future opportunities and challenges.

Robert B. Zoellick
President
The World Bank Group

Dominique Strauss-Kahn
Managing Director
International Monetary Fund

Acknowledgments

This report has been prepared jointly by the World Bank and the International Monetary Fund (IMF). In preparing the report, staff also consulted and collaborated with the African Development Bank (AfDB), the Asian Development Bank (ADB), the European Bank for Reconstruction and Development (EBRD), and the Inter-American Development Bank (IDB). The cooperation and support of staffs of these institutions are gratefully acknowledged.

Delfin S. Go was the lead author and manager of the report. Richard Harmsen led the team from the IMF. Principal authors of the various parts of the report included Jorge Arbache, Jean-Pierre Christophe Chauffour, Stefano Curto, John Elder, Vijdan Korman, Maureen Lewis, Hans Lofgren, and Mariem Malouche (World Bank); Andrew Berg, Chris Papageorgiou, Catherine Pattillo, and Jarkko Turunen (IMF); Malvina Pollock, Sherman Robinson, William Shaw, and Karen Thierfelder, (consultants). Sachin Shahria and Song Song were key members of the core team and assisted with the overall preparation and coordination of the report.

The work was carried out under the general guidance of Justin Lin, Senior Vice President and Chief Economist, and Hans Timmer, Director, Development Economics (DEC) Prospects Group, both of the World Bank. The circle of advisers included Shantayanan Devarajan, Shahrokh Fardoust, Deon Filmer, Ariel Fiszbein, Ann Harrison, Mohammad Zia Qureshi, Martin Ravallion, Augusto de la Torre, and Dominique van der Mensbrugghe.

Several staff members also made valuable contributions, including the following from the World Bank: Luca Bandiera, Uranbileg Batjargal, Shaohua Chen, Sie Chow, Lire Ersado, Elisa Gamberoni, Julien Gourdon, Hiau Looi Kee, Maria Hazel Macadangdang, Andrew Mason, Aaditya Mattoo, Israel Osorio-Rodarte, Claudio Enrique Raddatz Kiefer, Prem Sangraula, Nistha Sinha, Stacey Tai, Carolyn Turk, Marijn Verhoeven, and Hassan Zaman.

Other contributors from the IMF included John Brondolo and Mario Mansour; research assistance was provided by Emmanuel Hife and Ioana Niculcea.

Contributors from other institutions included Gaston Gohou and Timothy Turnere (AfDB); Indu Bhushan, Valerie Reppelin-Hill, Gina Marie Umali, and Edeena Pike (ADB); Yannis Arvanitis, Gary Bond, and James Earwicker (EBRD); and Susana Sitja Rubio and Luis F. Diaz (IDB).

Guidance received from the Executive Directors of the World Bank and the IMF and their staffs during discussions of the draft report is gratefully acknowledged. The report also benefited from many useful comments and suggestions received from the Bank and IMF management and staff in the course of its preparation and review. Additional information and data, including background papers, are available on the dedicated Web site, www .worldbank.org/gmr2010. The multilingual Web sites accompanying the report were produced by Roula Yazigi, Rebecca Ong, Swati Priyadarshini Mishra, and Mohamed Hassan. Rebecca Ong and Merrell Tuck-Primdahl managed the dissemination activities. The translation process was coordinated by Sheila Keane and Jorge del Rosario.

Bruce Ross-Larson was the principal editor. Martha Gottron did the final copyediting. From the World Bank's Office of the Publisher, Stephen McGroarty, Susan Graham, Aziz Gökdemir, and Denise Bergeron managed the design, production, printing, and distribution of the report.

Abbreviations and Acronyms

ADB   Asian Development Bank
AfDB   African Development Bank
AIDS   acquired immune deficiency syndrome
AfDF   African Development Fund
AsDF   Asian Development Fund
CIS   Commonwealth of Independent States
CPIA   Country Policy and Institutional Assessment
DAC   Development Assistance Committee
EBRD   European Bank for Reconstruction and Development
EU   European Union
FDI   foreign direct investment
G-8   Group of Eight
G-20   Group of Twenty
GDP   gross domestic product
GNI   gross national income
HIPC   heavily indebted poor country/countries
HIV   human immunodeficiency virus
IBRD   International Bank for Reconstruction and Development
IDA   International Development Association (World Bank Group)
IDB   Inter-American Development Bank
IFC   International Finance Corporation (World Bank Group)
IFI   international financial institution
IMF   International Monetary Fund
MCI   Monetary Conditions Index
MDGs   Millennium Development Goals
MIGA   Multilateral Investment Guarantee Agency (World Bank Group)
NGO   nongovernmental organization
ODA   official development assistance
OECD   Organisation for Economic Co-operation and Development
OPEC   Organization of the Petroleum Exporting Countries
PEPFAR   President's Emergency Plan for AIDS Relief
PPP   purchasing power parity
SDR   special drawing rights
UN   United Nations
WTO   World Trade Organization

Goals and Targets from the Millennium Declaration

GOAL 1	ERADICATE EXTREME POVERTY AND HUNGER
TARGET 1.A	Halve, between 1990 and 2015, the proportion of people whose income is less than $1.25 a day
TARGET 1.B	Achieve full and productive employment and decent work for all, including women and young people
TARGET 1.C	Halve, between 1990 and 2015, the proportion of people who suffer from hunger
GOAL 2	**ACHIEVE UNIVERSAL PRIMARY EDUCATION**
TARGET 2.A	Ensure that by 2015, children everywhere, boys and girls alike, will be able to complete a full course of primary schooling
GOAL 3	**PROMOTE GENDER EQUALITY AND EMPOWER WOMEN**
TARGET 3.A	Eliminate gender disparity in primary and secondary education, preferably by 2005, and at all levels of education no later than 2015
GOAL 4	**REDUCE CHILD MORTALITY**
TARGET 4.A	Reduce by two-thirds, between 1990 and 2015, the under-five mortality rate
GOAL 5	**IMPROVE MATERNAL HEALTH**
TARGET 5.A	Reduce by three-quarters, between 1990 and 2015, the maternal mortality ratio
TARGET 5.B	Achieve by 2015 universal access to reproductive health
GOAL 6	**COMBAT HIV/AIDS, MALARIA, AND OTHER DISEASES**
TARGET 6.A	Have halted by 2015 and begun to reverse the spread of HIV/AIDS
TARGET 6.B	Achieve by 2010 universal access to treatment for HIV/AIDS for all those who need it
TARGET 6.C	Have halted by 2015 and begun to reverse the incidence of malaria and other major diseases
GOAL 7	**ENSURE ENVIRONMENTAL SUSTAINABILITY**
TARGET 7.A	Integrate the principles of sustainable development into country policies and programs and reverse the loss of environmental resources
TARGET 7.B	Reduce biodiversity loss, achieving by 2010 a significant reduction in the rate of loss
TARGET 7.C	Halve by 2015 the proportion of people without sustainable access to safe drinking water and basic sanitation
TARGET 7.D	Have achieved a significant improvement by 2020 in the lives of at least 100 million slum dwellers
GOAL 8	**DEVELOP A GLOBAL PARTNERSHIP FOR DEVELOPMENT**
TARGET 8.A	Develop further an open, rule-based, predictable, nondiscriminatory trading and financial system (including a commitment to good governance, development, and poverty reduction, nationally and internationally)
TARGET 8.B	Address the special needs of the least-developed countries (including tariff- and quota-free access for exports of the least-developed countries; enhanced debt relief for heavily indebted poor countries and cancellation of official bilateral debt; and more generous official development assistance for countries committed to reducing poverty)
TARGET 8.C	Address the special needs of landlocked countries and small island developing states (through the Programme of Action for the Sustainable Development of Small Island Developing States and the outcome of the 22nd special session of the General Assembly)
TARGET 8.D	Deal comprehensively with the debt problems of developing countries through national and international measures to make debt sustainable in the long term
TARGET 8.E	In cooperation with pharmaceutical companies, provide access to affordable, essential drugs in developing countries
TARGET 8.F	In cooperation with the private sector, make available the benefits of new technologies, especially information and communications

Source: United Nations. 2008. *Report of the Secretary-General on the Indicators for Monitoring the Millennium Development Goals.* E/CN.3/2008/29. New York.

Note: The Millennium Development Goals and targets come from the Millennium Declaration, signed by 189 countries, including 147 heads of state and government, in September 2000 (http://www.un.org/millennium/declaration/ares552e.htm) and from further agreement by member states at the 2005 World Summit (Resolution adopted by the General Assembly–A/RES/60/1). The goals and targets are interrelated and should be seen as a whole. They represent a partnership between the developed countries and the developing countries "to create an environment—at the national and global levels alike—which is conducive to development and the elimination of poverty."

Overview: MDGs after the Crisis

What is the human cost of the global economic crisis? How many people will the crisis prevent from escaping poverty, and how many will remain hungry? How many more infants will die? Are children being pulled out of schools, not getting the education they need to become more productive adults and making it virtually impossible to reach 100 percent completion in primary education by 2015? What are the gender dimensions of the impacts? These are some of the questions as the global economy comes out of the worst recession since the Great Depression.

The questions do not have immediate answers—partly because the data to assess development outcomes are incomplete and collected infrequently but also because impacts can take several years to emerge. For example, deteriorating health and nutrition today could lead to higher mortality rates in subsequent years. Lower investments will hamper future progress in sanitation and water supply. Fewer children in school will lower completion rates in later years. And household incomes that fall far below the poverty line will delay escapes from poverty. This report uses indirect evidence to assess the impact of the crisis on several indicators, including the number of people who will not escape poverty, the increase in infant mortality, the number of children who will be denied education, and the increase in discrimination against women. Based on that assessment, the report identifies key policies necessary for the developing countries, donors, and the international financial institutions (IFIs) to reestablish progress toward the Millennium Development Goals (MDGs).

The MDGs provide powerful benchmarks for measuring global progress on key development outcomes, calling attention to the enormous challenges in low-income countries. The goals have likely contributed to the progress itself, galvanizing governments, donors, civil society, private agencies, and the media to support human development. But uniform goals—reducing poverty by half, infant mortality by two-thirds, maternal mortality by three-quarters—can underestimate progress in poor countries. Why? Because the greater the distance to the goals from low starting points in poor countries, the greater the improvement needed to reach the targets. While the extent to which countries are on track to achieve the MDGs in 2015 varies widely, recent improvements have been widespread, as have the losses caused by the crisis.

From the 1990s until the onset of the crisis in 2008, developing countries, including low-income countries, made significant progress in human development. However, the crisis attacked two critical drivers of progress toward the MDGs: faster growth and better service delivery. The impact was undoubtedly negative because of the severity of the recession and the tendency for indicators of human development to decline much more in bad times than they improve in good times. But these asymmetric effects are estimated from past crises, which were often driven by internal shocks, such as domestic policy failures, conflict, and institutional breakdowns. By contrast, the current crisis was driven by an external shock, and policies and institutions in developing countries have improved considerably in the past 15 years. Moreover, many countries have maintained social safety nets in the face of the income decline. That is why the impact on the MDGs could be more moderate than in past crises.

Even so, the analysis and projections discussed in this report indicate that the deterioration in human development is severe, with effects likely to last for several years. This grim outlook has been taken seriously by the international community. The International Monetary Fund (IMF), the World Bank, and the regional multilateral development banks have sharply boosted their assistance to developing countries. Despite some increase in protectionist measures, developing countries have largely maintained their access to markets, and the very real danger of widespread beggar-thy-neighbor policies has been avoided. Although aid expanded through 2008, it was at levels far below what is needed to meet donor commitments for total aid and aid to Sub-Saharan Africa.

Policy responses to the crisis have repercussions that must be dealt with. The expansion of fiscal deficits—required to sustain demand in the depths of the recession—must be reined in by developing and advanced countries alike. Additional resources will be required so that the frontloading of concessional assistance and the rapid expansion in lending by the multilateral development banks do not result in a sharp decline in multilateral flows in the coming years. And shifts in the organization and staff expertise of the IFIs may be required to confront the challenges in the new global economic environment.

Ten years after the adoption of the MDGs, the international community is intensifying its monitoring of the progress toward these goals. The United Nations has called on member states to convene a formal summit on the MDGs in 2010 to review implementation of the agreement, and the leaders of the Group of Eight (G-8), meeting in L'Aquila in 2009 renewed their commitment to mitigate the impact of the crisis on developing countries.

The MDG indicators showed significant progress before the crisis

When the crisis hit, many countries had already made considerable progress in reducing extreme poverty. Globally, poverty had fallen 40 percent since 1990, and the developing world was well on track to reach the global target of cutting income poverty in half by 2015. Thanks to rapid growth, especially in China, East Asia had already halved extreme poverty. Although Sub-Saharan Africa was unlikely to reach the target, poverty had been falling rapidly since the late 1990s. The goal was more ambitious for Africa than for other regions, because the 1990 incomes of a large part of the African population were far below the poverty line. And Africa implemented reforms later than other regions and therefore benefited later from accelerating income growth.

Progress on MDGs outside poverty was uneven. Developing countries were on track to achieve gender parity in primary and secondary education and access to safe water, although countries were falling behind on gender parity in tertiary education and empowerment of women. Progress was good on primary school completion, nutrition, maternal mortality and (less so) sanitation, even if results at the global level were expected to fall short of targets (figure 1). The health goals appeared most challenging. Most regions were off track, with East Asia, Latin America, and Europe and Central Asia doing better than other regions.

FIGURE 1   **Serious global shortfalls loom for the human development MDGs**

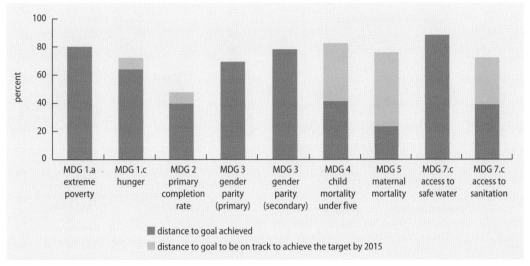

distance to goal achieved
distance to goal to be on track to achieve the target by 2015

Source: Staff calculations based on World Development Indicators database.
Note: Based on available data as of 2009, which can range from 2005 to 2009.

The crisis interrupted this progress, but the effects will not be apparent for many more years. Data needed to assess the degree of deterioration in development indicators will not be available for two or more years, and some impacts—for example, on mortality rates and school completion rates—will materialize only after several years. So this report uses historical examples and indirect evidence to assess the effects of the crisis on progress toward the MDGs.

Past crises generated exceptionally poor outcomes

The impact of economic cycles on MDG indicators is highly asymmetric. The deterioration in bad times is much greater than the improvement during good times (figure 2). Vulnerable groups—infants and children, especially girls, particularly in poor countries of Sub-Saharan Africa—are disproportionately affected during crises. For example, during contractions, female enrollment in primary and secondary education drops more than male enrollment. And the consequences of this disproportionate impact persist long into the future. Once children are taken out of school, future human capital is permanently lowered.

Several factors produce the asymmetric response.

- Economic indicators and quality of institutions and policy, such as political stability, voice and accountability, regulatory framework, rule of law, and government effectiveness, tend to decline sharply in downturns. Distinguishing cause and consequence is difficult, but vicious circles during crises are stronger than virtuous ones during prosperous times.
- Public and private spending on social services can easily be disrupted during economic crises, just when people need them most.
- Safety nets were uncommon in developing countries in previous crises.
- Donor funding also came under pressure if the crisis was global or if aid effectiveness declined during crises. But there is some evidence that official development assistance has provided countercyclical support since 2003.

Why this crisis may be different for low-income countries

Policies and institutions improved before the crisis. The economic performance of

FIGURE 2 **Key indicators plummet from their overall mean during growth decelerations, all countries**

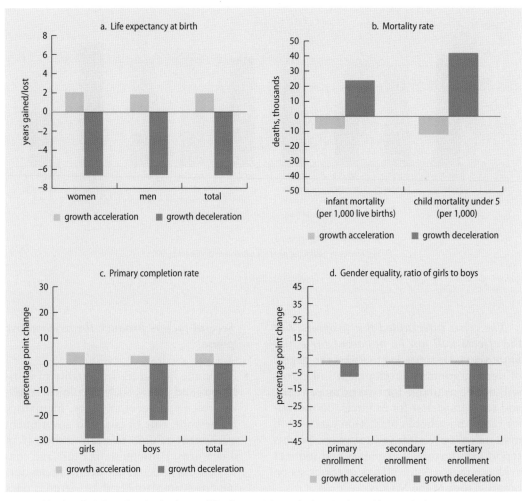

Source: World Bank staff calculations based on data from World Development Indicators database. See chapter 2 for more details.
Note: The panels show differences of averages during growth accelerations and decelerations from overall averages.

developing countries is highly correlated with the quality of policies. Many countries entered the crisis with better policies and fiscal positions than they had in previous episodes of contraction.

Unlike many previous crises, the current crisis was not caused by domestic policy failure. Historically, almost 90 percent of the output volatility in low-income countries has been generated by internal conditions and shocks, such as policy failures and conflicts. Since the 1990s output volatility in low-income countries has lessened, and the relative frequency of external shocks has increased. Stronger institutions and policies

in developing countries mean that they are better prepared to cope with shocks. Thus the impacts on human development outcomes may be less severe if conditions do not deteriorate and lead to widespread policy failures.

Spending on social safety nets has been relatively protected so far. Lower initial fiscal deficits and higher priorities for social spending have protected education and health spending in most countries. Up-to-date information is incomplete, but scattered information provides some examples. For example, of 19 programs initiated and monitored by the IMF and implemented in collaboration with the World Bank in 2008–09, 16 budgeted higher social spending for 2009. Of these, 9 were countries in Sub-Saharan Africa: Burundi, Republic of Congo, Côte d'Ivoire, Liberia, Malawi, Mali, Niger, Togo, and Zambia. Several African countries with poverty reduction strategies have protected their funding for social sectors. And some countries with fiscal space (Kenya and Nigeria) have protected capital expenditure, mainly for infrastructure. But there are also examples of forced contractions in social spending. Countries with precrisis fiscal and debt issues (such as Ethiopia and Ghana) had to undertake fiscal tightening. HIV/AIDS (human immunodeficiency virus/acquired immune deficiency syndrome) funding has been largely sustained, but with a new concern for the efficiency of resource use.

The international community responded strongly to the crisis

Despite widespread fears, developing countries' market access was not significantly reduced. At the end of 2009, 350 trade-restrictive measures had been put in place around the world, some 20 percent of them nontariff measures, such as quantitative restrictions, import licenses, standards requirements, and subsidies. Trade remedies were also on the rise. But in the aggregate, protectionism has been contained. The trade-restricting or -distorting measures introduced since October 2008 have amounted to only about 0.5 percent of world merchandise trade. Governments and multilateral development institutions supported developing countries' exports by bolstering trade finance. The Group of Twenty leaders pledged $250 billion in support of trade at their April 2009 London Summit; the World Bank Group provided guarantees and liquidity for trade finance through the International Finance Corporation's Global Trade Finance Program and Global Trade Liquidity Program. And export credit agencies stepped in to prevent a complete drying up of trade finance.

A massive IMF rescue was designed to limit economic contraction and contagion. The global nature of the crisis led the IMF to act swiftly to boost lending and modify conditionality frameworks. By the end of February 2010, the IMF had committed a record high $175 billion (including precautionary financing) to emerging and other developing countries with balance of payments difficulties; the commitments included a sharp increase in concessional lending to the world's poorest countries. The IMF also implemented a general allocation of special drawing rights equivalent to $250 billion, including almost $100 billion to emerging market economies and developing countries, $18 billion of it to low-income countries. Standard access to IMF financing has been doubled, a new flexible credit line without ex post policy conditions for countries with very strong track records has been adopted, and the provision of exceptionally large loans has become easier, while safeguards have been preserved.

Responses by multilateral development banks have sought to protect core development programs, strengthen the private sector, and assist poor households. More than $150 billion has been committed since the beginning of the crisis (two-thirds from the World Bank Group). International Bank for Reconstruction and Development (IBRD) lending almost tripled in fiscal 2009, and the first half of fiscal 2010 shows the strongest IBRD commitments in history ($19.2 billion, up from $12.4 billion in the same period in fiscal 2009). Commitments by the regional multilateral development banks also increased sharply, by more than 50 percent from 2007 to 2009. Low-income countries tapped more deeply into multilateral concessional resources in 2009, in part through frontloading multiyear allocations.

Donors increased aid volumes in real terms through 2009. Following an 11.7 percent increase in 2008, total net official development assistance (ODA) from the OECD's Development Assistance Committee (DAC) countries rose slightly by 0.7 percent in real terms in 2009. But in current U.S. dollars, it actually fell from $122.3 billion in 2008 to $119.6 billion in 2009. The 2009 figure represents 0.31 percent of members' combined gross national income (GNI). Aid from non-DAC donors, led by Saudi Arabia, rose

63 percent in real terms in 2008 to $9.5 billion. Development assistance from China will likely more than double in the next three years. Private aid, also substantial, is rising rapidly. And progress continued in reducing poor countries' debt burden through the Highly Indebted Poor Countries (HIPC) Initiative and the Multilateral Debt Relief Initiative. For 35 post-HIPC-decision-point countries, the debt burden will be reduced by 80 percent.

The recovery is stronger than expected, but the outlook for the MDGs remains worrisome

GDP growth in emerging market and developing economies is projected to accelerate to 6.3 percent in 2010. Most economies show signs of recovery (table 1), although many countries remain dependent on exceptional policy stimulus, and in most countries growth is not strong enough to undo the damage caused by the sharp deceleration in incomes and social conditions in 2009. Fiscal deficits in emerging market and developing economies rose by almost 3 percent of GDP in 2009 and are projected to remain high in 2010. Financial market conditions for these economies are improving and capital flows are returning, although international bank financing and foreign direct investment flows are projected to remain weak in 2010. The rebound of commodity prices in tandem with the global recovery in manufacturing production has

supported commodity exporters, but commodity prices remain below their precrisis levels.

Trade is recovering unevenly across regions. World trade contracted by 12 percent in 2009, and all regions experienced deep declines in imports. Signs of recovery are evident, but trade remains fragile. At the end of 2009 global trade was still below its precrisis level. Almost a year into the recovery, the dollar value of global trade remains 20 percent lower than it was before the crisis.

The impact of the crisis on poverty will be long lasting. Poverty rates will continue to fall after the crisis, but more slowly (table 2).[1] By 2015 the global poverty rate is projected to be 15 percent, not the 14.1 percent it would have been without the crisis. The crisis will leave an additional 64 million people in extreme poverty by the end of 2010. The recovery will not make up all the lost ground. And as a result of the crisis, 71 million fewer people will have escaped poverty by 2020. For Sub-Saharan Africa, the poverty rate is expected to be 38 percent by 2015, rather than the 36 percent it would have been without the crisis, lifting 20 million fewer people out of poverty.

The medium-term impact on other MDGs may also be considerable. Illustrative and indicative results from growth analyses[2] suggest persistent gaps between precrisis and postcrisis trends in 2015 (figure 3):

- An additional 55,000 infants might die in 2015. And 260,000 more children under

TABLE 1 **Global output**
percent change

Region	2007	2008	2009	Projections	
				2010	2011–13
World output	**5.2**	**3.0**	**−0.6**	**4.2**	**4.4**
Advanced economies	2.8	0.5	−3.2	2.3	2.4
Emerging and developing economies	8.3	6.1	2.4	6.3	6.6
Central and Eastern Europe	5.5	3.0	−3.7	2.8	3.8
Commonwealth of Independent States	8.6	5.5	−6.6	4.0	4.1
Developing Asia	10.6	7.9	6.6	8.7	8.6
Middle East and North Africa	5.6	5.1	2.4	4.5	4.8
Sub-Saharan Africa	6.9	5.5	2.1	4.7	5.7
Western Hemisphere	5.8	4.3	−1.8	4.0	4.2

Source: IMF World Economic Outlook. See chapter 3 for further discussions.

TABLE 2   **Poverty in developing countries, alternative scenarios, 1990–2020**

Scenario	1990	2005	2015	2020
Global level				
Percentage of the population living on less than $1.25 a day				
Postcrisis	41.7	25.2	15.0	12.8
Precrisis	41.7	25.2	14.1	11.7
Low-growth	41.7	25.2	18.5	16.3
Number of people living on less than $1.25 a day (millions)				
Postcrisis	1,817	1,371	918	826
Precrisis	1,817	1,371	865	755
Low-growth	1,817	1,371	1132	1053

Source: World Bank staff calculations.

FIGURE 3   **The long-run effect of slower growth on selected MDGs is worrisome**

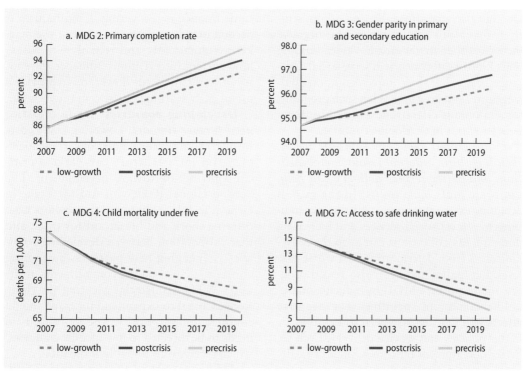

Source: World Bank staff calculations.

five could have been prevented from dying in 2015 in the absence of the crisis. The cumulative total from 2009 to 2015 could reach 265,000 and 1.2 million, respectively.

- An estimated 350,000 more students might be unable to complete primary school in 2015.
- Some 100 million more people might remain without access to an improved source of water.

Developing countries must maintain good policies and effective service delivery

Growth and institutional quality reinforce each other. Before the crisis, policy reforms triggered an impressive acceleration of growth in the developing world, which in turn helped to strengthen institutions and economic fundamentals. One of the dangers of the crisis is that reforms might be abandoned, leading to policy reversals and a deteriorating economy. It is important that all countries adopt credible medium-term fiscal adjustment plans to bolster confidence in macroeconomic policies and that they undertake policy reforms to secure long-term growth.

The effectiveness of safety nets should be enhanced given their importance in cushioning the effects of crises and in reducing poverty. Safety net programs in low-income countries are often small and fragmented, covering only a small percentage of the poor and vulnerable. There are real concerns about whether they are affordable and administratively feasible in light of the various negative incentives they might create. Understanding what kind of safety nets will serve social assistance best, what their implementation challenges are, and how to develop such programs for maximum effectiveness should inform policy reforms in developing countries.

If the global recovery remains weak, spending shifts, internal resource mobilization, and better service delivery can help, but these tools have limits. In the face of declining external revenues, shifting expenditures to protect social services and increasing domestic tax collections can keep the MDG indicators from deteriorating to a worst-case level. But higher taxes can also retard progress on the poverty MDG by reducing household income and spending. The negative effects of a tax increase need to be offset by better policies and service delivery. Even so, better development outcomes hinge critically not only on a better policy environment but also on a rapid global recovery that improves the export conditions, terms of trade, and capital flows for low-income countries.

The global community must continue to support developing countries

Multilateral cooperation in trade must be strengthened. Completion of the Doha Round is important in the aftermath of the crisis, because it would help governments resist protectionist pressures and keep markets open as expansionary policies unwind. Beyond Doha, there is a need to broaden cooperation on cross-border policy matters that are not on the Doha Development Agenda (climate change, and food and energy security). The crisis has also revealed the importance of strengthening monitoring and public reporting of government measures to increase transparency in the trading system (Global Trade Alert, Global Antidumping Database, World Trade Organization [WTO] monitoring reports).

Better monitoring of trade finance is needed. Although recent data indicate that trade finance is recovering, a mechanism is needed to collect data and monitor the market systematically and reliably—to assess how current interventions influence the supply of credit and trade flows, and to provide a useful early warning of stress in trade credit.

Developing countries' trade logistics need further support. Lowering trade costs through better trade regulations, trade logistics, and infrastructure can make a critical contribution toward development. The Second Global Review of Aid for Trade in Geneva in July 2009 found that donors were offering more and better aid for trade and that cooperation between developing countries is engaging new partners. Sustaining efforts to deliver on the commitments at the 2005 WTO Ministerial Meeting (in Hong Kong, China) to expand aid for trade should continue to be a priority. And more such aid needs to be directed to low-income countries, which receive only about half the total.

Aid has to expand to meet previous commitments. The expected medium-term impact of the crisis on low-income countries has heightened the urgency to scale up aid. But current donor spending plans leave a $14 billion shortfall in the commitments to increase aid by $50 billion by 2010 (in 2004 dollars). And the Group of Eight Gleneagles commitment to double aid to Africa by 2010 has yet to be reflected in core development aid to the region. Aid to Africa has grown 5 percent annually since 2000, but much of it has been in the form of debt relief or emergency and humanitarian assistance, not new finance. Reaching the 2010 target requires a further increase of $20 billion. Donor spending plans indicate that only an additional $2 billion is programmed, leaving a gap of $18 billion. Moreover, considerable scope remains for strengthening aid effectiveness by making aid more predictable; rationalizing the division of labor among donors; untying aid from the provision of goods and services in the donor country; increasing reliance on need and merit to guide aid allocations; and addressing the problem of countries that receive too little aid.

Necessary reactions to the crisis raise further policy challenges

Developing countries' fiscal positions deteriorate. Several developing countries maintained spending and expanded fiscal deficits to support domestic demand during the crisis. Indeed, more than one-third of these countries introduced discretionary fiscal stimulus plans in 2009. Absent such support, the impact on individual countries' growth and the shortfall in global demand would have been even greater than they were. But the rapid expansion of fiscal deficits and greater reliance on domestic finance in many countries may not be sustainable. The deterioration in debt ratios in low-income countries is particularly worrisome.

Optimal exit policies from policy support depend on country circumstances. Countries with weak private demand should continue policy support if they have the fiscal space. But countries facing financing constraints cannot delay adjustment. Donors should assist them by meeting their commitments to increase aid. All countries should adopt credible medium-term fiscal adjustment plans to bolster confidence in macroeconomic policies and undertake policy reforms to secure long-term growth.

The international financial institutions need to adapt to the new global environment. In the absence of increased resources from donors, the crisis-induced frontloading of concessional resources by the International Development Association and other multilateral agencies implies that concessional flows from these institutions must decline in the near future. Similarly, the sharp rise in IBRD commitments highlights the need for discussing a capital increase to avoid an eventual falloff in lending. Changes in responsibilities and organization of the IFIs are on the horizon: increased demand for technical services will shift requirements for staff expertise; coordination among the IFIs will need to be strengthened; and proposals to improve the responsiveness of the multilateral development banks (such as decentralization at the World Bank) are under consideration. The rapid response of the global economic community to the downturn helped avoid a new Great Depression, but decisive leadership still is required to ensure a rapid and sustainable recovery.

Notes

1. This projection is based on household surveys in more than 100 countries and on the effect of growth on household consumption.
2. These analyses are based on the estimated relationships between GDP growth and the MDGs, which can vary by country.

1

Millennium Development Goals: Significant Gains before the Crisis

What is the human cost of the global economic crisis? How many people will the crisis prevent from escaping poverty, and how many will remain hungry? How many more infants will die? Are children being pulled out of schools, making it virtually impossible to reach 100 percent completion in primary education by 2015? What are the gender dimensions of the impacts? These are some of the questions as the global economy comes out of the worst recession since the Great Depression.

The questions raised here are hard to answer immediately, partly because the data to assess development outcomes are incomplete and collected infrequently but also because impacts can take several years to emerge. For example, deteriorating health and nutrition now will lead to higher mortality rates later. Lower investments will hamper future progress in sanitation and water supply. Fewer children in school will lower completion rates in later years. And household incomes that fall far below the poverty line will delay escapes from poverty.

The Millennium Development Goals (MDGs) provide powerful benchmarks for measuring global progress on key development outcomes, calling attention to the enormous challenges in low-income countries. The goals have likely contributed to the progress itself, galvanizing governments, donors, civil society, private agencies, and the media to support human development.[1] But uniform goals—reducing poverty by half, infant mortality by two-thirds, maternal mortality by three-quarters—can underestimate progress in poor countries. Why? Because the pace of progress is inversely related to initial conditions, particularly the greater distance to the goals from low starting points in poor countries.[2] And although the extent to which countries are on track to achieve the MDGs in 2015 varies widely, recent improvements have been widespread. So, too, are the losses caused by the interruption in progress.

This chapter offers an overview of progress in the decade before the crisis. It serves as the starting point for a more forward-looking analysis and explains what is at stake when a period of strong growth in many developing countries, including the low-income countries in Africa, is interrupted.[3] Subsequent chapters examine economic forecasts, how development indicators responded to previous crises, and how the current crisis differs, thus providing the building blocks to answer the questions about the human costs of the crisis.

MAP 1.1   **Africa is the only region with high extreme poverty**

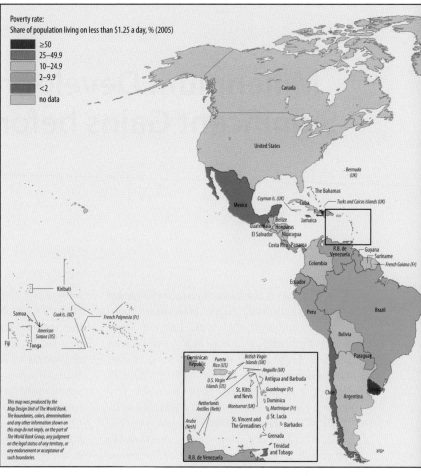

Source: PovcalNet, the World Bank.

Because the MDGs are more ambitious for poor countries, global progress is mixed

Before the global economic crisis in 2008–09, overall progress on the MDG targets were particularly strong on poverty reduction, even in Africa (figure 1.1). Progress was also made on gender parity in primary and secondary education, maternal mortality, and on reliable access to improved water. Progress was less encouraging on gender parity in tertiary education and other targets for the empowerment of women. Of greatest concern were the human development goals. Progress on most of them—especially for child mortality but also for primary school completion,

nutrition, and sanitation—was lagging at the global level (figure 1.2).

But substantial progress is evident in many areas

Economic growth is a key driver in reducing poverty and achieving other desired development outcomes, and it is there that progress has been most evident (figure 1.3). Economic growth in developing countries has accelerated, thanks to improved macroeconomic policies and a hospitable global environment—rapidly expanding world trade, favorable commodity prices, more foreign aid and debt relief, abundant low-cost capital, and large remittance flows. The 12 years before the

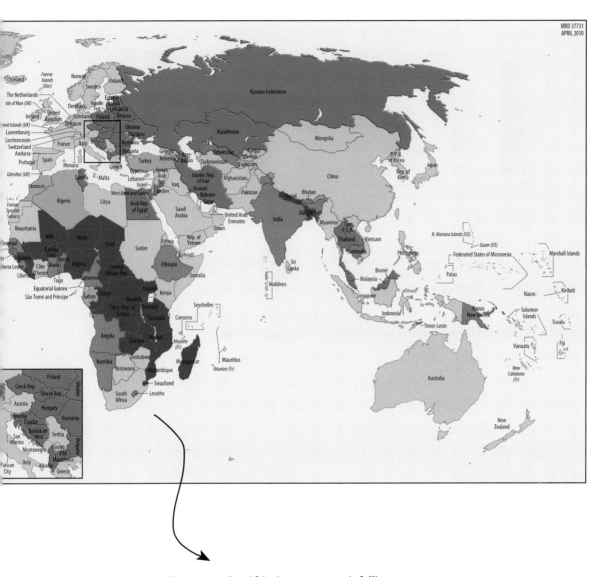

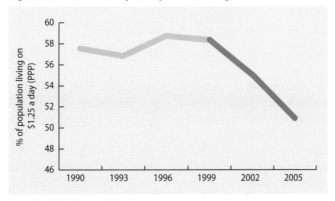

Figure 1.1   **But Africa's poverty rate is falling**

Source: World Development Indicators.

FIGURE 1.2   **At the global level, serious shortfalls loom for the human development MDGs**

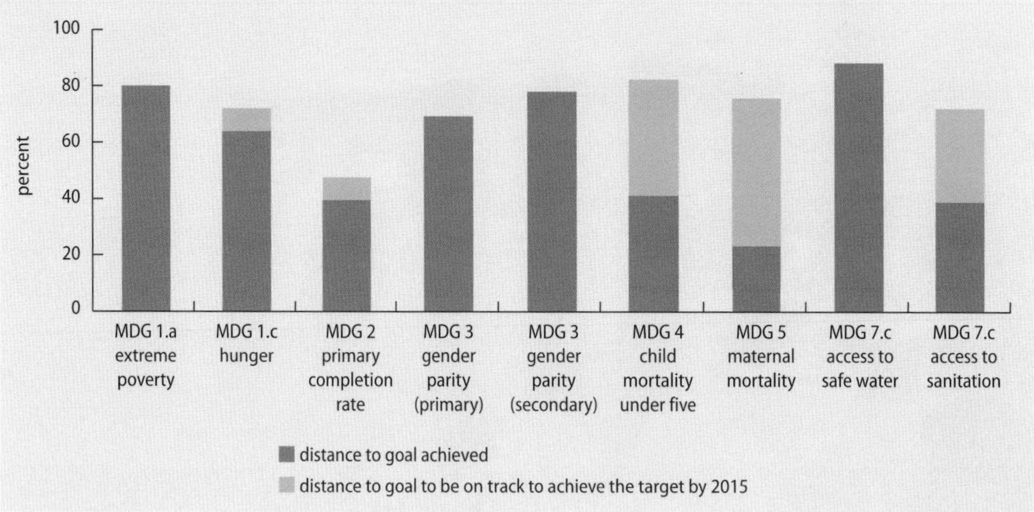

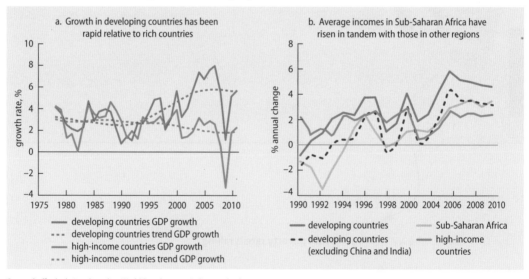

Source: Staff calculations based on latest available data as of 2009 from the World Development Indicators database.

FIGURE 1.3   **Since the 1990s growth in developing countries has accelerated**

Source: Staff calculations based on World Development Indicators database.

crisis capped a remarkable period of sustained economic growth, technological advances, and globalization that started in 1950, and spread to a widening number of developing countries in Asia and Latin America and finally to low-income countries in Africa.[4] Since the mid-1990s growth in Sub-Saharan Africa has been comparable to that in other regions. As a result, progress toward the MDGs has been greater for the goals most influenced by economic growth, such as income poverty.

Extreme poverty is falling rapidly. Despite growing populations, the number of poor people living on less than $1.25 a day in developing countries fell from about 1.8 billion in 1990 to 1.4 billion in 2005—from 42 percent of the population to 25 percent. The global MDG target of 21 percent poverty is

FIGURE 1.4   **Poverty reduction is substantial in all regions**

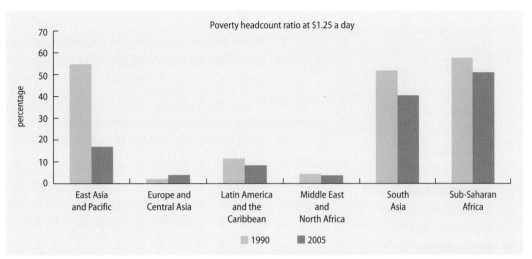

Source: PovcalNet, World Bank.
Note: Poverty rate is given as purchasing power parity (PPP) rate.

FIGURE 1.5   **Another view: Poverty rates and the number of poor people are falling rapidly**

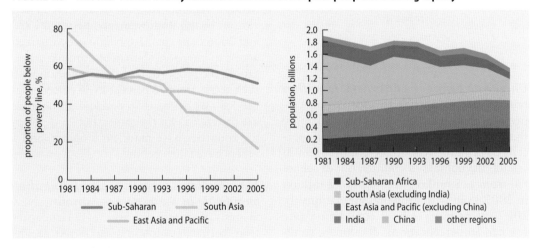

Source: PovcalNet, World Bank.

the one most likely to be exceeded, but the economic crisis adds new risks to prospects for reaching the goal.

Much of the progress is attributable to East Asia, which reduced the incidence of poverty from 55 percent in 1990 to 17 percent in 2005 (figure 1.4). China reduced its poverty rate from 60 percent to 16 percent, as the absolute number of extremely poor fell from 683 million to 208 million. India reduced the share of its population living in poverty from 51 percent to 42 percent, but because of population growth, the number of poor people actually rose from 436 million to 456 million.

With the precrisis surge of growth in Sub-Saharan Africa, the proportion of Africans living on less than $1.25 a day fell from 58 percent in 1990 to 51 percent in 2005, but the absolute number of poor people rose from 296 million to 388 million (figure 1.5). Despite Africa's recent progress, the pace of economic growth is still not fast enough there to cut the 1990 poverty rate by half in 2015. In almost every other region, it is.

FIGURE 1.6   Net enrollment rates are rising in many countries

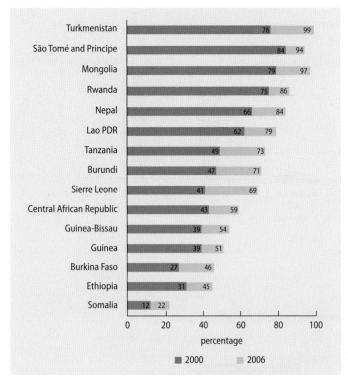

Source: UNICEF 2007.

Universal primary education is within reach. Many countries are close to providing universal primary education. In more than 60 developing countries, over 90 percent of primary-school-age children are in school; the number of children out of school fell from 115 million in 2002 to 72 million in 2007, even with growing populations. In 2007 the primary school completion rate reached 86 percent for all developing countries together—93 percent for middle-income countries but just 65 percent for low-income countries. Net enrollment rates are rising in several poor countries (figure 1.6). Because of the substantial improvements, the world will come close to the goal of universal primary school completion in 2015 (MDG 2) but still fall short. For Sub-Saharan Africa and South Asia the lower rates of 60 percent and 80 percent in 2007 still constitute advancement over the 51 percent and 62 percent, respectively, in 1991. But with 41 million primary-school-age children in Sub-Saharan Africa and 31.5 million in South Asia out of school, the task of meeting the target remains challenging.

Higher enrollments are shrinking the gender gap in education. Gender equality and female empowerment, the third MDG, are important not only in themselves but also because they improve progress on the other MDG targets related to poverty, hunger, disease, and education. As more girls than ever complete primary school, many countries have reached gender parity in primary education (figure 1.7). All told, almost two-thirds of developing countries reached gender parity at the primary school level by 2005, and the MDG 3 target of achieving gender parity in primary and secondary education can be met by 2015. Sub-Saharan Africa is making good progress but is far behind the global target.

Access to safe drinking water is on track globally and in most regions. Rapid expansions of infrastructure spending account for part of this increased access. Progress on this part of MDG 7 remains vital for child survival and various health improvements. Between 1990 and 2006 more than 1.6 billion people gained access to improved sources of drinking water, raising the proportion of the population with such access from 76 percent to 86 percent (figure 1.8). As many as 76 developing countries are on track to hit the target. But 23 developing countries have made no progress, and 5 others have fallen behind.

New findings suggest a significant drop worldwide in the maternal mortality. New analysis of maternal deaths in 181 countries from better data found a significant decline globally.[5] Aggregate maternal deaths decreased by over 35 percent from about 526,300 in 1980 to 342,900 in 2008. More than half of all maternal deaths were concentrated in six countries—India, Nigeria, Pakistan, Afghanistan, Ethiopia, and the Democratic Republic of Congo. All told, maternal deaths for every 100,000 live births decreased markedly from 422 in 1980 to 320 in 1990 and to 251 in 2008. The yearly rate of the decline in the global maternal mortality ratio since 1990 was 1.3 percent (with an uncertainty range of 1.0–1.5). Progress is still varied. The Arab Republic of Egypt, China, Ecuador, and Bolivia have been achieving rapid gains, and

FIGURE 1.7   Gender parity is close in primary education

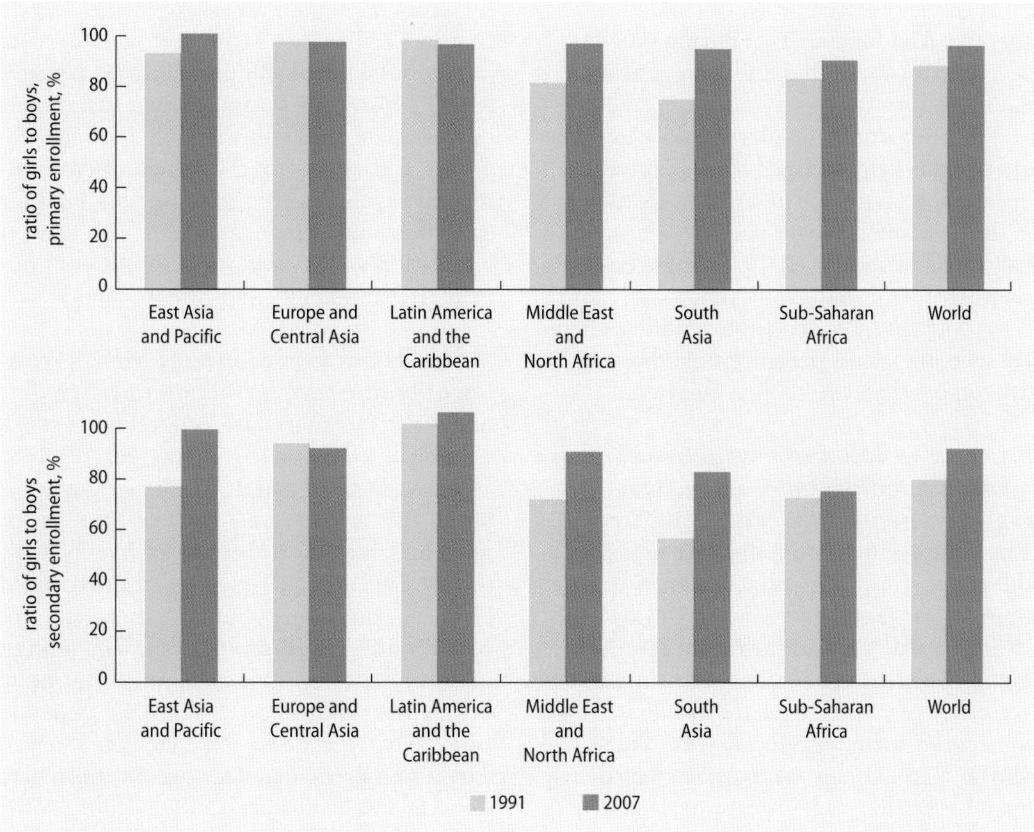

ratio of girls to boys, primary enrollment, %

| | East Asia and Pacific | Europe and Central Asia | Latin America and the Caribbean | Middle East and North Africa | South Asia | Sub-Saharan Africa | World |

ratio of girls to boys, secondary enrollment, %

| | East Asia and Pacific | Europe and Central Asia | Latin America and the Caribbean | Middle East and North Africa | South Asia | Sub-Saharan Africa | World |

■ 1991   ■ 2007

Source: World Development Indicators.

23 countries are on track with this MDG 5. In Sub-Saharan Africa, central and eastern regions showed some improvement since 1990, but southern and western regions showed deterioration because of the significant number of pregnant women who died from HIV infection. In southern Africa, the maternal mortality ratio increased from 171 in 1990 to 381 in 2008.

Where progress has been mixed or lacking

The recent food crisis has complicated progress on fighting malnutrition and hunger. The developing world is not on track to halve the proportion of people who suffer from hunger. Because reducing malnutrition is essential to success on several other MDGs, including infant mortality, maternal mortality, and education, it has a multiplier effect.

FIGURE 1.8   More people have improved sources of water

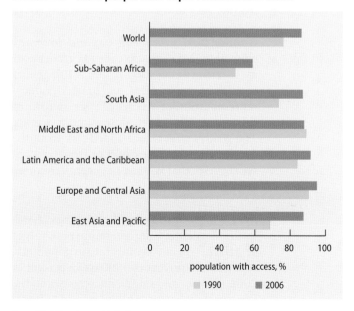

population with access, %

■ 1990   ■ 2006

Source: World Development Indicators.

Child malnutrition accounts for more than a third of the disease burden of children under age five. And malnutrition during pregnancy accounts for more than 20 percent of maternal mortalities.

The proportion of children under five who are underweight declined from 31 percent in developing countries in 1990 to 26 percent in 2007, a much slower pace than needed to halve malnutrition by 2015. Progress has been slowest in Sub-Saharan Africa and South Asia, with severe to moderate stunting affecting as many as 46 percent of children under five—more than 140 million children.

Progress on full and productive employment, especially for women, was lacking even before the crisis. (figure 1.9). The employment-to-population ratio is the proportion of a country's working-age population (ages 15 years and older) that is employed. Considerable underemployment in informal sectors and subsistent activities of rural areas are of course hard to account for in developing countries. The female employment ratios have consistently been lower than male ratios, particularly in the Middle East and North Africa and in South Asia. Nonetheless, progress is noted in the female ratios for Latin America and the Caribbean and to a slight extent in the Middle East and North Africa (figure 1.9).

Gender parity is weak beyond primary education. MDG 3 also calls for gender parity in tertiary education (figure 1.10), gender equality in employment, and greater political representation of women. Progress toward these targets has been slower and less even. The gender targets face added risk from the current crisis because evidence from past crises suggests that women in general are more vulnerable.

Access to sanitation has been elusive. Sanitation coverage, another important target of MDG 7 on environmental sustainability, rose from 43 percent in 1990 to 55 percent in 2006, in low- and middle-income countries. But the global target will be missed. Almost half the people in developing countries lack adequate sanitation. In Sub-Saharan Africa the proportion with access rose from 26 percent in 1990 to just 31 percent in 2006, and in South Asia, from 18 percent to 33 percent. MDG 7 also calls for integrating sustainable development into country policies and programs and reversing the losses of environmental resources. Progress on this broader environmental agenda, although fairly slow, is picking up as the world focuses on environmental sustainability and climate change.[6]

Prospects are worst for most MDGs relating to health, such as infant mortality. The under-five mortality rate in developing countries declined from 101 deaths per 1,000 to 74 between 1990 and 2007, showing notable but insufficient progress to meet MDG 4 for reducing child mortality under five by two-thirds. In 2006, 10 million children died before age five from preventable diseases, compared with 13 million in 1990. The human immunodeficiency virus/acquired immune deficiency syndrome (HIV/AIDS) epidemic and civil conflicts have impeded Sub-Saharan Africa's progress. Its under-five mortality rate stood at 144 deaths per 1,000 in 2008, down from 185 in 1990. Sub-Saharan Africa has 20 percent of the world's children under age five but 50 percent of all child deaths. Progress in reducing infant mortality is also well short of the target in South Asia.

The situation is similar for universal access to reproductive health (MDG 5.b). For example, the contraceptive prevalence rate has increased for all income groups between 1990 and 2007 but is still quite low at only 33 percent for low-income countries in 2007 (figure 1.11).

Progress in halting the spread of major communicable diseases has been mixed (MDG 6). An estimated 33.4 million people were living with HIV/AIDS in 2008; there were 2.7 million new infections and about 2 million AIDS-related deaths. The rapidly rising trends of HIV spread and related deaths that were recorded in the 1990s were halted in the 2000s and were showing some signs of decline in recent years (figure 1.12). However, further actions are still necessary to achieve

FIGURE 1.9 **Progress lacking on ratio of employment to population**

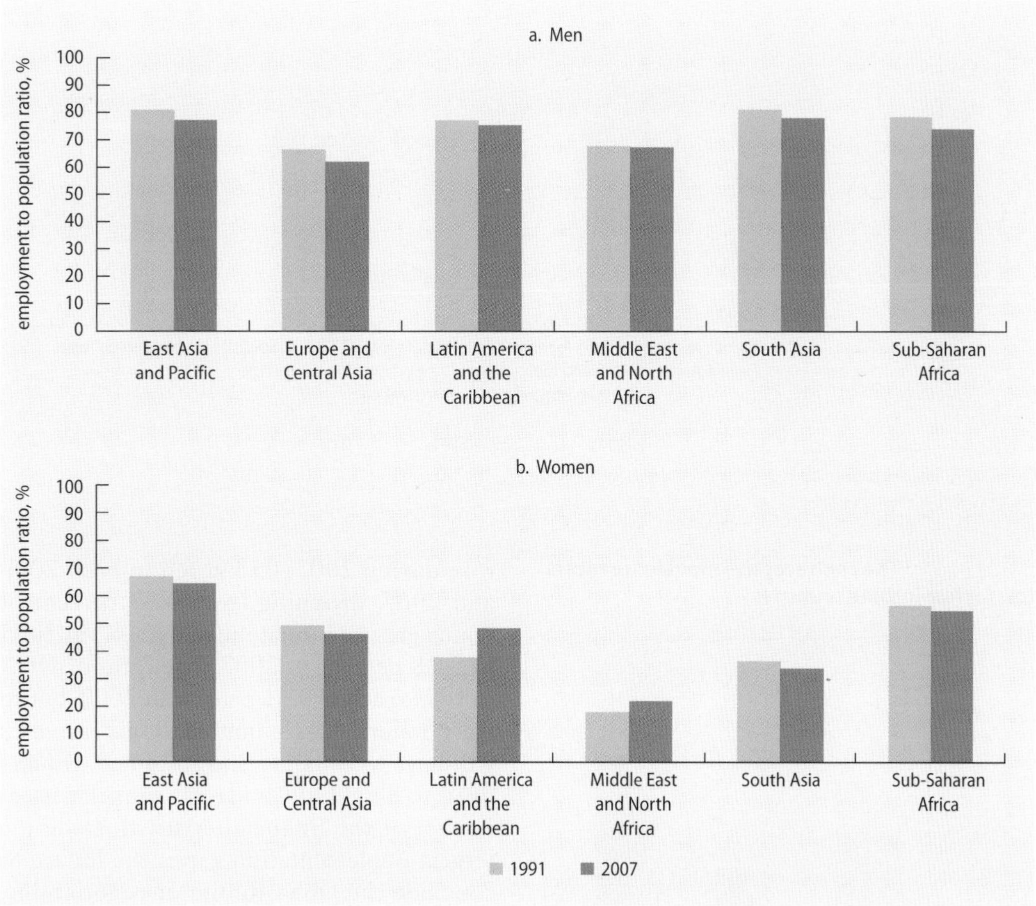

Source: World Development Indicators.

significant reversals. Sub-Saharan Africa remains the region most heavily affected by HIV worldwide, accounting for over two-thirds of all people living with HIV and for nearly three-fourths of AIDS-related deaths in 2008. HIV prevalence has declined in recent years in Sub-Saharan Africa (map 1.2), but it has risen in other regions, albeit from much lower levels.

Antiretroviral treatment (ART) now reaches almost a third of people living with HIV/AIDS in developing countries (figure 1.13). But few countries will meet the target of universal access to treatment anytime soon.

The prevalence of tuberculosis, which killed 1.3 million people in 2008, has been declining in all regions except Sub-Saharan Africa. Mortality from malaria remains high—at

about 1 million people annually, 80 percent of them children in Sub-Saharan Africa.

More attention should be given to achieving environmental goals. According to the World Bank's 2010 *World Development Report* on development and climate change, developing countries can shift to lower-carbon paths while promoting development and reducing poverty, as long as they receive financial and technical assistance from high-income countries. High-income countries, which produced most of the greenhouse gas emissions of the past, must act to shape our climate future, taking actions quickly to reduce their own carbon footprints and boost development of alternative energy sources. The costs for getting there will be high but still manageable. A key way

FIGURE 1.10   **Female enrollment in tertiary education lags in Sub-Saharan Africa and South Asia, 2007**

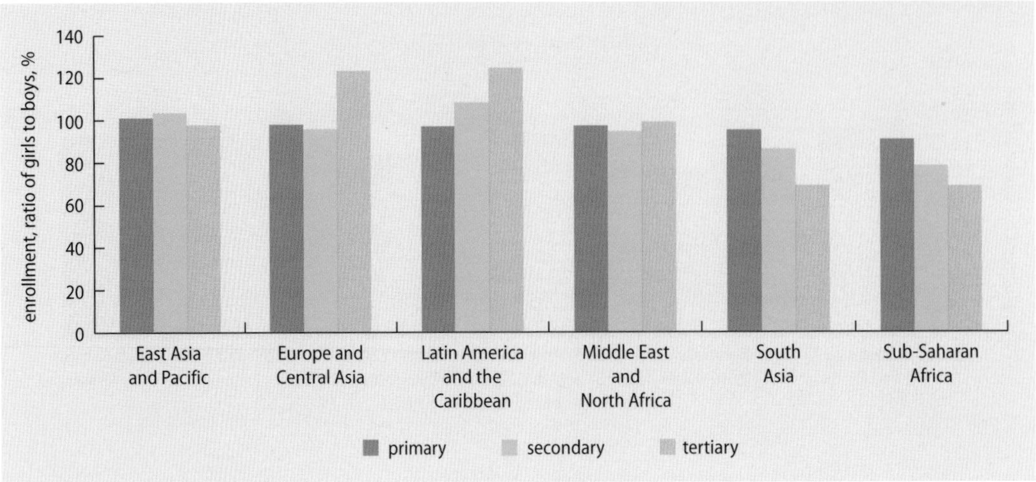

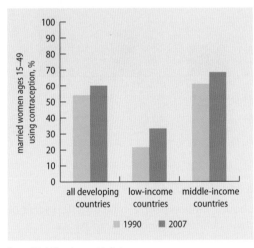

Source: World Development Indicators.

FIGURE 1.11   **The contraceptive prevalence rate is low for low-income countries**

Source: World Development Indicators.

rose during 2003–05 but fell in both 2006 and 2007, dropping from 0.33 percent of donor gross national income (GNI) in 2005 to 0.28 percent in 2007. The ratio of ODA to GNI reached 0.31 percent in 2009, but to meet donors' aid commitments, aid increases will have to be larger and sustained. Donors need to shield aid budgets from the fiscal impact of the financial crisis. In trade the largest implementation gap is the failure to conclude the Doha Round of negotiations. Progress has been greater in providing debt relief to poor countries, thanks to the Heavily Indebted Poor Countries Initiative and the Multilateral Debt Relief Initiative. The lack of specific targets is hampering the transfer of technology to developing countries and their access to essential drugs.[8]

to slow climate change is to ramp up funding for mitigation in developing countries, where most future growth in emissions will occur.[7]

More progress is needed on developing a global partnership for development. MDG 8 covers cooperation in aid, trade, debt relief, and access to technology and essential drugs. Net disbursements of official development assistance (ODA) from the Development Assistance Committee of the Organisation for Economic Co-operation and Development

Progress varies by type of country

Inside the global picture is considerable variation across income groups, regions, and countries. Middle-income countries have progressed fastest toward the MDGs. As a group, they are on track to achieve the target for poverty reduction. But many of them still have large concentrations of poverty, in part reflecting great income inequality. These concentrations of poverty, together with large populations in some countries, mean that middle-income countries remain home to a majority of the world's poor in absolute numbers. Many middle-income countries also continue to face major challenges in achieving the nonincome human development goals.

Progress has been weaker in low-income countries, with considerable variability. It has been slowest in fragile and conflict-affected states (figure 1.14). Wracked by conflict and hampered by weak capacities, these states—more than half of them in Sub-Saharan Africa—present difficult political and governance contexts for the effective delivery of development finance and services. Fragile states account for close to a fifth of the population of low-income countries but more than a third of their poor people. Much of the challenge of achieving the MDGs will be concentrated in low-income countries, especially fragile states.

Most regions are progressing rapidly toward the goals. Thanks to rapid economic growth, especially in China, East Asia has already halved extreme poverty. South Asia is on track to do the same, but it is seriously off track on most human development goals. For the health goals most regions are off track, although the rate of progress varies substantially, with East Asia and the Pacific, Latin America and the Caribbean, and Europe and Central Asia doing better than the other regions.

Sub-Saharan Africa is a special case. It is easy to see that Sub-Saharan Africa lags on all the MDGs, including poverty reduction. But that is only half the story—because the region has made progress. Practically all the MDG curves for Sub-Saharan Africa (figure 1.15) have been headed in the right direction for more than 10 years, but the progress required looks steeper in direct comparisons with other regions because of Africa's lower starting points. Achievements are more apparent when viewed against the severe economic stagnation that afflicted the region from the 1970s to the early 1990s.

MAP 1.2 Proportion of population living with HIV is still high but declining in Sub-Saharan Africa, 1990, 2001, and 2007

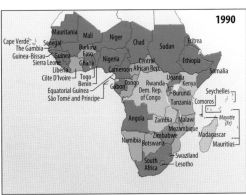

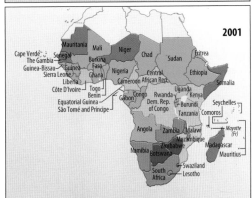

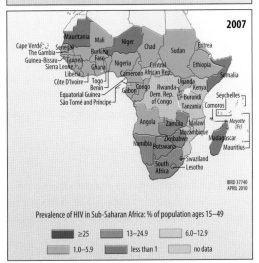

Prevalence of HIV in Sub-Saharan Africa: % of population ages 15–49

≥25   13–24.9   6.0–12.9   1.0–5.9   less than 1   no data

Source: United Nations 2009.

Many countries are likely to fall short of most of the goals. Among countries for which there are data, the proportion off track exceeds that of countries on track for

FIGURE 1.12   **HIV prevalence rates and estimated deaths are showing signs of decline**

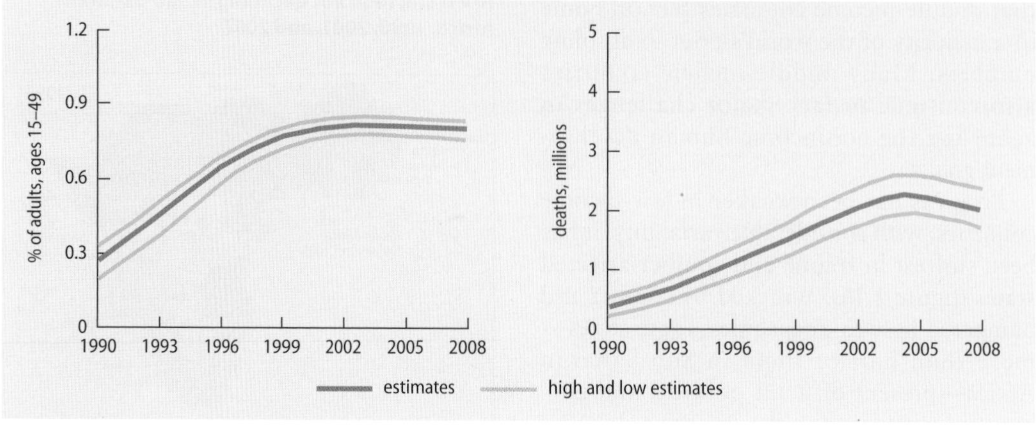

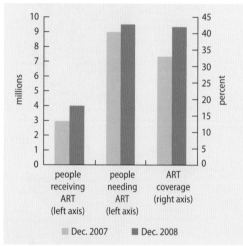

— estimates   — high and low estimates

Source: UNAIDS/WHO.
Note: The HIV adult prevalence rate is defined as the proportion of people ages 15 and above who are infected with HIV.

FIGURE 1.13   **Improving access to antiretroviral treatment is still far from universal**

Source: UNAIDS/WHO.
Note: ART - antiretroviral treatment.

all MDGs except poverty reduction and gender parity in school (figure 1.16). This result likely comes from low starting points in poor countries.

How starting points affect results

Progress varies positively with income growth but is conditioned by starting points or country circumstances. This phenomenon is best illustrated for poverty reduction. In general, the elasticity, or responsiveness, of poverty

with respect to economic growth depends on how the incomes of poor people move with average growth; whether growth is in broad terms reaching poor people; and how any increase in incomes interacts with the income distribution and the poverty line. However, when a common poverty goal like the MDG 1 is applied to all developing countries against a uniform poverty yardstick (such as $1.25 a day), starting points or country circumstances matter greatly. Starting points thus help explain why, despite the precrisis progress in growth and poverty reduction, low-income countries are still far from reaching the poverty MDG.

Recent empirical analysis reveals that a high initial poverty incidence slows progress against poverty at any given growth rate.[9] Analysis of more than 600 household surveys in 116 countries since 1980 confirms the story: in two countries with the same economic growth rate, poverty reduction will be slower in the country that begins with the higher poverty rate (figure 1.17). There are some data and observation issues to consider. At low poverty rates, there is considerable noise, and elasticity becomes volatile, especially at the $1.25-a-day poverty threshold. Some more advanced countries have no computable observations in this range. Twelve countries with zero poverty rates in the initial period have zero or irregular elasticity; seven

FIGURE 1.14   **Fragile states have made the least progress toward the MDGs**

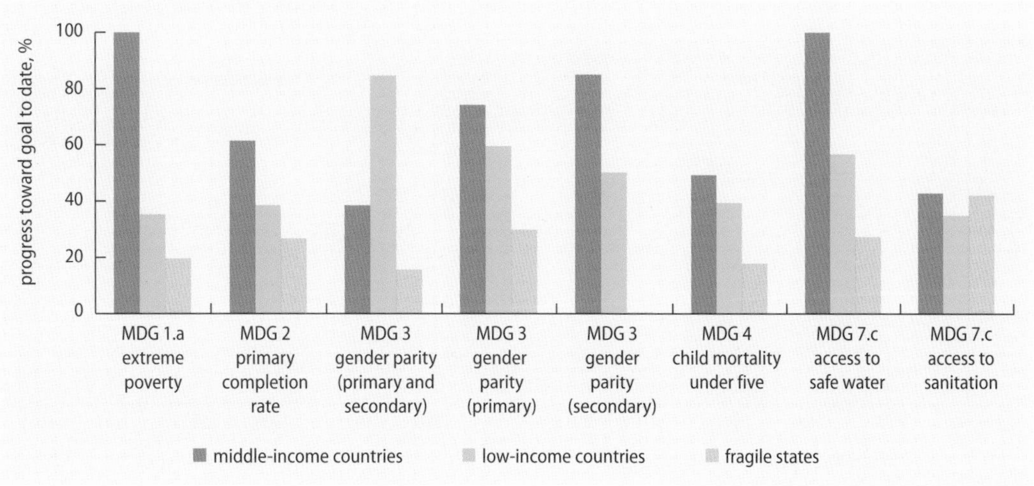

Source: Staff calculations based on World Development Indicators database.
Note: Most recent data as of 2009.

other countries with nonzero poverty rates have zero elasticity. Almost all these outliers belong to transitional economies in Eastern Europe and include the turbulent years in the 1990s when their economies, incomes, and income distributions were undergoing fundamental changes. Even at a $2.00-a-day poverty line, seven countries have zero elasticity. When the initial poverty rate is greater than 10 percent, the pattern becomes broadly more regular.[10]

At the aggregate or regional level, the responsiveness (median elasticity) of poverty to growth is generally lower in low-income countries, which tend to have higher initial poverty rates for both the $1.25-a-day and the $2.00-a-day international thresholds (table 1.1). Elasticity also depends on the choice of a global poverty threshold, although the pattern holds in general. For middle-income countries, particularly upper-middle-income ones, the lower $1.25 threshold becomes less meaningful as the median poverty rate falls below 4 percent. The regional numbers are summarized in table 1.2.

The pattern clearly reflects the more difficult circumstances in poor countries and fragile states. For example, in fragile states the median elasticity of extreme poverty to growth is lowest at the $1.25 a day poverty line. One explanation is that the poverty gap, which reflects the depth of poverty as well as its incidence, is greater in poor countries. A related "distance" measure is the percent ratio of the average income of the poor to the poverty line; the distance between the average income of the poor and the poverty line is greater in many low-income countries. In 2005 Sub-Saharan Africa's poverty gap and its mean ratio of the average income of the poor to the $1.25-a-day poverty line are 20.1 percent and 59.7 percent, respectively. These numbers are worse than comparable figures for other regions (table 1.3). Middle-income countries tend to have better numbers. The two large countries, China and India, are exceptions in the sense that, despite their starting points in income and poverty rates, poverty reduction has been rapid not just because of the high growth rates but also because the poverty gap and the average income distance from the poverty line have been relatively low. For all these countries, many of the poor are already close to the $1.25-a-day threshold and growth can more easily raise their incomes over the poverty line. In contrast, in African countries like Liberia, Mozambique, Rwanda, and Tanzania, which have very high poverty gaps and greater distance to the thresholds, the same

FIGURE 1.15   Progress in Sub-Saharan Africa is significant but still insufficient—partly because of low starting points

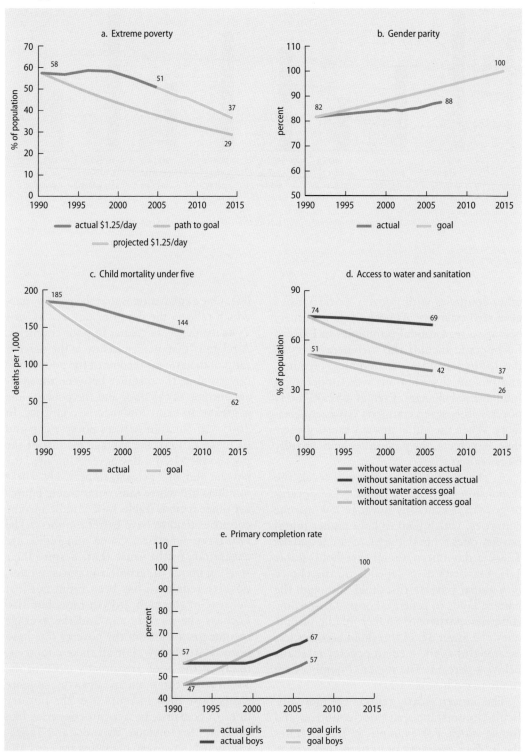

Source: World Development Indicators.
Note: PPP is purchasing power parity.

FIGURE 1.16   **Many countries are falling short of most MDGs, 2009**

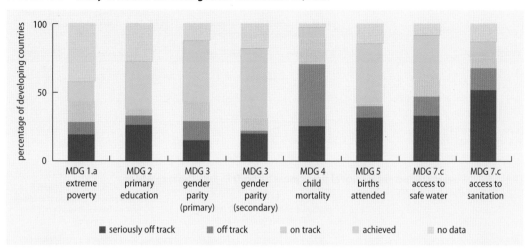

Source: Staff calculations based on World Development Indicators database.
Note: The data cover 144 developing countries and the latest available information as of 2009.

FIGURE 1.17   **Poverty responds less to growth when the initial poverty rate is high**

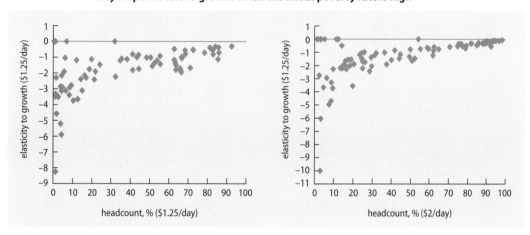

Source: Staff calculations from PovcalNet, the World Bank.
Note: There are data or observation issues especially when the poverty rate is low; see text for details.

level of growth would be unlikely to push many households above the poverty line in a short period of time.

Another explanation is simply arithmetic, having to do with the way the poverty MDG is defined.[11] It is easier for a middle-income country to halve its poverty rate from, say, 10 percent to 5 percent than for a poor country to cut its rate by even less than half, say, from 50 percent to 35 percent. Although the rate of reduction is lower in the poorer country than in a richer country of comparable population size, the number of people to move out of poverty will be much larger in the poor country.

All this simply means that a long period of sustained and shared growth will be crucial to meet the poverty MDG in many poor countries. To really achieve rapid progress, growth may have to reach the rates in China and India. Although a pro-poor growth rate will raise the income of the poor, the high

TABLE 1.1   Poverty reduction is more difficult in poor countries

Country group	Median growth elasticity of poverty with respect to poverty line		Median poverty headcount at initial year with respect to poverty line (%)	
	$1.25 a day	$2.00 a day	$1.25 a day	$2.00 a day
Low-income countries	−1.01	−0.53	66.02	85.77
Fragile states	−0.81	−0.54	51.46	74.99
Lower-middle-income countries	−1.65	−0.88	15.11	29.54
Upper-middle-income countries	−1.04	−1.41	3.60	11.32

Source: World Bank staff calculations from PovcalNet.
Note: The values in the table are the medians of {ln(H2/H1/ln(M2/M1)} in each category.

TABLE 1.2   Poverty reduction is several times more difficult in Sub-Saharan Africa

Region	Median growth elasticity of poverty with respect to poverty line		Median poverty headcount at initial year with respect to poverty line (%)	
	$1.25 a day	$2.00 a day	$1.25 a day	$2.00 a day
East Asia and Pacific	−1.43	−0.79	48.6	77.9
Europe and Central Asia	−2.00	−1.12	3.7	10.2
Latin America and the Caribbean	−2.03	−1.44	8.8	20.9
Middle East and North Africa	−2.89	−2.06	4.6	19.6
South Asia	−1.05	−0.48	66.5	88.1
Sub-Saharan Africa	−0.76	−0.36	66.0	83.9
Total	−1.18	−0.81	18.4	39.4

Source: World Bank staff calculations from PovcalNet.
Note: The values in the table are the medians of {ln(H2/H1/ln(M2/M1)} in each category.

TABLE 1.3   Poverty gaps and ratio of mean income of the poor to the $1.25-a-day poverty line are worse for low-income regions or countries, 2005

	Poverty gap with respect to $1.25 a day (%)	Ratio of mean income of those below $1.25 a day to the poverty line (%)
Sub-Saharan Africa	20.1	59.7
South Asia	9.2	75.9
East Asia and Pacific	5.6	71.3
Latin America and the Caribbean	4.9	65.1
Middle East and North Africa	1.4	84.1
Europe and Central Asia	1.1	67.8
Middle-income countries		
Albania	0.1	91.7
Brazil	2.8	65.6
Mexico	0.1	89.6
Thailand	0.01	96.4
Large countries		
China: urban	0.2	90.2
China: rural	6.5	75.2
India	10.0	76.1
African countries		
Tanzania	48.6	45.1
Mozambique	42.0	48.1
Liberia	40.7	50.7
Rwanda	38.2	49.9

Source: PovcalNet, World Bank.

poverty gaps imply that it will take longer or more effort for the poor to cross the poverty line. In light of the finding that the poverty rate itself may take more time to evolve, what low-income countries achieved before the crisis is indeed remarkable.

The full impact of the global economic crisis still lies ahead

It is likely that the world has not yet seen the full impact of the crisis on the MDG indicators. A slow global recovery could imply that progress on MDG indicators will stray further from the path it was on before the crisis. Will economic growth and development deteriorate because of a less hospitable global economic environment brought about by the global economic crisis? Chapters 2, 3, and 4 look at lessons from past crises, the current economic situation, the prospects for growth, and the outlook for the MDGs. Chapter 5 focuses on the actions and policies for attaining the MDGs—and beyond.

Notes

1. See, for example, Sachs 2005.
2. A point raised by Clemens and Moss (2005); Clemens, Kenny, and Moss (2007); Easterly (2009); and Vandemoortele (2009).
3. This observation is documented in several recent studies. See, for example, World Bank (2008) on the decoupling of trend growth for developed and developing countries. For Africa, see IMF (2008), Go and Page (2008), Ndulu (2008), and World Bank (2000).
4. Rodrik 2009.
5. Hogan and others 2010. Weak vital registration systems in developing countries make the maternal mortality ratio one of the hardest things to measure, and previous estimates showed very little change over time. The new study supplemented national vital registration data with other sources, such as sibling histories in household surveys, census data, and death surveys. It also carefully examined uncertainty in the expected maternal death rate from five sources—stochastic variance in the input data, nonsampling error in data systems, errors in the covariates (such as GDP per capita, educational attainment, HIV seroprevalence, and the like), and estimation error from using simulation methods.
6. Environmental sustainability and its links to the MDGs were a major focus of Global Monitoring Report 2008 (World Bank and IMF 2008). The 2010 World Development Report also focused on development and climate change (World Bank 2010).
7. See World Bank (2010) for an in-depth discussion and treatment of this issue.
8. United Nations 2008.
9. Ravallion 2009.
10. The $1.25-a-day relationship can be approximated by a logarithmic regression: log(elasticity) = −1.0634 + 0.4725 (initial poverty rate), n = 101, which is significant at 1 percent (t = 5.13). See Ravallion (2009) for careful estimation and testing of convergence.
11. Easterly 2009.

References

Clemens, M. A., and T. J. Moss. 2005. "What's Wrong with the Millennium Development Goals?" Brief. Center for Global Development, Washington, DC.

Clemens, M. A., C. J. Kenny, and T. J. Moss. 2007. "The Trouble with the MDGs: Confronting Expectations of Aid and Development Success." *World Development* 35 (5): 735–51.

Easterly, W. 2009. "How the Millennium Development Goals Are Unfair to Africa." *World Development* 37 (1): 26–35.

Go, D., and J. Page, eds. 2008. *Africa at a Turning Point?* Washington, DC: World Bank.

Hogan, M., K. Foreman, M. Naghavi, S. Ahn, M. Wang, S. Makela, A. Lopez, R. Luzana, and C. Murray. 2010. "Maternal Mortality for 181 Countries, 1980–2008: A Sytematic Analysis of Progress towards Millennium Development Goal 5." *Lancet.* www.lancet.com, April 12, 2010.

IMF (International Monetary Fund). 2008. *Regional Economic Outlook: Sub-Saharan Africa.* Washington, DC (October).

Ndulu, B. J. 2008. *The Political Economy of Economic Growth in Africa, 1960–2000.* Cambridge, U.K.: Cambridge University Press.

Ravallion, M. 2009. "Why Don't We See Poverty Convergence?" Policy Research Working Paper 4974. World Bank, Washington, DC.

Rodrik, D. 2009. "Growth after the Crisis." Paper prepared for the Commission on Growth and Development, Harvard Kennedy School, Cambridge, MA.

Sachs, J. 2005. *The End of Poverty.* New York: Penguin Books.

UNICEF 2007. *Progress for Children, A World Fit for Children, Statistical Review* (6, December). New York.

United Nations. 2008. "Delivering on the Global Partnership for Achieving the Millennium Development Goals." MDG Gap Task Force Report. New York.

———. 2009. *The Millennium Development Goals Report.* New York.

Vandemoortele, Jan. 2009. "The MDG Conundrum: Meeting the Targets without Missing the Point." *Development Policy Review* 27 (4): 355–71.

World Bank. 2000. *Can Africa Claim the 21st Century?* Washington, DC: World Bank.

———. 2008. *Global Development Finance 2008: The Role of International Banking.* Vol. 1. *Review, Analysis, and Outlook.* Vol. 2. *Summary and Country Tables.* Washington, DC: World Bank.

———. 2010. *World Development Report 2010: Development and Climate Change.* Washington, DC: World Bank.

World Bank, and IMF. 2008. *Global Monitoring Report 2008: MDGs and the Environment: Agenda for Inclusive and Sustainable Development.* Washington, DC: World Bank.

2

Lessons from Past Crises—and How the Current Crisis Differs

Historically, periods of sharp contraction have been extremely harmful for human development. Social indicators tend to deteriorate rapidly during economic downturns and improve slowly during economic booms. Moreover, vulnerable groups, such as children and women, are more exposed to the effects of growth volatility.

The asymmetric response of social indicators to the growth cycle likely results from contractions associated with conflict or weak institutions that impair government services. With global crises, donor spending may also come under pressure.

There are several reasons, however, why this crisis may be different from previous crises for low-income countries—social spending has been largely protected so far; precrisis policies and institutions were better; and external shocks, not domestic policy failures, were the main cause of the current crisis for developing countries.

Nonetheless, the impact on the Millennium Development Goals (MDGs) is worrisome. In particular, several rapid and qualitative assessments find that households are already making painful adjustments, particularly in middle-income countries.

How growth volatility affects human development and gender indicators

It is commonly observed that human development indicators deteriorate during growth downturns. Also true, but more difficult to calculate, is that deteriorations in human development indicators during downturns tend to exceed improvements during economic booms (box 2.1 explains the definition of growth cycles used here). For example, life expectancy is 2 years longer during growth accelerations than the overall average, but 6.5 years shorter during decelerations (figure 2.1). Infant mortality is 8 per 1,000 lower during accelerations, and 24 per 1,000 higher during decelerations. The primary school completion rate is 4 percent higher during accelerations but 25 percent lower during decelerations. Further evidence for asymmetry is the size of correlation coefficients relating social indicators with upturns and downturns (table 2.1). In general, the correlation between social indicators and periods of deceleration is stronger than the correlation between social indicators and periods of acceleration (for details, see annex 2A.1).

BOX 2.1   Defining growth cycles in developing countries

The historical growth patterns considered in this study are derived from a dataset for 163 countries covering 1980–2008. A growth acceleration episode meets three conditions for at least three consecutive years:

- The four-year forward-moving average growth rate minus the four-year backward-moving average growth rate exceeds zero for each year.
- The four-year forward-moving average growth rate exceeds the country's average growth rate, meaning that the pace of growth during accelerations is faster than the country's trend. Thus the definition of episodes of growth acceleration (or deceleration) is endogenous to each country's long-run rate of growth.
- Average GDP per capita during the four-year forward-moving period exceeds the average during the four-year backward-moving period, ensuring

that the growth acceleration episode is not a recovery from a recession.

A growth deceleration episode meets these three conditions in reverse. The framework is from Arbache and Page (2007), which extends the methodology in Hausmann, Pritchett, and Rodrik (2005) by examining both accelerations and decelerations and by making each country's long-run growth rate endogenous. Testing the sample means of development indicators for significant differences during periods of growth acceleration and deceleration can show whether countries that experience more growth fluctuations face slower progress on the MDGs and identify how growth cycles affect changes in development indicators.

Source: Arbache and Page 2007; Arbache, Go, and Korman 2010.

Economic downturns also have a disproportionate impact on girls relative to boys. Life expectancy of girls and boys increases by two years during good times but decreases by about seven years for girls and six years for boys during bad times. The primary education completion rate rises 5 percent for girls and 3 percent for boys during good times but decreases 29 percent for girls and 22 percent for boys during bad times. The female-to-male enrollment ratios for primary, secondary, and tertiary education rise about 2 percent during growth accelerations but fall 7 percent (primary), 15 percent (secondary), and 40 percent (tertiary) during decelerations. These differences may result from household time and resource allocations that favor boys over girls when household budgets shrink.[1] The differential impact on child schooling and child survival is greatest in low-income countries, while gender differences are smaller in middle-income countries. Economic downturns also have different effects on the labor force

participation of women and men, with important implications for how families adjust to economic crises (box 2.2).

Despite some commonalities, the relationship between growth volatility and development outcomes varies across countries and regions. Initial conditions, regional spillovers, trade arrangements, economic geography, and other factors are associated with how countries and regions respond to economic downturns. For example, human development indicators in Sub-Saharan Africa are among the lowest in the world: infant and under-five mortality rates are almost three times higher than the global average, life expectancy is 29 percent lower, primary school completion is 66 percent lower, and the ratio of female to male tertiary enrollment is about half the global mean. But the difference between the average level of social indicators in good and bad times is smaller for Sub-Saharan Africa than it is for developing countries as a whole (compare figures 2.1 and 2.2). This finding may imply that at low levels

FIGURE 2.1   Key human development and gender indicators plummet from their overall mean during growth decelerations, all countries

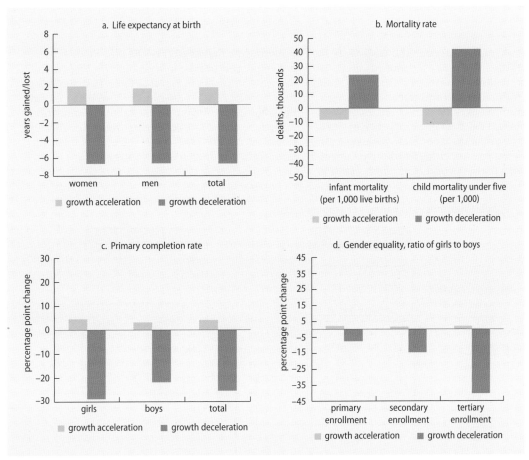

Source: World Bank staff calculations based on data from World Development Indicators. See annex table A2.1 for levels and Arbache, Go, and Korman (2010) for more details.
Note: Differences of sample averages during growth accelerations and decelerations from overall sample means.

TABLE 2.1   Correlation coefficients between growth acceleration and deceleration and human development indicators

Indicator	Growth acceleration		Growth deceleration	
	Coefficient	Significance level	Coefficient	Significance level
Life expectancy at birth, women (years)	0.13	**	−0.22	**
Life expectancy at birth, men (years)	0.12	**	−0.25	**
Life expectancy at birth, total (years)	0.13	**	−0.23	**
Infant mortality rate (per 1,000 live births)	−0.17	**	0.21	**
Child mortality under five rate (per 1,000)	−0.15	**	0.22	**
Primary completion rate, girls (% of relevant age group)	0.16	**	−0.26	**
Primary completion rate, boys (% of relevant age group)	0.13	**	−0.23	**
Primary completion rate, total (% of relevant age group)	0.16	**	−0.26	**
Ratio of girls to boys, primary enrollment	0.17	**	−0.22	**
Ratio of girls to boys, secondary enrollment	0.1	**	−0.19	**
Ratio of women to men, tertiary enrollment	0.06		−0.18	**

Source: World Bank staff calculations based on data from World Development Indicators.
Note: Tests for differences in the means of these variables among growth accelerations, decelerations, and all country-year observations show that they are almost all statistically significant at the 1 percent level (**).

BOX 2.2   Aggregate economic shocks and gender differences: A review of the evidence

The labor market for nonagricultural wage work by women (often used as a proxy for women's access to decent work) tends to behave very differently from the market for nonagricultural wage work by men. While the unemployment rate rarely differs between men and women, a much smaller proportion of working-age women are in the labor force (whereas most men of working age are either working or unemployed, women may be working at home). Thus in analyzing the impact of crises (see the figure below), it is important to take into account the response of women who are not in the labor force. In some crises, for example, in Indonesia in 1997, women entered the labor force to maintain household consumption (called the added-worker effect). In the Republic of Korea during the 1997 crisis, some women left the labor force (the discouraged-worker effect).

Possible transmission channels of economic crisis

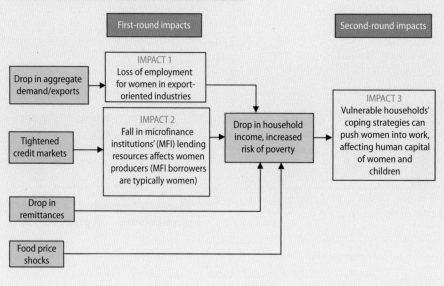

of income, the ability to improve social indicators is particularly limited—and therefore so is the likely deterioration.

Explaining the pattern of past crises

Several factors contributed to negative human development outcomes during past economic downturns, including the high frequency of downturns in low-income countries; the poor policy environment in many countries during past crises, particularly in low-income countries; shrinking social spending during contractions and the lack of social safety nets; and declines in aid during crises that also affect high-income countries.

Poor countries suffer from frequent economic contractions and high growth volatility

One reason for the low levels of human development in low-income countries is that they experience numerous crises. Of all country-year observations for low-income, International Development Association (IDA)-eligible, and Sub-Saharan African countries, nearly

BOX 2.2   (continued)

The table below summarizes country studies of the impact of crises on women's labor market participation and health and education outcomes.

Previous crises: Available evidence by country

Income level at time of crisis	Country	Labor market effects for women	Schooling	Health
Low-income country	Côte d'Ivoire		Decline in student enrollment for both boys and girls.	Deteriorating child health for both boys and girls.
	Pooled survey data from several low-income countries			Girls' infant mortality more sensitive than boys' infant mortality to fluctuations in GDP.
Lower-middle-income country	Indonesia	Added-worker effect in 1997–98.	Decline in student enrollment for young boys and girls and older girls.	Higher neonatal mortality, but overall not much effect on child health. Lower body mass index for adults.
	Peru	Added-worker effect in Lima.	Increase in student enrollment for both boys and girls.	Higher infant mortality rate.
	Philippines	Added-worker effect.	Drop in high school enrollment for both boys and girls. Drop in elementary school enrollment, more for girls than boys. Increase in child labor, more for boys than girls.	
Upper-middle-income country	Argentina	Added-worker effect in urban areas during 1990s.		
	Brazil	Both added- and discouraged-worker effect in São Paulo during 1980s.		
	Costa Rica		Decline in student enrollment for both boys and girls in rural areas; higher for girls than boys in urban areas.	
	Mexico	Added-worker effect during 1980s.	Increase in student enrollment in 1995–96, stronger for boys than girls.	Higher child mortality during crises.
	Russian Federation			Deterioration in weight for height for both boys and girls.
High-income country	Korea, Rep.	Discouraged-worker effect in Seoul in 1997–98.		
	United States	No effect.	Increase in student enrollment during Great Depression.	Improved child health outcomes.

Source: Sabarwal, Sinha, and Buvinic 2009.

FIGURE 2.2 **Key human development and gender indicators also fall below their overall means during growth decelerations in Sub-Saharan countries, if less so**

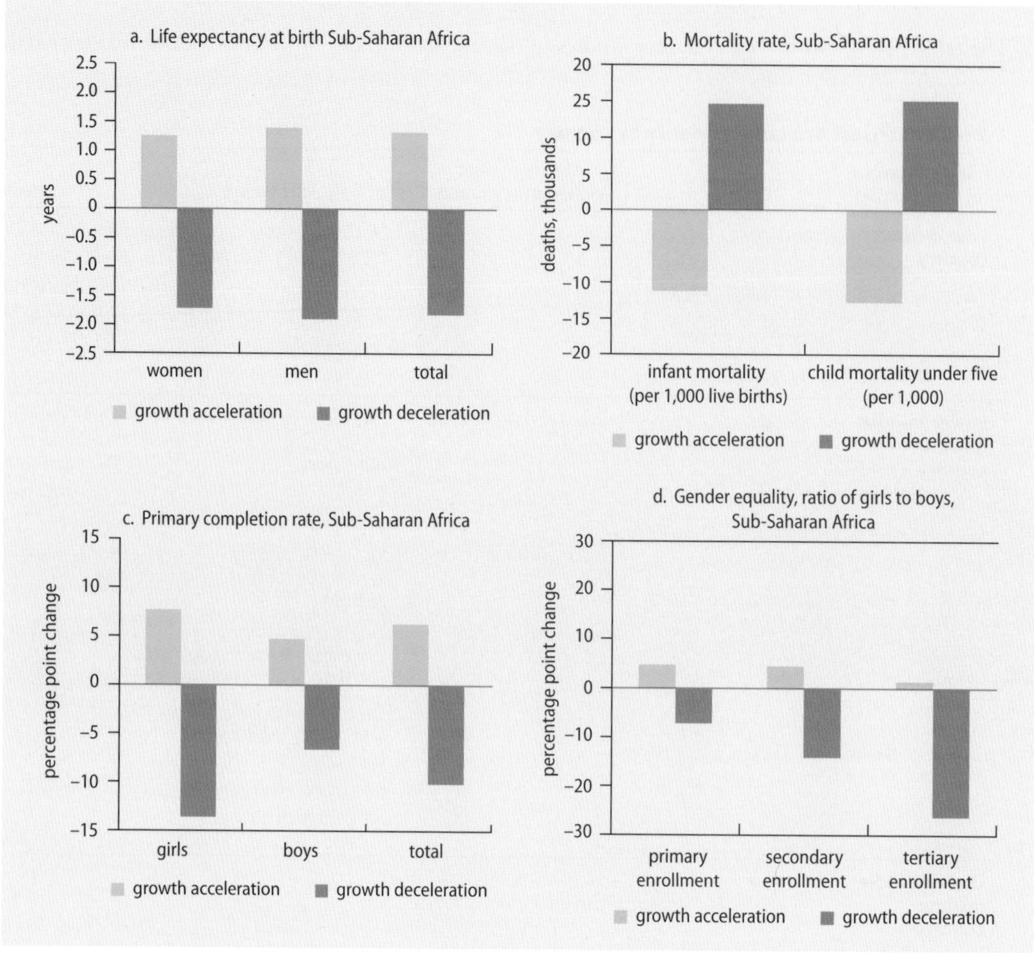

a. Life expectancy at birth Sub-Saharan Africa

b. Mortality rate, Sub-Saharan Africa

c. Primary completion rate, Sub-Saharan Africa

d. Gender equality, ratio of girls to boys, Sub-Saharan Africa

growth acceleration   growth deceleration

Source: World Bank staff calculations based on data from World Development Indicators. See annex table A2.1.2 for levels and Arbache, Go, and Korman (2010) for more details .
Note: Differences of sample averages during growth accelerations and decelerations from the overall sample means.

a quarter are decelerations; for the middle-income countries in East Asia, Europe and Central Asia, and Latin America, less than 10 percent are decelerations (table 2.2). Similarly, the share of accelerations is 37–39 percent for poorer countries but 43–53 percent for middle-income countries.[2] In addition, overall growth volatility is greater in low-income countries and in Sub-Saharan Africa than in middle-income countries (see table 2.2). The regional pattern suggests growth spillovers at the geographic level, which may be associated with economic geography, regional trade arrangements, natural disasters, regional migration, and regional conflicts.

Differences in the frequency of economic contraction explain a significant share of the differences in the average growth rate of different groups of countries. Growth in GDP per capita during 1980–2008 was 0.6 percent a year in low-income countries and more than 2 percent a year in middle-income countries. The slower growth in low-income countries stems from the greater frequency of decelerations,[3] not from a marked difference in growth rates during booms and busts. For example, during periods of acceleration, low-income countries' per capita GDP rose 3.75 percent, slightly less than the 4.5 percent growth rate for middle-income countries. During decelerations, low-

TABLE 2.2   Frequency of growth acceleration and deceleration, growth rates, and GDP per capita, 1980–2008

Region, income	GDP		Growth acceleration		Growth deceleration	
	GDP per capita growth rate (%)	Standard deviation of growth	Frequency (country years)	GDP per capita growth rate (%)	Frequency (country years)	GDP per capita growth rate (%)
World	1.89	6.03	0.47	4.27	0.11	−3.81
Region						
East Asia and Pacific	3.09	4.45	0.46	5.01	0.09	−2.75
Europe and Central Asia	2.20	6.65	0.53	4.79	0.08	−7.19
Latin America and the Caribbean	1.63	4.65	0.53	3.72	0.07	−2.78
Middle East and North Africa	1.41	5.51	0.43	2.89	0.06	−3.44
South Asia	3.72	2.87	0.36	4.69	—	—
Sub-Saharan Africa	1.02	7.28	0.39	4.19	0.22	−3.17
Country Income category						
Developing countries	1.67	6.37	0.46	4.33	0.14	−3.87
IDA countries	0.99	6.28	0.39	3.82	0.21	−3.47
Low-income countries	0.63	6.74	0.37	3.75	0.23	−3.50
Lower-middle-income countries	1.98	5.89	0.47	4.52	0.13	−4.99
Upper-middle-income countries	2.34	6.43	0.55	4.54	0.08	−2.76
High-income, non-OECD countries	3.02	7.41	0.42	5.90	0.02	−4.62
High-income OECD countries	2.19	2.59	0.54	3.31	0.03	−2.32

Source: World Bank staff calculations based on data from World Development Indicators.
Note: — = not available. OECD = Organisation for Economic Co-operation and Development.

income countries' per capita GDP fell 3.5 percent, somewhat less than in middle-income countries. Thus "defensive" policies that prevent collapses should have substantial impacts on average growth by avoiding multiple collapses and their negative outcomes.[4] The finding that the elasticity of poverty to growth is lower in high-poverty countries (see chapter 1) suggests that low-income countries, where poverty rates are high, need a long period of sustained growth to reduce poverty and improve other human development indicators.

Contractions tend to occur in severely unfavorable economic and policy environments

Contractions have a grave impact on human development because they are marked by an overall deterioration in government effectiveness. Similar to human development indicators, indicators of institutional quality (political stability, voice and accountability, regulatory framework, rule of law, and government effectiveness) in developing countries perform asymmetrically over the growth cycle. In other words, the deterioration during bad times is much greater than the improvement during good times relative to the sample averages for

all times (figure 2.3). Causality likely moves in both directions: a deterioration in institutions impairs growth, which leads to further institutional weaknesses, and so on. In many cases both institutions and growth are affected by domestic violence or foreign wars. In Sub-Saharan Africa, for example, the frequency of major and minor conflicts is about 23 percent during growth deceleration and 13 percent during growth acceleration. In oil- and mineral-dependent economies, defects in institutional quality may be masked by the revenues generated by favorable commodity prices. These defects become clear when prices turn down and revenues dry up.[5]

Macroeconomic variables such as investment, savings, exports, imports, external finance, and inflation deteriorate more during downturns than they improve during upturns (see figure 2.3). During decelerations, both savings and investment, particularly fixed private investment, decline relative to average levels (as a share of GDP) by much more than they rise during accelerations. The increase in foreign direct investment as a share of GDP during accelerations is twice as large as the drop during decelerations (relative to the sample mean). The very high values for inflation during growth decelerations reflect the incidence of hyperinfla-

FIGURE 2.3 During growth decelerations, economic and institutional indicators diverge far from the overall means

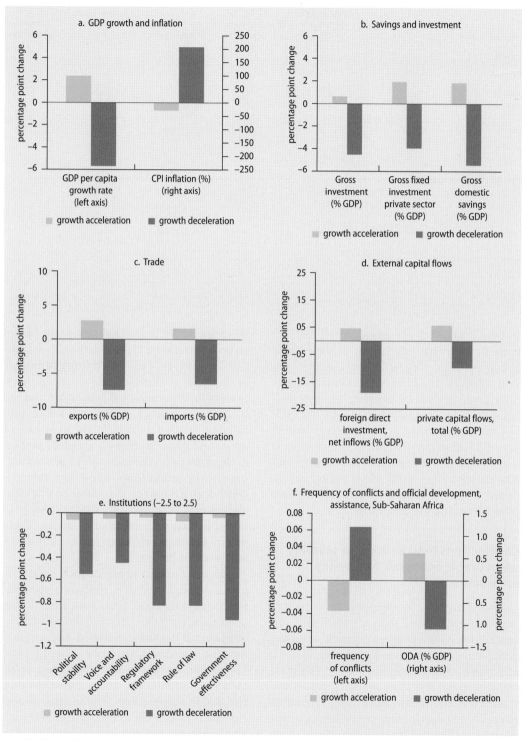

Source: World Bank staff calculations based on data from World Development Indicators. See annex table A2.3 for levels and Arbache, Go, and Korman (2010) for more details.
Note: Differences of sample averages during growth accelerations and decelerations from the overall sample means.

TABLE 2.3   Correlation coefficients between economic cycles and economic and institutional indicators

Indicator	Growth acceleration		Growth deceleration	
	Coefficient	Significance level	Coefficient	Significance level
Final consumption (% GDP)	−0.1	**	0.13	**
Government consumption (% GDP)	−0.07	**	0.04	**
Gross capital formation (% GDP)	0.09	**	−0.17	**
Gross domestic savings (% GDP)	0.1	**	−0.13	**
Gross private fixed capital formation (% GDP)	0.19	**	−0.19	**
Imports (% GDP)	0.06	**	−0.09	**
Exports (% GDP)	0.09	**	−0.11	**
Trade (% GDP)	0.08	**	−0.11	**
Net foreign direct investment (% GDP)	0.03		−0.04	*
Private capital flows, total (% GDP)	0.04	*	−0.04	*
Inflation (%)	−0.06	**	0.13	**
Institutions				
Political stability	−0.07	**	−0.12	**
Voice and accountability	−0.07	**	−0.1	**
Regulatory framework	−0.06	*	−0.19	**
Rule of law	−0.1	**	−0.18	**
Government effectiveness	−0.05	*	−0.21	**

Source: World Bank staff calculations. Indicators on institutions are from the World Bank Institute's Worldwide Governance Indicators database, which relies on 33 sources, including surveys of enterprises and citizens, and expert polls, gathered from 30 organizations around the world.
* Significant at the 5 percent level; ** significant at the 1 percent level.

tion during several growth collapses in Africa before the 1990s and incidents of high inflation in the early 1990s (such as in Angola, Armenia, Azerbaijan, Belarus, Brazil, Democratic Republic of Congo, Peru, and Ukraine).[6]

Aid to poor countries is procyclical, suggesting that donors respond to an emerging policy failure by giving less aid. Macroeconomic and institutional variables are more closely correlated with the incidence of deceleration than of acceleration (table 2.3)—further evidence of the asymmetric behavior of these indicators over the economic cycle and of the extremely poor economic environment characterizing downturns in developing countries.

Social spending under pressure

Drops in spending on social services like education and health care are an important reason for the sharp deterioration in human development indicators during crises. Cutbacks in social spending are more worrisome during crises because that is when people need these services most. Cutbacks during crises are also harmful because such disruptions have long-lasting effects. This section draws on evidence of the impacts of GDP downturns on public

and private domestic spending on health and public education for over 108 developing countries for 1995–2007.[7]

The analysis points to three key results. First, social spending growth rates tended to be volatile. Second, per capita social spending levels nonetheless showed a steady upward trend. Third, social spending in poor countries was subject to more pressures than in richer countries during contractions in GDP. The last result confirms that it is the low-income countries that are more likely to need help in protecting social expenditures during crises.

The volatility of public and private health spending is evident from the unweighted average of growth rates of social spending by country over time, a calculation that gives equal weight to changes for each country and does not allow the larger countries to dominate the pattern. In particular, changes in public health spending are more volatile than GDP growth trends over time (figure 2.4). Historically, a drop in GDP growth of 2 percent or more has had a greater than proportional effect on the growth of public health spending. Growth of private health spending (insurance and out-of-pocket payments) responds in a similar way, although the pattern is more vola-

FIGURE 2.4   Health spending growth rate is more volatile than its per capita level or GDP growth

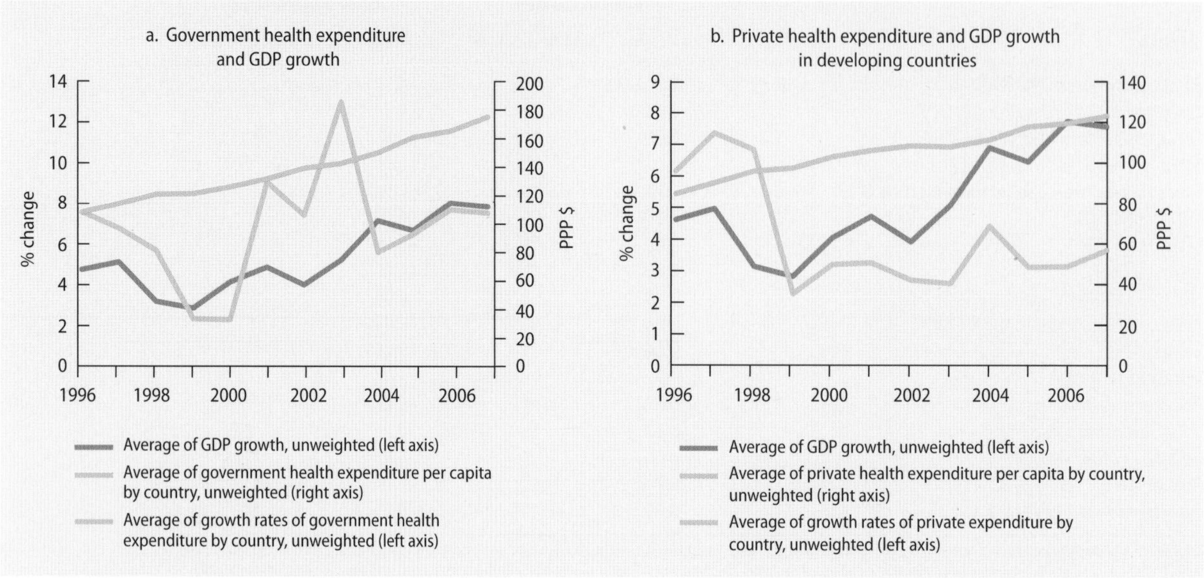

a. Government health expenditure and GDP growth

b. Private health expenditure and GDP growth in developing countries

Average of GDP growth, unweighted (left axis)

Average of government health expenditure per capita by country, unweighted (right axis)

Average of growth rates of government health expenditure by country, unweighted (left axis)

Average of GDP growth, unweighted (left axis)

Average of private health expenditure per capita by country, unweighted (right axis)

Average of growth rates of private expenditure by country, unweighted (left axis)

Source: Lewis and Verhoeven 2010.

FIGURE 2.5   Public education spending is less closely tied to GDP growth than is health spending

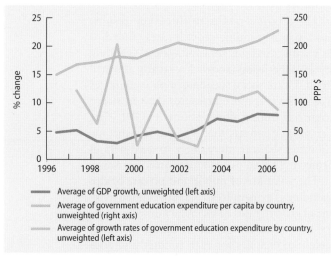

Average of GDP growth, unweighted (left axis)

Average of government education expenditure per capita by country, unweighted (right axis)

Average of growth rates of government education expenditure by country, unweighted (left axis)

Source: Lewis and Verhoeven 2010.

ing level (which is also an unweighted average across countries) suggests that the volatility of spending growth rates was affecting countries with lower levels of per capita spending more than countries with higher spending levels. Indeed, the data confirm that the negative impacts of crises on health spending are much stronger in the lowest-income countries, where growth in health spending is more likely to fall in response to a decline in GDP.

Education spending in developing countries appears to be less closely tied to GDP growth than is health spending (figure 2.5). In absolute terms, the public sector spends more, on a per capita basis, on education than on health. There is also a modest rising trend. The data on education spending are weak, however, so any conclusions concerning cross-country trends are subject to considerable uncertainty.[8]

Donor funding under pressure

Does aid to developing countries rise during crises? The sharp deterioration in human development indicators and the decline in social spending during growth decelerations highlight a potentially important role for donors. Aid's contribution to welfare in developing countries could be bolstered by increasing aid in

tile than for government spending, especially before 2005.

Despite the fluctuations in growth rates of GDP and health spending, the trends in absolute per capita health spending continue to rise over time. In general, private health spending rises more slowly than public health spending. The steady rise of the mean per capita spend-

FIGURE 2.6   Aid to education and health does not appear to be closely related to GDP growth, 1998–2007

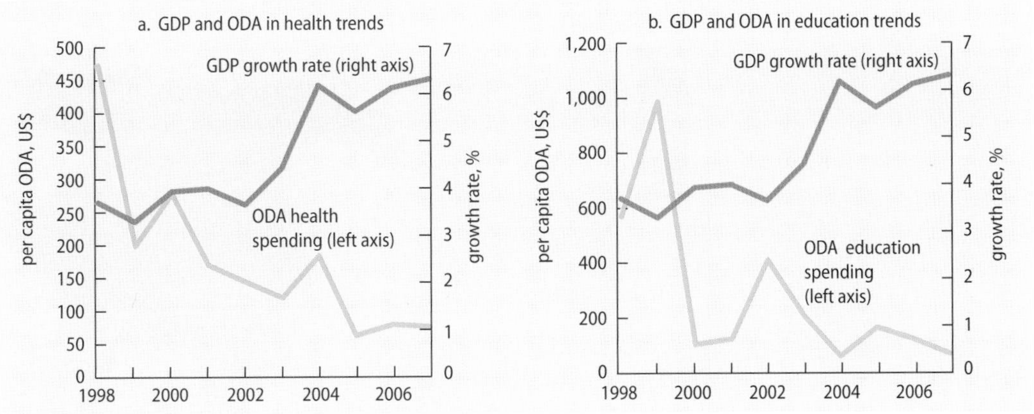

Source: Lewis and Verhoeven 2010.

bad times to compensate for shortfalls in government resources. The evidence on whether aid plays such a countercyclical role is mixed. Overall, aid to individual countries appears to be procyclical, increasing when growth rises and falling when growth slows. And growth in aid to health and education sectors does not appear to be closely related to GDP growth in developing countries (figure 2.6). However, after 2003, aid to education shows a small response to growth, with donor financing rising and falling as national education resources fall and rise. This countercyclical financing suggests that donor spending is modestly compensating for GDP growth shifts.

Evidence on aid funding during financial crises in donor countries is limited. A recent study that tracked donor allocations during and after banking crises (1998–2007) in developed countries suggests that donor funding is tied to economic prosperity in those countries.[9] Aid flows decline 20–25 percent during banking crises in member countries of the Organisation for Economic Co-operation and Development (OECD) and take significant time to recover. Not all donor programs are equally affected. But some combination of the fiscal costs of crises, debt overhang after the crisis ends, and perhaps erosion in public support reduces aid flows from affected donor countries. To the extent that aid recipients and donors are simultaneously affected by crises (as in the recent crisis), cutbacks in donor

funding could deepen the economic deterioration in developing countries.

Two deviations from these aggregate trends are instructive—and encouraging. During the Southeast Asian crisis of 1997, donors (most notably the U.K. Department for International Development) supported core social programs in Indonesia, slowing the declines in education and health spending and permitting social services to continue.[10] During the current crisis, Mexico sought loans from the World Bank to compensate for budget reductions and to expand temporary safety nets. Latvia, Lithuania, Poland, and Romania all received policy loans or technical assistance from the World Bank to support reforms and continued financing of safety nets and education and health programs. These aid responses provided necessary finance for income support and social service programs—both critical for bridging financial gaps during a downturn.

Safety nets were uncommon in developing countries before previous crises

Few countries facing previous macroeconomic and financial crises in Asia (1997–99), Europe (Russian Federation 1998, Turkey 2001), and Latin America (1980s, 1994–95, 1999, 2001–02) had strong safety nets in place before the crisis. Countries had to scale up programs, regardless of the fit between the original target

MAP 2.1   **Around 9 million young children die before their fifth birthday**

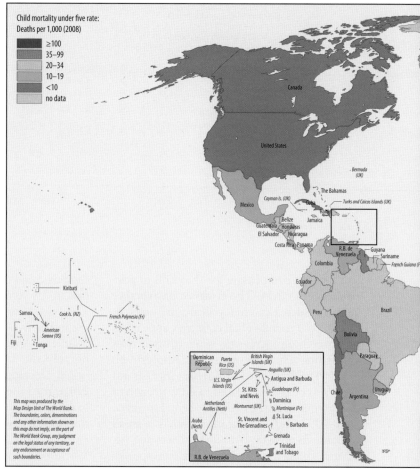

Source: World Development Indicators.

population and the population affected by the crisis, or quickly start new ones. Mexico scaled up retraining and employment programs and targeted food distribution in response to the "tequila" crisis, even though these programs probably did not target the most affected populations. Safety net programs set up after a crisis starts often suffer from poor initial implementation, as with Indonesia's Labor-Intensive Public Works (JPS Padat Karya) program, or take too long to scale up, as with Colombia's Families in Action (Familias en Acción) program.[11]

Despite the difficulties, however, countries have managed to start effective safety net programs in response to crises. Argentina established a new workfare (Jefes de Hogar) program

in response to the 2002 crisis and extended it to 2 million participants within a year. Incidence and coverage were good, with about 80 percent of the benefits concentrated among the poorest 40 percent of the population. Argentina benefited from extensive experience with an earlier, smaller workfare program. The Republic of Korea was able to quickly introduce a public works program in response to the Asian financial crisis, reaching more than 400,000 people within six months.[12]

Beyond emergency responses to natural disasters and humanitarian crises, safety nets have been uncommon in low-income countries, partly because they were viewed as taking away from more productive expenditures. But support for social safety nets in the poorest

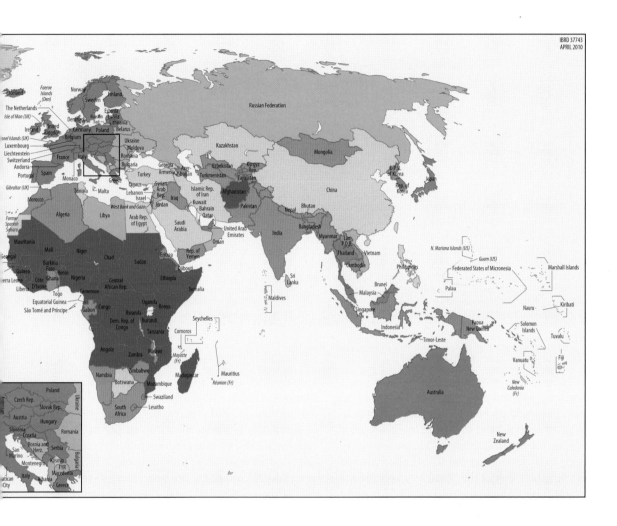

countries has risen as their importance in protecting the poor and vulnerable during crises has become evident. Low-income and fragile countries are devoting a larger share of lending to public works programs and increasing cash transfers and in-kind safety nets, with a renewed focus on school feeding programs.

A key lesson in previous crises is the importance of well-functioning safety nets in responding to a crisis and promoting growth and development afterward. When already in place, safety nets can be scaled up to meet increased needs and then scaled back as the crisis subsides. They can provide temporary protection for households by cushioning unemployment, contractions in public services, and falling demand for formal and informal work.

But if safety nets are not in place when shocks strike, governments might respond with price subsidies or other suboptimal policies, which can leave an unwanted legacy of fiscal burden, economic distortions, lower growth, and greater poverty.

What is happening in the current crisis—and what is different?

There is some hope that human development indicators have not deteriorated as much during the current crisis as in previous crises. Because the current economic crisis did not reach most developing countries until 2009, it is too early to arrive at a definitive conclusion on its impact. However, rapid surveys and dis-

FIGURE 2.7   **Despite intense fiscal pressures, Mexico's federal funding for health and education is set to rise in 2009–10**

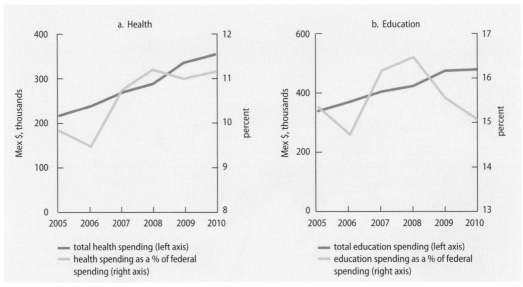

Source: Mexican government statistics.
Note: Data are estimated for 2005–07, approved for 2008 and 2009, and projected for 2010.

cussions with governments have yielded preliminary evidence showing that social spending may have held up better during this crisis than in previous ones and that there has been more reliance on social safety nets. Moreover, policy regimes in developing countries had improved considerably before the crisis, so governments might have had greater success in protecting their populations from the worst effects of the growth downturn.

Social spending held up in some regions

Impacts on social sector budgets for 2008–10 varied by country circumstances, specifically according to how the global downturn affected the economy and public revenues and whether countries prepared for a possible contraction.

Latin America and the Caribbean. In Latin America social spending has remained strong, partly because of the relatively modest size and scope of the downturn in much of the region and partly because of efforts to protect social spending. Some of the larger economies (such as Brazil and Chile) instituted social measures aimed at financing temporary

employment and transfers to vulnerable populations. Chile's Social and Economic Stabilization Fund provided a countercyclical boost in spending, blunting the effect of the external shock.[13] In Mexico, the severe contraction imposed intense fiscal pressure, but education and health funding are nevertheless set to rise 10 percent in 2009–10 (although spending on education is expected to fall sharply as a share of total government expenditures; figure 2.7). El Salvador is not cutting education funding despite the severe recession, but health spending is expected to fall from 3.4 percent to 3.0 percent of GDP, largely because of reductions in the Social Security Institute's health expenditures.[14]

Eastern Europe and Central Asia. Because Eastern Europe was the hardest hit of emerging market regions, countries there were the first to cut all areas of public spending. Neither education nor health has necessarily been spared. However, aggregate trends in social spending alone are not an accurate indication of the impact of the crisis on outcomes. Some countries have directed spending reductions to sectors with overcapacity, thus improving

BOX 2.3   Crises as opportunities for reform

Crises can present opportunities to achieve reforms in social sector spending that will improve efficiency and welfare over the long term. The current crisis sharply reduced GDP in many countries in Eastern Europe—by more than 15 percent in Latvia—making it impossible to sustain social spending at precrisis rates. Across-the-board cuts in education spending would have greatly impaired access to education, with dismal implications for the quality of the workforce and long-term productivity. Instead, Latvia and Romania directed spending cuts at areas of overcapacity, through reforms that previously had been blocked by political opposition.

Latvia is using the stringencies imposed by the crisis to right-size its teaching force. By shifting teacher financing and management to local governments and providing them with per capita student transfers, the central government is tackling overcapacity. This reform translates into an average 34 percent reduction in the number of teachers and a 45 percent reduction in teacher salaries. In the health sector, the government has embraced sources of efficiency gain through restructuring. Drawing on diagnostic work with the World Bank, the government has eliminated excess hospital beds, invigorated outpatient care,

and prioritized the financing of effective health care procedures by adjusting the list of ineligible health services. The crisis made all these needed reforms possible, and policy research informed strategic investment decisions, largely avoiding across-the-board reductions or random cuts in social programs.

Romania responded to declining school enrollments and tighter budgets by substantially reducing education personnel (teaching and nonteaching positions) in 2009 and by curtailing supplements to base salaries. Some 18,000 teachers (6 percent) were laid off following adjustments in teaching norms and substantial cuts in the funds allocated to each county. The Ministry of Education, Research, and Innovation cut 15,000 additional public positions, consolidated schools, and reduced the number of scholarships for higher education. The staffing reductions will allow much needed adjustments to class size and better alignment of teachers, students, and budgets. The ministry also has reduced the number of fee-paying students, which shrinks the overall resource envelope for higher education at the same time that budgets are being cut.

Source: Lewis and Verhoeven 2010.

long-term efficiency and limiting the welfare impact of expenditure cuts (box 2.3).

By contrast, some countries had increased planned spending heading into the crisis, necessitating painful reductions as government resources dwindled. In Moldova, education sector employees make up about 60 percent of public employees. During two election campaigns in 2009, the outgoing government raised teachers' salaries 25–30 percent to align entry-level salaries with average national earnings but made no commensurate increases in class size or shifts in teaching loads. Other measures were contemplated that would further raise real wages if implemented. The new government's challenge will be to implement corresponding increases in class size or shifts in teaching loads. Ukraine adopted a social standards law in November 2009 that calls for

large increases in minimum wages and social standards throughout 2009–10. Public wages were adjusted accordingly at the end of 2009, but the subsequent wage hikes have not taken place because of challenges to the law in the Constitutional Court. More recently, the Cabinet of Ministers approved salary top-ups for secondary, vocational, and university teachers (equivalent to 20 percent of base salary). With no budget yet in place for 2010, budget operations are being executed on the basis of an operational budget that limits current monthly spending to one-twelfth of the 2009 appropriations.

One indicator of the impact of the crisis on health expenditures is that pharmaceutical spending (a good proxy for health sector spending) has declined sharply in Eastern Europe. World demand continued to rise from

FIGURE 2.8   **Average pharmaceutical expenditures fall in Eastern Europe, especially in the Baltics, before beginning to rise again**

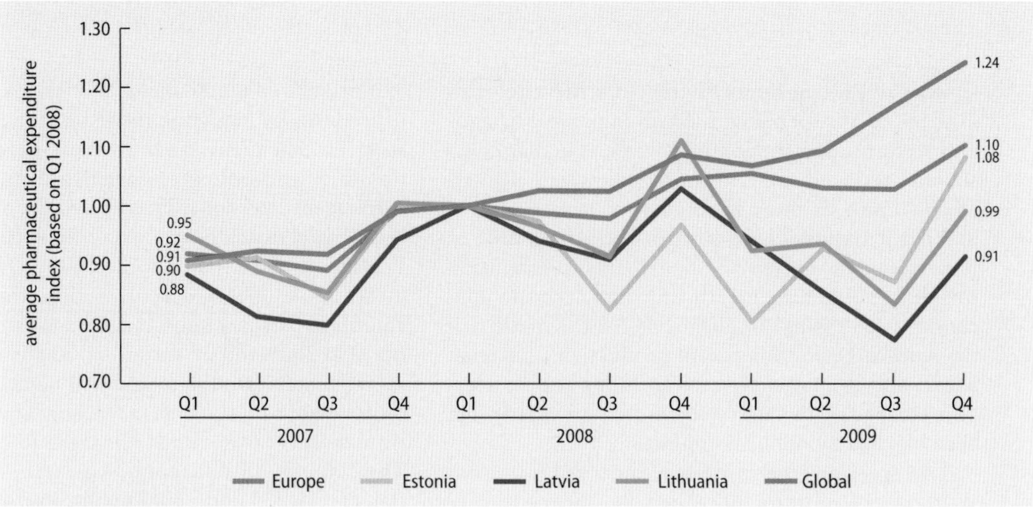

Source: Laing and Buysse 2010.

the first quarter of 2007 through the last quarter of 2009 (with the first quarter of 2008 considered the last quarter before the worldwide financial crisis), but expenditures in Eastern Europe declined in the first quarter of 2009 before beginning to rise again. The decline was most dramatic in the Baltics, with Latvia cutting back pharmaceutical expenditures by more than 25 percent between the fourth quarter of 2008 and the end of 2009 (figure 2.8).

Information on social sector spending in other regions is extremely limited, but scattered information provides some examples. For example, 16 of 19 country programs initiated and monitored by the International Monetary Fund and implemented with the World Bank in 2008–09 budgeted higher social spending for 2009; 9 of those countries were in Sub-Saharan Africa (Burundi, Republic of Congo, Côte d'Ivoire, Liberia, Malawi, Mali, Niger, Togo, and Zambia.[15] Several African countries with poverty reduction strategies have protected funding for social sectors. Some countries with adequate fiscal space (Kenya and Nigeria) have protected capital expenditure, mainly for infrastructure. But there are also examples of forced contractions in social spending. Countries with precrisis fiscal and debt problems (such as Ethiopia and Ghana)

had to undertake fiscal tightening.[16] The effects of the crisis have been relatively modest in East Asia, although qualitative evidence in six countries suggests that informal work has surged and that migrants have returned home temporarily, lowering overall income and reducing households' ability to pay for social services. Households have responded by transferring children from private to public schools and reducing food consumption, although parents contend that they have tried to shield children's nutrition.[17]

Spending to combat HIV/AIDS (human immunodeficiency virus/acquired immune deficiency syndrome) is a special case. Big increases in funding have made HIV/AIDS one of the most important items on the development agenda. Funding for HIV/AIDs programs during the current crisis has been largely sustained. The uptick in donor spending in 2008–09, when the economic crisis was accelerating in donor countries, is encouraging. The Global Fund to Fight AIDS, Tuberculosis, and Malaria (the Global Fund) disburses quickly once allocations are decided, but recipient country spending has been slow. So the issue is sluggish disbursement and a new concern for efficiency of resource use (see annex 2.2 for a detailed discussion). Almost 40 percent of the Global

FIGURE 2.9   **Undisbursed HIV/AIDS grants from the Global Fund to Fight AIDS, Tuberculosis, and Malaria, Rounds 1–7**

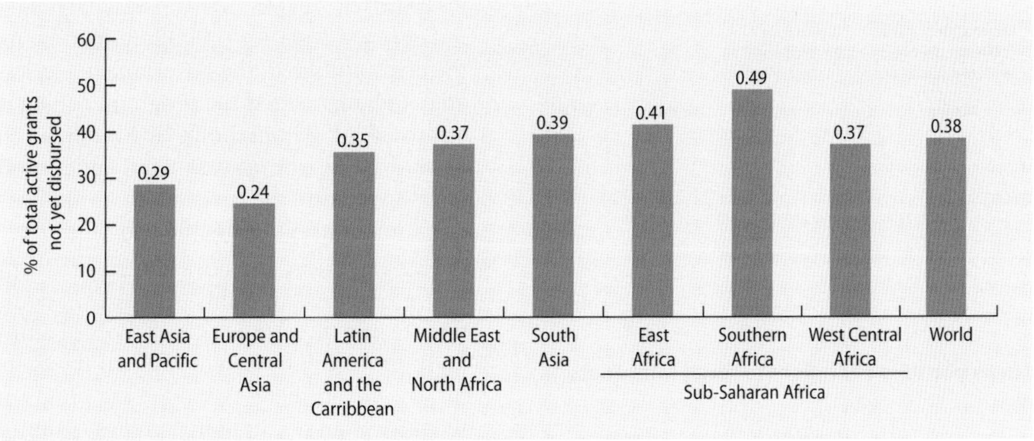

Source: Lewis 2009.

Fund resources remain undisbursed, a possible source of additional resources if there is a shortfall or delay in funding flows. Almost half the allocations to Sub-Saharan Africa are undisbursed (figure 2.9). The $900 million allocated in late 2009 under Round 9 is also unlikely to have been disbursed yet.[18]

The recent buildup of social safety nets

Safety nets have been a crucial part of the response to the crises in the hardest-hit countries. Many countries that responded most effectively already had safety nets, which governments were able to quickly modify and expand. Evidence on the distribution of safety net programs shows that programs vary considerably across regions. For example, food-based programs are more common in Africa than in other regions (figure 2.10).[19]

Another sign of the importance of safety nets in responding to the crisis is the dramatic increase in World Bank lending for safety nets after the crisis struck—topping $3 billion in 29 countries in fiscal 2009. Elevated activity is expected to continue in 2010–11, particularly in low-income countries and fragile and postconflict settings (table 2.4).[20] The regional distribution of lending activities reflects the dominance of Latin America, which had the greatest number of effective safety nets in

place before the crisis that could be scaled up (table 2.5). Less funding to Africa and South Asia reflects the fact that existing safety nets were smaller and less able to absorb funds. Thus, where capacity was in place, lending could be quickly leveraged. Some countries have been reluctant to introduce safety net programs because of the costs involved, although reducing across-the-board subsidies

FIGURE 2.10   **Food-related safety net programs are more common in Africa than elsewhere**

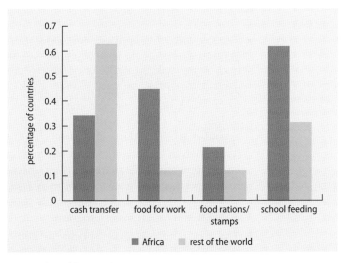

Source: Wodon and Zaman 2010.
Note: Based on a March 2008 survey of 120 World Bank country teams.

TABLE 2.4 World Bank lending for safety nets before and since the food, fuel, and financial crises, 2006–11
US$ billions

Period	International Bank for Reconstruction and Development Loans	International Development Association Loans	Grants	Total
2006–08 (precrisis)	0.57	0.62	0.03	1.23
2009–11 (postcrisis)	4.48	1.38	0.03	5.89

Source: Data from the World Bank Business Warehouse project database for projects classified as social safety nets (54).
Note: Data do not include interventions funded under the Global Force Crisis Response Program.

TABLE 2.5 World Bank portfolio allocations to social safety nets, by region, 2009–10

Region	Amount (US$ millions)	Number of projects
Latin America and the Caribbean	2,917	21
Europe and Central Asia	926	21
East Asia and Pacific	618	9
Sub-Saharan Africa	574	23
South Asia	373	9
Middle East and North Africa	19	8

Source: Data from the World Bank Business Warehouse project database for projects classified as social safety nets.
Note: Data do not include interventions funded under the Global Force Crisis Response Program.

while augmenting targeted safety nets can help reduce poverty without a significant drain on revenues (box 2.4).

Several countries expanded existing or planned safety net programs in response to the crisis.

- *The Republic of Yemen*, hard hit by the global food crisis (drought has forced imports of more than three-quarters of its food), expanded safety net programs with support from the World Bank and the European Union. The cash-for-work program was extended to an additional 22,000–26,000 households in communities most affected by higher food prices, the share of cash transfers to the poorest beneficiaries was increased, and 40,000–50,000 more households were added to the cash transfer program.

- The food and fuel price shocks in 2008, the global economic crisis, and a recent typhoon have sharply increased poverty in *the Philippines*. The government had begun

planning for a pilot conditional cash transfer program (Pantawid Pamilyang Pilipino Program, or 4Ps) in 2007. It was launched in February 2008 for 6,000 households. As the crisis unfolded, the government accelerated and augmented the program, rolling it out to 376,000 households by March 2009. In mid-2009, the government announced plans to expand the program to as many as 1 million households by the end of 2009.

- Before the crisis, the government of *Brazil* had established a highly successful conditional cash transfer program, Bolsa Familia, to protect poor families. When the crisis hit, the government expanded the program to more than 12 million families, using a new methodology of poverty maps and an income volatility index, and raised the benefit level 10 percent to compensate for higher food prices. The program was expanded in regions where poverty reduction has been slow—in urban municipalities and in the mid-south region—reaching 1.3 million families in those areas in 2009. Another 600,000 families within poverty belts or in specific vulnerable groups are expected to join the program in 2010.

- In response to the food, fuel, and financial crises, *Chile* announced in April 2009 the strengthening of multiple safety net programs. Family allowances of about $45 were distributed to 1.4 million families, including all families in the Chile Solidario program (around 300,000), families in the Family Subsidy program, and families whose monthly income was $555 or less. In all, some 5.6 million people in the bottom 40 percent of the income distribution will benefit, at a cost of $62 million.

- The government of *Ethiopia* established the Productive Safety Net Program in 2005 to pay for participation in labor-intensive public works and provide direct support to elderly or incapacitated household members. The program has been expanded since, providing immediate assistance to 1.5 million households when the food and fuel crises struck, and providing additional transfers to 4.4 million people as the crisis deepened. Evaluations find a positive impact on use of

BOX 2.4   Using safety nets to lower the cost of reducing poverty

Some countries have hesitated to establish safety nets because of the cost. Safety net expenditures in developing countries average 1–2 percent of GDP. Expenditures on programs that are to scale and that have been evaluated as delivering significant positive impacts, such as Mexico's Oportunidades and Brazil's Bolsa Familia, average 0.4 percent of GDP. Ethiopia's largest safety net program, the Productive Safety Net, costs about 1.7 percent of GDP.

The introduction of a well-targeted safety net can provide the political space to reduce or eliminate expensive and poorly targeted general price subsidies, freeing up resources to fund the targeted programs. The potential for such reallocations is considerable because many countries have large and costly price subsidies. More than a third of countries recently surveyed by the International Monetary Fund raised subsidies an average of 1 percent of GDP in response to higher food and fuel prices. Several examples illustrate successful country experiences in switching from universal subsidies to targeted safety nets.

In the late 1990s *Mexico* progressively moved funding from price and in-kind food subsidy programs to the Oportunidades conditional cash transfer program, probably the most positively evaluated safety net program in a developing country. Fifteen years later, as food prices rose dramatically, the government was able to protect the poor by issuing a one-time top-up benefit to those already in the pro-

gram. The response was easy, fast, and affordable because of the earlier investment.

In 2005 *Indonesia* cut its fuel subsidies by $10 billion, using a quarter of the released funds for a targeted cash transfer that more than compensated poor recipients for their losses. Another quarter of the savings went to basic health and education programs for the poor.

In 2008 *the Philippines* found itself short of effective policy instruments to protect the poor against escalating rice prices. A key part of its multipronged response package, which cost some 1.3 percent of GDP, was a program of loosely targeted and distortive rice subsidies. Realizing that this approach is expensive and regressive, the government is working on better safety net options—unifying administration under a new umbrella program, scaling up a proxy means test for targeting households, reforming and expanding the school feeding program, and accelerating rollout and scaling up of a conditional cash transfer program.

Source: Data for 87 countries for which data on safety net expenditure were available from World Bank public expenditure reviews, safety net assessments, social protection strategy notes, and other studies. Data coverage is low for Sub-Saharan Africa, where government spending on safety nets may be low, but where donor funding may compensate considerably. See also IMF 2005.

health services and caloric availability and reductions in negative coping behaviors, such as child labor and withdrawal from school.

Safety nets are important not only in cushioning the effects of the crisis but also as part of a broader poverty reduction strategy interacting with social insurance; health, education, and financial services; the provision of utilities and roads; and other policies for reducing poverty and managing risk. Many challenges remain, however. Safety net programs in low-income countries are often slight and fragmented and cover only a small percentage of poor and vulnerable populations. There are real concerns over whether they are affordable

and administratively feasible or desirable, considering the negative incentives they might create. Thus a part of policy reforms in developing countries should be understanding what kind of safety net program best serves various social assistance activities, what the implementation challenges are, and how to develop programs for maximum effectiveness.[21]

Informal safety nets and remittances

Households manage risk through informal safety nets (such as crop diversification), informal savings and credit associations, burial societies, labor exchange arrangements, migration, and emigration. Informal safety nets are generally more effective against idiosyncratic

MAP 2.2 **An infant in a developing country is ten times more likely to die than a newborn in a developed country**

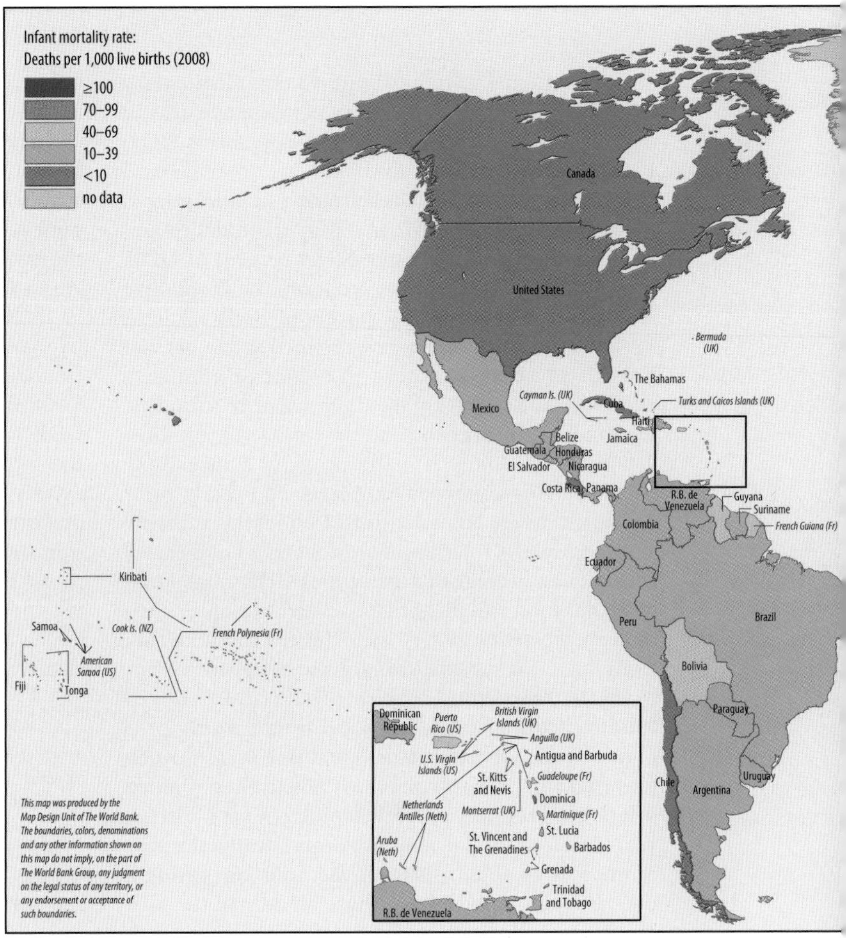

Infant mortality rate:
Deaths per 1,000 live births (2008)

≥100
70–99
40–69
10–39
<10
no data

Source: World Development Indicators.

shocks that affect only one or a few households than against systemic shocks that affect whole communities. Thus it is not clear whether such risk-mitigation strategies were any more effective during the recent crisis than they had been previously.

Remittances have played an important countercyclical role in crises that affected individual developing countries.[22] Because remittances are unaffected by idiosyncratic shocks or even local or national systemic shocks, they are an important part of the household safety net for many poor households. More than tripling since earlier in the past decade, remittances constitute important monetary flows

to developing countries; they reached $338 billion in 2008 before the full impact of the financial crisis was felt. [23]

The global nature of the current crisis has likely reduced the support that remittances can provide. Remittance flows to developing countries are estimated at $317 billion for 2009, a 6.1 percent decline from 2008. Analysis of the first nine months of 2009 shows that the financial crisis has affected remittance flows unevenly. Remittances to Latin America and the Caribbean have suffered large declines (down 13 percent in Mexico, for example), mainly because of the early effects of the crisis in the United States and Spain. Similarly, remit-

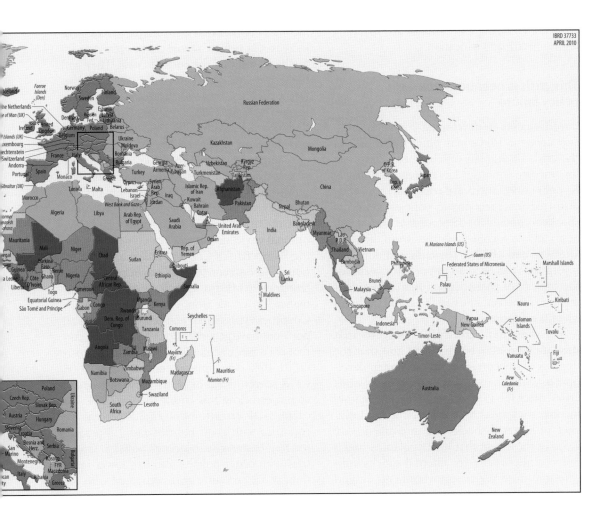

tances to the Middle East and North Africa have declined more than expected, plunging 20 percent in the Arab Republic of Egypt and Morocco. The situation is even more serious in Europe and Central Asia, where many countries are among the top recipients of migrant remittances as a percentage of GDP. Tajikistan, where remittances make up 50 percent of GDP, experienced a decline of more than 30 percent in the first half of 2009. Many other countries in the region have experienced similar declines. By contrast, in Sub-Saharan Africa the decline has been less steep and in some countries, such as Uganda, flows have increased. In South Asia, remittances have remained strong, even increasing in some cases (up 24 percent in Pakistan, 16 percent in Bangladesh, and 13 percent in Nepal). In East Asia and the Pacific, flows were also stronger than expected (up 4 percent in the Philippines).

A study by the World Food Programme found that families that rely on remittances from abroad were among groups most affected by the current financial crisis.[24] In Armenia, where remittances make up 20 percent of GDP and are the main source of income for 25 percent of households, the impact was felt immediately, with remittances slumping 30 percent in the first quarter of 2009. In Nicaragua, a country highly dependent on remittances and vulnerable to economic downturns in the U.S. economy, food consumption patterns are changing and families are spending less on health and education.

This crisis is not about domestic policy failure

Improvements in developing countries' policies since the 1990s may blunt the impact of the crisis on human development. Crises in low-income countries have often been driven by poor governance, civil conflicts, or severely distorted macroeconomic policies. (Internal shocks accounted for 89 percent of output volatility in low-income countries from the early 1960s to mid-1990s.) The failure of domestic institutions has been an important reason for the severity of past crises on human development, macroeconomic variables, and the quality of institutions.

But some indirect evidence suggests that this situation may be changing and that the impacts of the current crisis on human development could be less severe than in previous crises. Since the 1990s output volatility in low-income countries has lessened, and the influence of external shocks has intensified (box 2.5). To the extent that lower volatility and a reduced importance for internal shocks indicate improved policies, governments should be better placed to protect their people from the most severe impacts of the crisis.

Assessing the quality of policies and institutions over time is difficult, but external evidence does indicate an improvement in many developing countries since the 1990s. Inflation rates have declined substantially, fewer countries have unsustainable debt positions, more countries have access to private capital markets and have attracted substantial foreign direct investment, financial intermediation has risen as a share of output, trade barriers have come down, black market exchange rate premiums have shrunk, and civil conflict has subsided in many countries. The pace of policy reform has varied. In Latin America weak currencies, banking sectors, and poor fiscal management tended to amplify the impact of past crises, whereas improvements in the policy and institutional framework have cushioned the impact

of the current crisis—a first for the region. By contrast, in Europe and Central Asia middle-income countries that were unable to halt large increases in private sector credit growth were the hardest hit by the current crisis. They had higher growth rates before the crisis but also larger declines after the crisis, and on balance they experienced lower average growth rates than countries with more modest increases in private sector credit growth.

Comparing the economic performance of countries according to the quality of their policies and institutions shows the importance of policy reform. Although there is no perfect measure of the quality of the policy and institutional environment in developing countries, the World Bank's Country Policy and Institutional Assessment (CPIA) provides a consistent framework for assessing country performance (on a scale from 1, worst, to 6, best).[25] Countries with better policies or initial fiscal positions have generally done better in the current crisis (see chapter 3). And before the crisis (2001–07), developing countries with 2008 CPIA scores of 3.2 or better grew faster than countries below this cutoff (figure 2.11). Per capita GDP growth averaged 3.9 percent for countries with good policies and 1.9 percent for fragile states with poorer policies. Countries with better policies also had lower inflation, at 5.2 percent a year, compared with 6.6 percent for countries with poorer policies. The pattern is the same for countries in Sub-Saharan Africa.[26] Before the current crisis, countries with better policies tended to have better outcomes for MDG indicators such as under-five mortality, gender equality in primary and secondary education, primary school completion, and access to an improved water source. Several empirical studies also showed that better policies and institutions improve the marginal contribution of growth to progress on human development indicators.[27]

The impact of the current crisis is still worrisome

The crisis has generated predictions of rising mortality rates and closed schools as governments reduce services in response to falling output and public revenues. These fears are

BOX 2.5   Are external shocks becoming more important than internal shocks for developing countries?

Historically, developing countries have endured greater macroeconomic volatility than have industrial economies. A simple look at the data shows that output volatility (measured as the standard deviation of real GDP growth) has been two to three times greater in developing countries than in industrial countries in the last 20 years.

Because developing countries are highly dependent on primary commodities and foreign capital and have greater exposure to natural disasters, policy makers often blame external shocks, such as terms-of-trade fluctuations, natural disasters, and aid volatility, for countries' uneven macroeconomic performance.

However, research shows that external shocks account for only a small fraction of the variance in real per capita GDP in low- and middle-income countries. Among low-income countries, external shocks, including terms-of-trade fluctuations, global economic growth, international financial conditions, natural disasters, and aid volatility, explain no more than 11 percent of output volatility. The 89 percent residual is probably related to internal conditions, such as the volatility of macroeconomic management. Among middle-income countries, external shocks account for about 20 percent of output volatility.

Since the 1990s, however, many developing countries have undergone structural transformations that may have calmed internal volatility and increased the importance of external factors. Research shows that external shocks have become more important for developing countries in several regions during the past two decades (see the figure at the right). In African countries this shift has resulted not from an increase in the volatility of external shocks, or in countries' vulnerability to them, but rather from the taming of internal sources of volatility. In these countries—among the most volatile—standard indicators of democratic accountability, economic man-

External shocks have become more important since the 1990s

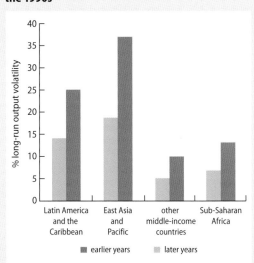

agement, and control of corruption have improved since the early 1990s. Many middle-income countries have also strengthened their fiscal position by reducing deficits and accumulating reserves; tamed inflation through independent central banks; and promoted local bond markets after the Asian and Russian financial crises of 1997–98.

Source: Raddatz 2007, 2008a, 2008b.
Note: The data for Latin America and the Caribbean, East Asia and Pacific, and other middle-income countries correspond to 1974–1985 (earlier) and 1986–2004 (later). The bars for Africa correspond to 1963–89 (earlier) and 1990–2003 (later). External shocks explaining long-run output volatility include the state of the world business cycle, international financial conditions, terms of trade, natural disasters, and aid flows.

grounded in the experience of past crises, when, as noted earlier and in box 2.6, poverty, hunger, health outcomes, and access to education deteriorated sharply. Despite policy improvements and efforts to sustain social spending and ramp up safety nets, preliminary indications of the impact of the crisis on human

development point to serious problems. An important reason is the size of the shock—it is the largest global downturn since the Great Depression. Thus while developing countries' efforts have been important in mitigating the impact of the crisis, the crisis nevertheless has been a severe setback to poverty reduction.

FIGURE 2.11 **Economic performance and MDG outcomes are better with good policy**

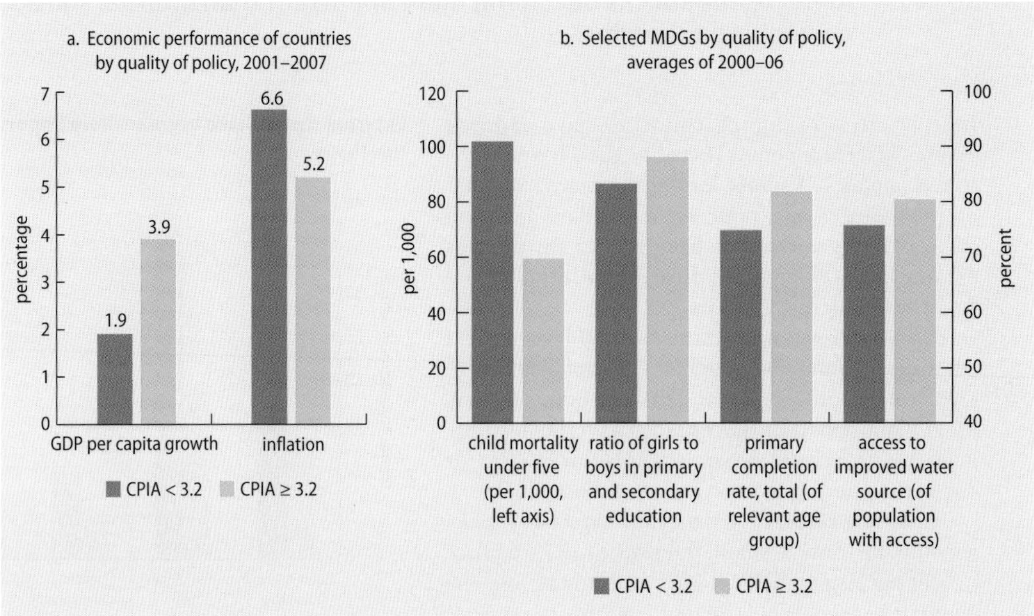

Source: World Bank staff calculations.
Note: CPIA is the World Bank's Country Policy and Institutional Assessment framework for assessing country performance; ratings range from 1 (worst) to 6 (best). Countries with a CPIA score of 3.2 or better have better policies than countries that score under 3.2.

The recent deterioration in human development indicators began with the food and fuel price shocks of 2007. In some countries food prices almost doubled with no adjustment in earnings.[28] In Mozambique incomes were almost halved and food consumption fell by a fifth; children's weight for age and body mass index were reduced with no change in height for age, indicating that the price rise has seriously compromised nutrition. The effects spilled over into the efficacy of HIV/AIDS treatment, with lower-income households showing slower improvements than households with higher incomes and better access to adequate nutrition, which reinforces the beneficial effects of antiretroviral therapies. Recent analysis finds that the 2008 global food price spike may have increased global undernourishment by some 6.8 percent, or 63 million people, relative to 2007.[29] Moreover, the analysis shows that the sharp slowdown in global growth in 2009 might have contributed to 41 million more undernourished people compared with the number there would have been without the economic crisis.

The problems were compounded by the global economic crisis. A poverty monitoring study of 13 countries suggests that in countries like the Central African Republic and Ghana, parents were forced to take their children out of school and that in other countries they scrambled to finance their children's continuing attendance.[30] In Serbia, Roma children dropped out of school because of a lack of clean clothes and soap. Poor households in Cambodia and the Philippines reported cutting overall consumption in response to income shocks to protect children's school attendance. Although little information exists on the differential impact of the crisis on women and men, recent surveys of East Asia do not show that women have been disproportionately affected (box 2.7).

Recent surveys in Armenia, Montenegro, and Turkey give a sense of how declines in income induced by the crisis are reducing household consumption.

BOX 2.6   Human development suffered severely during crises in developing countries

Household studies from past crises suggest that the impact on human development can be serious. In the lowest-income countries, poverty rises, people eat lower-quality food, school enrollments fall, health care use drops, and infant mortality rises. Even modest reductions in food consumption for children between birth and age two can have lasting deleterious effects on cognitive and physical development. In South Africa and Zimbabwe, the nutritional deprivation of young children led to lower height for age and shorter stature in adulthood.

Analysis of the effects of downturns on infant mortality in Sub-Saharan Africa shows that a 1-percent reduction in per capita GDP is associated with a rise in the infant mortality rate of 0.34–0.48 per 1,000 live births, or 34–39 percent of the average annual change in the infant mortality rate. Infant girls are more likely than boys to die during downturns, and both rural and less educated women are at higher risk of losing their infants.

For middle-income countries the picture is less consistent. In Latin America school attendance has increased during crises, possibly because children are not needed for economic activity, but infant mortality appears to have risen. In Indonesia the crisis of the late 1990s had little measurable impact on schooling or health, possibly because the country was better off and perhaps because education and health services were better protected. But the impacts of recession are far more severe for child health than for education, even in middle-income countries.

Source: Wodon and Zaman 2010; Ferreira and Schady 2009; Dinkelman 2008; Alderman, Hoddinott, and Kinsey 2006; and Gottret and others 2009.

Food consumption in Armenian households has fallen 41 percent, and health care spending is down 47 percent. Some 50–60 percent of households in the four lowest income quintiles have cut back on health care services and drug purchases. Household reductions in food consumption are inversely related to income, with 20 percent of the wealthiest households cutting back (noteworthy in itself) and more than 55 percent of the poorest 20 percent doing so. Even bigger cuts are seen in spending on entertainment and expensive foods. There is some evidence that these cutbacks have helped protect education spending.

In Montenegro unemployment figures suggest that cutbacks affect almost a quarter of households. Safety nets cover only 18 percent of the poorest 20 percent of households, and informal private transfers are disappearing as remittances shrink and informal safety nets unravel. Private investments in education, health insurance, and preventive health care have fallen, reducing resilience to further shocks (figure 2.12). Overall, 9 percent of households reduced preventive care visits, but 25 percent of poor households did, and the same percentage of poor households canceled health insurance. In education the wealthiest households cut back the most—20 percent compared with 11 percent for the lowest-income households.

In Turkey, the poorest households have experienced the largest reductions in wages and self-employment income. Some 91 percent of the poorest 20 percent of households lost income, but even the wealthiest 20 percent experienced some income loss. Safety nets cover only 20 percent of the poorest households, requiring the rest to sell assets, draw down savings, and find other informal sources of support. Among the poorest households, 75 percent have reduced children's food consumption, 29 percent have curtailed health care use, and 14 percent have cut back on education spending. Even middle-class households have trimmed spending, especially in education.

The data now available on the impact of the crisis on human development are still much too limited to draw any conclusions on the overall impact. But there is certainly evidence of suffering as a result of the severe global

BOX 2.7   **Gender differences in impacts of the crisis: Evidence from East Asia**

Although the effects of the crisis have clear gender dimensions, it is not clear that women in East Asia have been disproportionately affected. Gender-specific impacts would be expected because of the gender division of labor in the labor market and in the home, gender disparities in access to productive resources, and gender dimensions of household resource allocation. But precise impacts are unclear because they depend on multiple factors including the size of the shock, the economic structure of the country, the nature of government responses, and the speed of economic recovery. Identifying the gender impacts of the crisis is thus an empirical issue.

Empirical analysis is complicated by a lack of data. High-frequency data on the social impacts of the crisis is generally not available, and the lack is particularly intense for gender-disaggregated data. Thus multifaceted approaches are needed, such as

rapid qualitative assessments (including focus group discussions), ex ante simulations using precrisis household survey data, analysis of labor force survey data as available, and triangulation across data sources.

Data indicate that unemployment in East Asia has barely changed during the crisis, for men or women, but that women's participation has tended to rise. In some countries unemployment has fallen more for women than for men, while increases in labor force participation have been more marked for women than for men (see the figures below), particularly in poorer countries, where female labor has shifted from unpaid work to self-employment. Both quantitative and qualitative data indicate longer working hours as men and women take on additional jobs to compensate for falling earnings from primary jobs.

Labor force participation by gender in selected East Asian countries, 2007–09

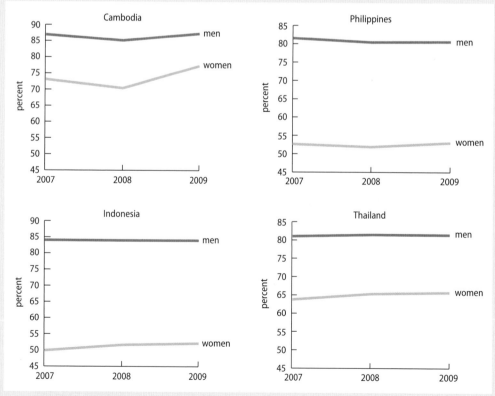

Source: World Bank staff calculations.

BOX 2.7   (continued)

The impact of labor market shocks is driven by several factors, of which gender is only one. Both quantitative and qualitative findings suggest that simple interpretations of labor market data may be misleading. As an example, well-publicized data show layoffs from enterprises producing garments and other products for export to shrinking markets, sectors where female employment tends to dominate. Less well-documented is the contraction in hours and earnings in sectors serving domestic markets, where purchasing power is closely linked to the health of the export sector. These sectors may be dominated by men. Women laid off from formal sector work may be better off than men facing highly restricted earnings in informal sector jobs. Quantitative and qualitative evidence from Cambodia suggests that more male workers in the construction sector have been affected by the crisis than female workers in the garment sector. Moreover, male construction workers are more likely to be poor and have fewer economic fallbacks than female garment workers.

There is no consistent cross-country pattern in differences in hours of paid work by gender. In some countries, such as Cambodia, both men and women have greatly increased their hours of paid work. In other countries, such as Indonesia, women have overtaken men in hours of paid work in the past two years. And in other countries, such as the Philippines, men and women appear to work the same number of paid hours. However, focus group discussions suggest

that women's total work burden (paid plus unpaid domestic work) has increased over the past year. In urban Thailand, women explain that their time on unpaid domestic work has declined a little but not enough to offset rising labor market hours. In rural Cambodia and the Philippines, research teams noted that an increased dependence on common property resources, including firewood, has increased women's time on domestic chores.

The welfare impacts of the crisis, by gender, also appear to be nuanced. Microsimulations of the poverty impacts of the crisis in Cambodia suggest that male-headed households were more affected in urban areas, while female-headed households were more affected in rural areas (see the figure below). For urban male-headed households, this finding likely reflects the impacts of the crisis on male jobs in construction and tourism. The effects for rural female-headed households appear to reflect the loss of remittance income in addition to more direct crisis impacts on household earnings. Findings from rapid assessments in rural Cambodia indicate that female-headed households commonly cut back consumption sharply and increased their indebtedness to cope with loss of income as remittances from urban areas fell. Male migrant workers—often migrant spouses—reported being unable to return home as often as before because of increased transportation costs and reduced earnings, meaning less male labor on the farm during peak periods.

Impacts of the global financial crisis on male- and female-headed households in Cambodia

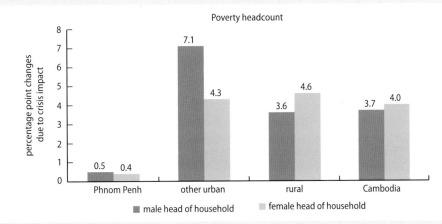

Source: Bruni and others forthcoming.

FIGURE 2.12   **Spending cutbacks in crisis-affected households are jeopardizing future welfare in Armenia, Montenegro, and Turkey**

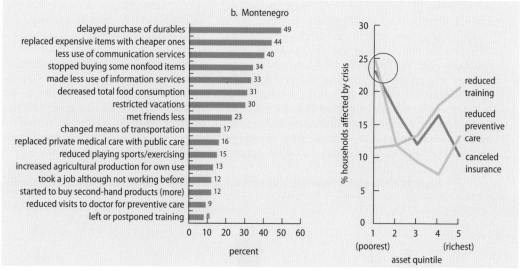

a. Armenia

less use of entertainment — 64
fewer meetings with friends — 59
cheaper instead of more expensive food items — 58
reduced or stopped visits to healthcare centers — 47
reduced or stopped buying medicines — 41
reduced amount of food consumed — 41
stopped buying some nonfood items — 40
increased use of public transport or walking — 33
work odd jobs — 13
increased own food production — 12
migration for work — 10
bought second-hand items — 9
other mitigation measures — 3
withdrew or postponed admission to school — 2

0 10 20 30 40 50 60 70
percent

percent — stopped visiting health centers / stopped buying medicine / decreased food consumption
1 (poorest) 2 3 4 5 (richest)
income quintile

Source: Armenia Integrated Living Conditions Survey 2009. See Ersado, forthcoming.

b. Montenegro

delayed purchase of durables — 49
replaced expensive items with cheaper ones — 44
less use of communication services — 40
stopped buying some nonfood items — 34
made less use of information services — 33
decreased total food consumption — 31
restricted vacations — 30
met friends less — 23
changed means of transportation — 17
replaced private medical care with public care — 16
reduced playing sports/exercising — 15
increased agricultural production for own use — 13
took a job although not working before — 12
started to buy second-hand products (more) — 12
reduced visits to doctor for preventive care — 9
left or postponed training — 8

0 10 20 30 40 50 60
percent

% households affected by crisis — reduced training / reduced preventive care / canceled insurance
1 (poorest) 2 3 4 5 (richest)
asset quintile

Source: Montenegro Crisis Monitoring Survey 2009. See Hirshleifer and Azam, forthcoming.

downturn. Even if the deterioration in human development indicators has not been as severe as in previous crises (as speculated above), the human suffering will be considerable.

Although many people in middle-income countries are above the threshold of the poverty MDG, they are also the hardest hit by adjustments in wage earnings and employment.[31]

Early evidence in 41 middle-income countries indicates that the impact on the labor market has been severe, especially in wealthier middle-income countries of the Europe and Central Asia region. Although the number of jobs and their growth have been negatively affected, the impact has been mostly on the quality and earnings of employment (figure 2.13).

FIGURE 2.12 (continued)

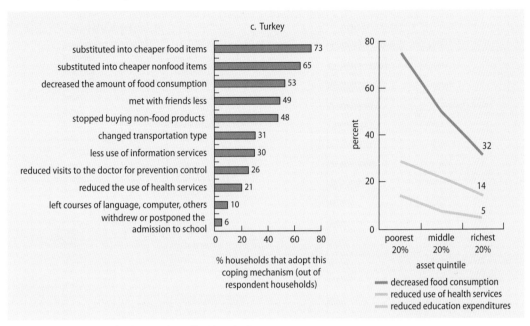

Source: TEPAV, UNICEF, and World Bank 2009; Turkey Welfare Monitoring Survey.

- Three-quarters of the labor market adjustment stems from slower growth in take-home pay, only one-quarter from less job creation.
- Earnings in most middle-income countries are falling mainly because people are working fewer hours. Hourly wages have changed little except in Europe and Central Asia, where they have declined.
- The crisis severely affected labor markets, with few countries spared. It caused a sharp slowdown in wage-bill growth, which fell by an average of 8 percentage points. The exceptions were Argentina, China, and the former Yugoslav Republic of Macedonia, where wage-bill growth accelerated.
- Employment has shifted away from industrial employment into services, where jobs tend to be of lower productivity and offer lower wages.
- For a given decline in GDP growth, the labor market impact was more severe in upper-middle-income countries and in countries with fixed exchange rates.

The large impact in Europe and Central Asia resulted mainly from sharp drops in GDP growth. But fixed exchange rates worsen the labor market impact. On average, countries with fixed currency regimes witnessed a decline in employment of 1.7 percentage points, compared with only 0.4 in countries with floating rates. The slowdown in the wage-bill growth was also less severe for the countries with moderate levels of development.

The nature of recent labor market adjustments in these countries suggests that effective policy packages should also focus on supporting earnings and household income, not just generating employment. Responses taken in developed European countries—such as partial unemployment insurance, expanded cash transfers to poor workers, and temporary wage subsidies—may be priority interventions in those countries where hours and earnings adjustments dominated.

Conclusions

Because crises have very negative effects on human development indicators, good policies and institutions are essential in developing countries to avert downturns in the first

FIGURE 2.13   **The crisis sharply reduced wage earnings in middle-income countries**

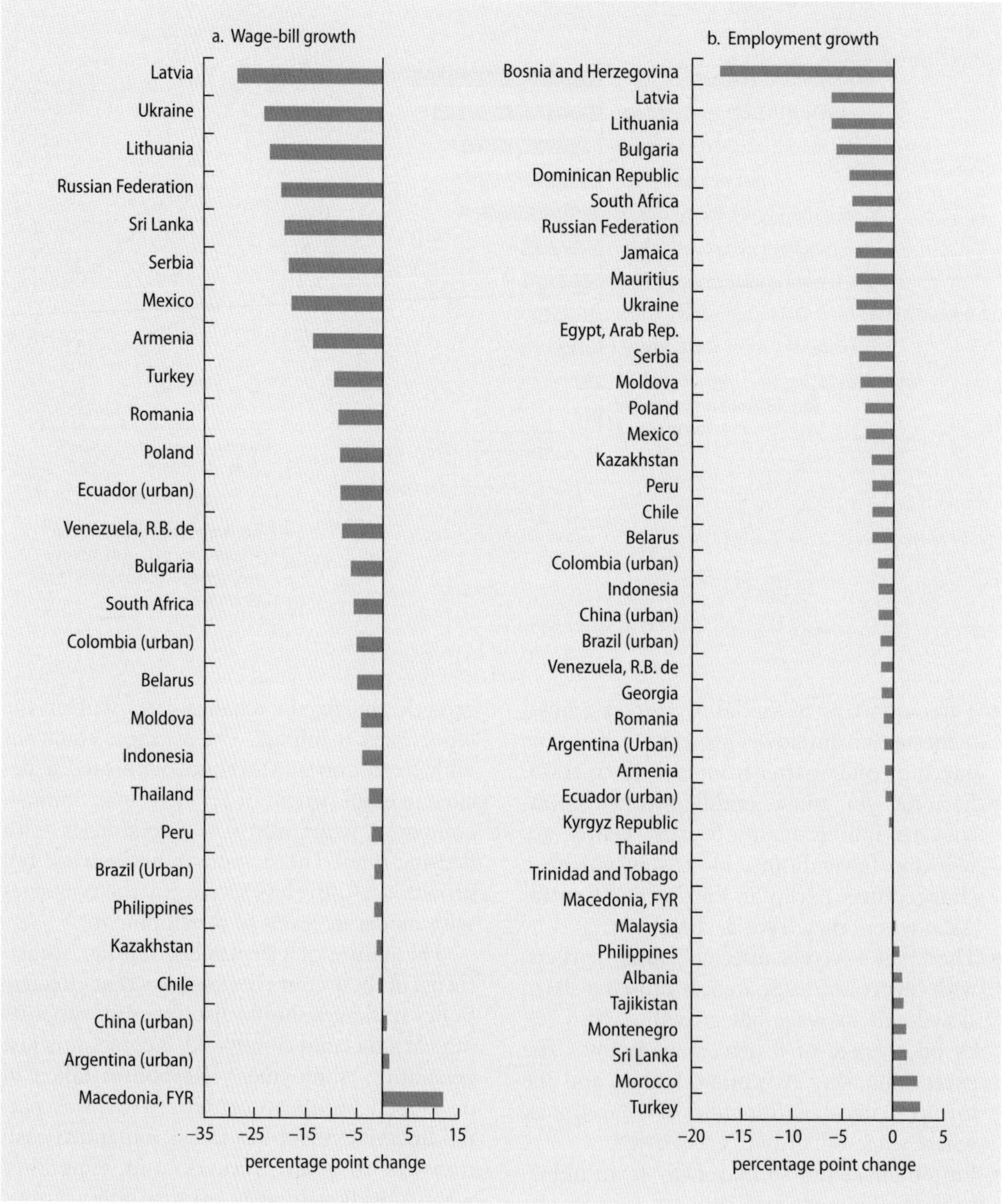

a. Wage-bill growth

b. Employment growth

percentage point change

Source: Khanna, Newhouse, and Paci, forthcoming.

place, dampen their negative effects when they do occur, and reduce the potential for reversal of reforms. Policy failures, particularly in low-income countries affected by corruption and violent conflict, have been a major reason for the sharp deterioration in human development indicators in past crises.

There are some reasons for hope that the current crisis may be different for low-income countries. A great deal of social spending has been protected so far. Policies and institutions had improved before the crisis. And external shocks, not domestic policy failures, were the main causes of the current crisis. Nonetheless, the impacts on progress toward the MDGs are already worrisome.

While recovery of the global economy appears to be stronger than expected, small reductions in growth could still have lasting negative consequences for poverty and human development. The contraction was so sharp that a long period of strong growth is needed to undo the damage inflicted on development outcomes. The next chapter examines the growth outlook and macroeconomic challenges, including the fiscal tensions created by temporary stimulus measures and protection of social spending.

Annex 2.1 Human and economic indicators during growth cycles

This annex presents more detailed information on the asymmetric impact of growth decelerations on human development indicators, macroeconomic variables, and institutional quality in developing countries. Tables 2A.– –2A.3 show the average level of each indicator during growth accelerations, growth decelerations, other periods, and across all times. Tests for differences in the means of these variables between growth accelerations, decelerations, and all country-year observations show that they are all statistically significant at the 1 percent level.

The conclusion that these indicators tend to deteriorate more in bad times than they improve in good times does not stem from composition effects. It is important to examine these effects because the averages for each period (accelerations, decelerations, and other) do not reflect the same number of observations or equal participation by different income groups—there are more accelerations than decelerations, and low-income countries have greater representation in the sample means during bad times because of the higher frequency of decelerations in these countries (see main text). Because

TABLE 2A.1   **Differences between sample averages: Human development and gender indicators**

Variable	Growth acceleration	Growth deceleration	Otherwise (not in acceleration or deceleration)	Sample period
Life expectancy at birth, women (years)	72.1	63.4	69.4	70.0
Life expectancy at birth, men (years)	66.6	58.1	64.2	64.7
Life expectancy at birth, total (years)	69.2	60.7	66.7	67.3
Infant mortality rate (per 1000 live births)	27.7	59.7	39.9	35.9
Child mortality under-five rate (per 1,000)	42.4	96.3	59.3	54.3
Primary completion rate, girls (% of relevant age group)	83.2	49.8	76.3	78.6
Primary completion rate, boys (% of relevant age group)	84.5	59.6	80.2	81.4
Primary completion rate, total (% of relevant age group)	84.4	54.8	78.1	80.2
Ratio of girls to boys, primary enrollment	95.6	86.1	92.5	93.6
Ratio of girls to boys, secondary enrollment	96.9	80.7	94.8	95.3
Ratio of women to men, tertiary enrollment	107.3	65.1	106.2	105.4

Source: World Bank staff calculations based on data from World Development Indicators.
Note: Tests for differences in the means of these variables between growth accelerations, decelerations, and all country-year observations show that they are all statistically significant at the 1-percent level.

TABLE 2A.2   **Differences between sample averages: Sub-Saharan Africa**

Variable	Growth acceleration	Growth deceleration	Otherwise (not in acceleration or deceleration)	Sample period
Life expectancy at birth, girls (years)	55.2	52.3	53.4	54.0
Life expectancy at birth, boys (years)	52.2	48.9	50.1	50.8
Life expectancy at birth, total (years)	53.7	50.5	51.7	52.3
Infant mortality rate (per 1.000 live births)	80.7	106.6	97.3	91.9
Child mortality under-five rate (per 1,000)	133.5	161.3	154.3	146.2
Primary completion rate, girls (% of relevant age group)	55.1	33.8	42.1	47.4
Primary completion rate, boys (% of relevant age group)	59.8	48.4	50.9	55.0
Primary completion rate, total (% of relevant age group)	57.4	41.0	46.5	51.1
Ratio of girls to boys, primary enrollment	89.7	77.9	82.4	85.0
Ratio of girls to boys, secondary enrollment	82.3	63.6	76.1	77.7
Ratio of women to men, tertiary enrollment	60.2	32.5	64.4	58.7

Source: World Bank staff calculations based on data from World Development Indicators.
Note: Tests for differences in the means of these variables between growth accelerations, decelerations, and all country-year observations show that they are all statistically significant at the 1-percent level.

TABLE 2A.3   **Differences between sample averages: Economic and institutional indicators**

Variable	Growth acceleration	Growth deceleration	Otherwise (not in acceleration or deceleration)	Sample period
Final consumption (% GDP)	81.45	88.78	83.74	83.30
Government consumption (% GDP)	15.41	16.68	16.61	16.10
Gross capital formation (% GDP)	23.76	18.57	23.35	23.10
Gross domestic savings (% GDP)	18.58	11.23	16.26	16.70
Gross fixed capital formation private sector (% GDP)	16.35	10.43	13.75	14.40
Imports (% GDP)	45.80	37.45	43.85	44.10
Exports (% GDP)	40.43	30.05	36.52	37.60
Trade (% GDP)	86.23	67.50	80.37	81.70
Foreign direct investment. net inflows (% GDP)	4.48	2.07	3.56	4.00
Private capital flows, total (% GDP)	2.99	1.40	2.03	2.40
CPI inflation (%)	14.88	251.32	37.90	43.90
Institutions (−2.5 to 2.5)				
Political stability	−0.16	−0.65	0.03	−0.10
Voice and accountability	−0.07	−0.47	0.09	−0.02
Regulatory framework	−0.03	−0.82	0.15	0.01
Rule of law	−0.14	−0.90	0.12	−0.07
Government effectiveness	−0.04	−0.96	0.14	0.00
Frequency of conflicts (Sub-Saharan Africa)	0.13	0.23		
Aid to poor countries (Sub-Saharan Africa)				
ODA (% GDP)	13.80	12.10		
ODA per capita (US$)	69.50	41.80		

Source: World Bank staff calculations. Data for Sub-Saharan Africa from Arbache, Go, and Page (2008). Indicators on institutions are from the World Bank Institute's Worldwide Governance Indicators database, which relies on 33 sources, including surveys of enterprises and citizens, and expert polls, gathered from 30 organizations around the world; they each range from −2.5 (worst) to 2.5 (best).
Note: Tests for differences in the means of these variables between growth accelerations, decelerations, and all country-year observations show that they are all statistically significant at the 1 percent level. ODA = official development assistance.

human development indicators are generally lower in low-income than in middle-income countries, the greater frequency of low-income country observations drops the averages for decelerations, which could account for the asymmetric relationship. However, even after controlling for the sample composition effects by comparing the sample means of countries undergoing growth decelerations and accelera-

tions with their own sample means when not in growth decelerations (the column "otherwise" in the three tables), decelerations still have an asymmetric effect.[32] Furthermore, the averages for periods not in acceleration or deceleration (normal times) are close to the averages for the entire sample (the last column in each table), providing evidence that the economic cycles are being correctly identified.

Annex 2.2   The special case of HIV/AIDS spending

Large increases in funding have made HIV/AIDS (human immunodeficiency virus/acquired immune deficiency syndrome) one of the most important items on the development agenda. In less than a decade the international community has mobilized talent and financing to address HIV/AIDS with new institutions and long-term financial commitments to countries suffering from an established and growing epidemic. This attention and financing have produced data that outstrip that available for health care generally, allowing a more thorough examination of trends. The 2008–09 recession is the first global crisis to affect international support for HIV/AIDS spending, and the responses are instructive.

Roughly 33 million people have HIV/AIDS, but only a third of those are on antiretroviral therapy that will extend their life. There is no cure for AIDS. Discontinuities in treatment create resistance to the basic ("first line") antiretroviral treatment, which can lead to broader drug resistance. The alternative "second line" treatment is 10–20 times more expensive. Thus antiretroviral therapy is central to meeting the MDG 6A to combat HIV/AIDS. Equally important to treating those who have contracted HIV/AIDS is strengthening prevention—the only way to stem the pandemic.

Likely short-term effects of the crisis

Funding for HIV/AIDS has risen sharply over the past decade. During 2001–05, aid commitments for HIV/AIDS programs rose almost 30 percent ($4.75 billion), fueled by the establishment of the Global Fund and by philanthropic efforts by the Clinton Foundation, the Bill & Melinda Gates Foundation, and others. New sources of funding have come onstream since 2005 with the U.S. President's Emergency Plan for AIDS Relief (PEPFAR) and UNITAID, which disburses much of its resources through the Global Fund.

In 2008 public and private entities allocated $15.8 billion for global HIV/AIDS programs, $6.7 billion of it from bilateral and European Union contributions.[33] Pledges to the Global Fund rose from $2.5 billion in 2007 to $3.0 billion in 2008, and then declined to $2.6 billion in 2009. In the last funding cycle (Round 9), demand from countries also fell.[34] The U.S. PEPFAR program increased its contributions from $4.5 billion in 2007 to $6.2 billion in 2008 and has subsequently increased its annual budgets. The 2010 fiscal year allocation is just shy of $7 billion, suggesting that U.S. support is continuing.[35]

Fueled largely by increased donor resources, public health spending in the high-prevalence countries of eastern and southern Africa has risen rapidly in absolute and per capita terms (see map 1.2). As a share of GDP, the increases have gone disproportionately to people with HIV/AIDS.[36] Government spending in countries that formerly had high HIV/AIDS prevalence, like Brazil and Thailand, has financed both prevention and treatment. Other countries, such as Ghana, have legally binding commitments ensuring treatment for people with AIDS.

Of 77 countries recently surveyed, most indicated that they had adequate funding from governments, donors, and other sources to finance their current HIV/AIDS programs, but they raised concerns about the future.[37] Prevention was identified as the likely victim if funding fell. A further concern was the increased cost of imported drugs and supplies resulting from currency devaluations in some countries.[38] The Clinton Foundation recently obtained price concessions from manufacturers that could compensate for the exchange rate penalty.

The impact of the current downturn is not entirely clear, but the uptick in donor spending in 2008 and 2009, when the economic crisis was accelerating in donor countries, is encouraging. The Global Fund disburses quickly once allocations are decided, but recipient country spending has been slow. Almost 40 percent of the Global Fund resources remain undisbursed, a possible source of additional resources if there is a shortfall or delay in funding flows. Almost half the allocations to Sub-Saharan Africa are undisbursed (see figure 2.9). The $900 million allocated in late 2009 under Round 9 is unlikely to have been disbursed yet.[39]

Although countries may appear to have "adequate" funding for HIV/AIDS, the situation is more nuanced: Some donor funds cannot be applied flexibly, leaving countries with important gaps even when they appear to be highly funded in aggregate terms. This is where the unearmarked flexibility of the International Development Association becomes critical.

The highest-prevalence regions of Africa receive the bulk of external funding (figure 2A.1), but financing per current AIDS patient paints a different picture (figure 2A.2). Although there is a general correlation between the number of patients and funding across countries, financing available for each patient still lags in the highest-prevalence regions of Africa.

Greater efficiency is imperative because the agenda has broadened and the pace of infection has not slowed. Targeting high-risk groups and improving management and efficiency in delivery can raise quality and efficiency. The Bahamas plan greater use of generic drugs, better patient adherence to treatment protocols, and a sharper focus on the cost effectiveness of purchases and service delivery. While not costless, such improvements will boost effectiveness and reduce waste, which are equivalent to reducing costs. They also raise the quality of services including health care services.

And what of prevention?

Most international resources are earmarked for treatment. But the only way to stem the need for treatment and save lives is to expand prevention initiatives.

An in-depth evaluation of the U.S. PEPFAR program concluded that it reduced deaths by 5 percent but had no effect on prevention.[40] The recent multimillion dollar evaluation of the Global Fund noted the organization's neglect of prevention.[41] A more modest assessment of the programs of the World Bank, Global Fund, and PEPFAR also concluded that prevention was the weak link.[42] The challenge is that for every HIV/AIDS patient placed on treatment, two or three newly infected people will need treatment for life.[43]

Countries that have prioritized prevention—Brazil, Rwanda, and Thailand—have seen prevalence decline or remain low, despite spiraling levels in the early 1990s. Prevalence rates in these countries contrast with those in Botswana and Swaziland, which have struggled to initiate effective prevention programs as prevalence reached epidemic proportions. The long-term trends reflect lack of attention to prevention 5–10 years ago. But current prevention efforts remain inadequate, and the crisis could further curtail such efforts if constrained

FIGURE 2A.1   **Projected Global Fund to Fight AIDS, Tuberculosis, and Malaria and U.S. PEPFAR HIV/AIDS grants as of April 2009**

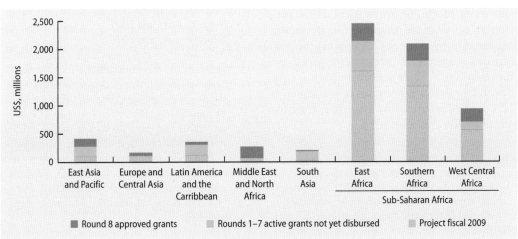

Source: Lewis 2009.

FIGURE 2A.2   Projected Global Fund to Fight AIDS, Tuberculosis, and Malaria and U.S. PEPFAR HIV/AIDS grants per AIDS patient as of April 2009

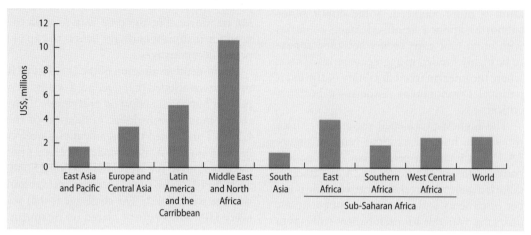

Source: Lewis 2009.

budgets force cutbacks in prevention. It is a dynamic problem; new infections occur daily, and so a continuous, uninterrupted response is required. It may take 7–10 years for a person to become symptomatic, but even people without evident symptoms can pass on the virus and infect others. Actions now will reduce the rate at which people with the virus can pass it on, underscoring the importance of antiretroviral therapy as a prevention measure.

The Bill & Melinda Gates Foundation and others are financing extensive efforts in prevention technologies, and considerable ongoing research is exploring how to discourage risky behaviors. But equal attention must go to actually promoting behavior change and rolling out promising approaches where prevention lags. Because programs for prevention are dwarfed by those for treatment, the balance deserves some recalibration to spare those not yet infected. While neither simple nor easy, a push to expand prevention is warranted if there is to be progress on Goal 6A: halting the spread of HIV/AIDS by 2015.

Notes

1. Arbache, Go, and Korman 2010. Although the aggregate figures show girls' education is affected by growth cycles, there is still a lack of microstudies that show girls are disproportionately more likely to be pulled out of

schools during covariate shocks. However, some of these more adverse effects may be occurring in conflict or disastrous situations with institutional breakdowns so that microstudies are not available.

2. For the entire sample of developing countries, 47 percent of the 4,415 country-year observations are classified as growth accelerations while 11 percent are classified as growth decelerations. The remaining 42 percent of observations are for years in which countries experienced neither growth acceleration nor deceleration episodes.

3. To some extent this pattern may be endogenous, because average income per capita tends to rise in countries with more frequent growth accelerations and fall in countries with more frequent collapses.

4. Arbache and Page 2007.

5. Arbache and Page 2010.

6. Arbache, Go, and Page 2008. The inflation figure would have been higher had Zimbabwe been included; it was excluded from the analysis because of missing data for other variables.

7. The analysis is taken from Lewis and Verhoeven (2010) and relies on data from the International Monetary Fund (IMF), the World Bank, United National Educational, Scientific, and Cultural Organization (UNESCO, education spending), and the World Health Organization (WHO) National Health Accounts (health spending).

8. The absence of a consistent time series in education spending data required the integra-

tion of data from UNESCO, the IMF, and the World Bank. This is in contrast to the consistent and much higher quality data from WHO National Health Accounts.

9. Dang, Knack, and Rogers 2009.
10. Gottret and others 2009.
11. Grosh and others 2008.
12. Blomquist and others 2002.
13. Ferreira and Schady 2009.
14. World Bank forthcoming.
15. IMF 2009.
16. High-Level Seminar on Africa Fiscal Policy for Growth in Light of the Global Crisis, Maputo, December 2009, sponsored by the World Bank and various governments.
17. Turk 2009.
18. Global Fund (www.theglobalfund.org/programs/search/?lang=en&round=9).
19. Wodon and Zaman 2010.
20. These data do not include safety net and nutrition interventions under the World Bank's Global Food Crisis Response Program, which has funded an estimated $380 million for safety net interventions in 21 countries, including grant funding for small, targeted projects in 17 low-income IDA-eligible countries (totaling $95 million).
21. See Grosh and others (2008) for detailed discussion of the design and implementation challenges of effective safety nets.
22. World Bank 2006.
23. Ratha, Mohapatra, and Silwayl 2009.
24. World Food Programme 2009. The study analyzes 126 countries and focuses on five case studies.
25. Countries are rated according to performance in 16 areas grouped into four clusters: economic management, structural policies, policies for social inclusion and equity, and public sector management and institutions.
26. Arbache, Go, and Page 2008.
27. See, for examples, Wagstaff and Claeson (2004); Rajkumar and Swaroop (2008); and Filmer and Pritchettt (1999).
28. de Walque and others 2010.
29. Tiwari and Zaman 2010.
30. Turk and Mason 2009.
31. Khanna, Newhouse, and Paci, forthcoming.
32. See Arbache, Go, and Korman (2010) for more discussion.
33. The figure includes international and domestic philanthropic contributions, World Bank financing, government expenditures, and household spending, but it excludes other multilateral and private sector funding.

34. The Global Fund has initiated a new $2.6 billion funding window for the next two years, which it estimates is insufficient. These requirements are not addressed here because the focus is on financing HIV/AIDS prevention and treatment.
35. Kaiser Family Foundation (2009) and www.KKF.org provide updates of spending.
36. Case and Paxson 2009.
37. A survey of UNAIDS and WHO country offices by the World Bank, UNAIDS, and WHO (2009) asked about possible issues as the crisis evolved and the likely impact on HIV/AIDS programs over the next 6–12 months.
38. UNAIDS 2009.
39. Global Fund (www.theglobalfund.org/programs/search/?lang=en&round=9).
40. Bendavid and Bhattacharya 2009.
41. Sherry, Mookherji, and Ryan 2009.
42. Ooman, Bernstein, and Rosenzweig 2007.
43. Revenga and others 2006.

References

Alderman, H., J. Hoddinott, and B. Kinsey. 2006. "Long-Term Consequences of Early Childhood Malnutrition." *Oxford Economic Papers* 58 (3): 450–74.

Arbache, J., D. Go, and V. Korman. 2010. "Does Growth Volatility Matter for Development Outcomes? An Empirical Investigation Using Global Data." Background paper for *Global Monitoring Report 2010*. World Bank, Washington, DC.

Arbache, J., D. Go, and J. Page, eds. 2008. *Africa at a Turning Point? Growth, Aid, and External Shocks.* Washington DC: World Bank.

Arbache, J., and J. Page. 2007. "More Growth or Fewer Collapses? A New Look at Long-Run Growth in Sub-Saharan Africa." Policy Research Working Paper 4384. World Bank, Washington, DC.

———. 2010. "How Fragile Is Africa's Recent Growth?" *Journal of African Economies* 19 (1): 1–25.

Bendavid, E., and J. Bhattacharya. 2009. "The President's Emergency Plan for AIDS Relief in Africa: An Evaluation of Outcomes." *Annals of Internal Medicine* 150 (10): 688–95.

Blomquist, J., J. P. Cordoba, M. Verhoeven, C. Bouillon, and P. Moser. 2002. "Social Safety Nets in Response to Crisis: Lessons and Guidelines from Asia and Latin America." In *Towards Asia's Sustainable Development: The Role of Social Protection,* pp. 297–332. Paris: OECD.

Bruni, A. Mason, Pabon, and C. Turk. Forthcoming. "Gender Dimensions of the Crisis in East Asia and the Pacific." World Bank, Washington, DC.

Case, A., and C. Paxson. 2006. "Stature and Status: Height, Ability, and Labor Market Outcomes." NBER Working Paper 12466. National Bureau of Economic Research, Cambridge, MA.

Dang, H., S. Knack, and H. Rogers. 2009. "International Aid and Financial Crises in Donor Countries." Policy Research Working Paper 5162. World Bank, Washington, DC.

De Walque, D., H. Kazianga, M. Over, and J. Vaillant. 2010. "The Impact of the Food Crisis on HIV/AIDS Treatment and Health Outcomes in Mozambique." Paper presented at World Bank Development Economics Development Research Group Workshop, January 13, Washington, DC.

Dinkelman, T. 2008. "The Long-Term Effects of Being Born in a Drought: Evidence from the Cape Area Panel Study 2002–06." Paper presented at the Northeastern Universities Development Consortium Conference, November 8–9, Boston University, Boston, MA.

Ersado, L. Forthcoming. "The Global Economic Crisis in Armenia: Policy Responses and Household Coping Strategies." World Bank Working Paper. Washington, DC.

Ferreira, F., and N. Schady. 2009. "Aggregate Economic Shocks, Child Schooling, and Child Health." *World Bank Research Observer* 24 (2): 141–81.

Filmer, D., and L. Pritchett. 1999. "The Impact of Public Spending on Health: Does Money Matter?" *Social Science and Medicine* 49 (10): 1309–23.

Gottret, P., V. Gupta, S. Sparkes, A. Tandon, V. Moran, and P. Berman. 2009. "Protecting Pro-poor Health Services during Financial Crises: Lessons from Experience." In *Innovations in Health System Finance in Developing and Transitional Economies: Advances in Health Economics and Health Services Research,* vol. 21, ed. Dov Chernichovsky and Kara Hanson. Bingley, U.K.: Emerald Group Publishing.

Grosh, M., C. del Ninno, C. Tesliuc, and A. Ouerghi. 2008. *For Protection and Promotion: The Design and Implementation of Effective Safety Nets.* Washington, DC: World Bank.

Hausmann, R., L. Pritchett, and D. Rodrik. 2005. "Growth Accelerations." *Journal of Economic Growth* 10 (4): 303–29.

Hirshleifer, S., and M. Azam. Forthcoming. "Impact of the Economic Crisis in Montenegro: Evidence from Crisis Response Survey." ECSHD Working Paper. World Bank, Europe and Central Asia Region, Human Development Unit, Washington, DC.

IMF (International Monetary Fund). 2005. "Petroleum Product Subsidies: Costly, Inequitable, and Rising." IMF Staff Position Note SPN/10/05. Washington, DC.

———. 2009. "Fiscal Policy in Sub-Saharan Africa in Response to the Impact of the Global Crisis." IMF Staff Position Note SPN/09/10. Washington, DC.

Kaiser Family Foundation. 2009. Updates of various information, including "The U.S. President's Emergency Plan for AIDS Relief (PEPFAR)," Fact sheet on U.S. Global Health Policy. Washington, DC (November) (www.kff.org).

Khanna, G., D. Newhouse, and P. Paci. Forthcoming. "Fewer Jobs or Smaller Paychecks? Labor Market Impacts of the Financial Crisis in Middle Income Countries." World Bank, Washington, DC.

Laing, R., and I. Buysse. 2010. "Impact of the Global Crisis on the Global Pharmaceutical Sector." Paper presented (January 7) at University of Utrecht, the Netherlands.

Lewis, M.. 2009. "Likely Impacts of the Crisis on HIV/AIDS Programs." Paper presented to HIV/AIDS Economics Reference Group Meeting, April 21, Washington, DC.

Lewis, M., and M. Verhoeven. 2010. "Financial Crises and Social Spending: The Impact of the 2007–2009 Crisis." Background paper for *Global Monitoring Report 2010.* World Bank, Washington, DC.

Ooman, N., M. Bernstein, and S. Rosenzweig. 2007. *Following the Funding for HIV/AIDS.* Washington, DC: Center for Global Development.

Pritchett, L. 2000. "Understanding Patterns of Economic Growth: Searching for Hills among Plateaus, Mountains, and Plains." *World Bank Economic Review* 14: 221–50.

Raddatz, C. 2007. "Are External Shocks Responsible for the Instability of Output in Low-Income Countries?" *Journal of Development Economics* 84 (1): 155–87.

———. 2008a. "External Shocks and Macroeconomic Volatility in Latin America." World Bank, Washington, DC.

———. 2008b. "Have External Shocks Become More Important for Output Fluctuations in African Countries?" In *Africa at a Turning Point? Growth, Aid, and External Shocks,* ed. J. Arbache, D. Go, and J. Page. Washington, DC: World Bank.

Rajkumar, A., and V. Swaroop. 2008. "Public Spending and Outcomes: Does Governance Matter?" *Journal of Development Economics* 86 (1): 96–111.

Ratha, D., S. Mohapatra, and A. Silwal. 2009. "Migration and Remittance Trends 2009: A Better-than-Expected Outcome So Far, but Significant Risks Ahead." Migration and Development Brief 11. World Bank, Washington, DC.

Revenga, A., M. Over, E. Masaki, W. Peerapatanapokin, J. Gold, V. T. Sathien, and S. Thanprasertsuk. 2006. "The Economics of Effective AIDS Treatment Evaluating Policy Options for Thailand." World Bank, Washington, DC.

Sabarwal, S., N. Sinha, and M. Buvinic. 2009. "Aggregate Economic Shocks and Gender Differences: A Review of the Evidence." World Bank, Washington, DC.

Sherry, J., S. Mookherji, and L. Ryan. 2009. *The Five-Year Evaluation of the Global Fund to Fight AIDS, Tuberculosis and Malaria.* Calverton, MD: ICF Macro International.

TEPAV (Economic Policy Research Foundation), UNICEF (United Nations Children's Fund), and World Bank. 2009. "The Economic Crisis and the Welfare of Families: Results from the Five Urban Centers in Turkey." Ankara.

Tiwari, S., and H. Zaman. 2010. "The Impact of Economic Shocks on Global Undernourishment." Policy Research Working Paper 5215. World Bank, Washington, DC.

Turk, C. 2009. "Rapid, Qualitative Assessments of the Impacts of the Economic Crisis: Overview of Findings from Eight Countries." Internal discussion paper. World Bank Social Development Department, Washington, DC.

Turk, C., and A. Mason. 2009. "Impacts of the Economic Crisis in East Asia: Findings from Qualitative Monitoring in Five Countries." Paper presented at the 3rd China–ASEAN Forum on Social Development and Poverty Reduction and 4th ASEAN +3 High Level Seminar on Povery Reduction, September 28–30, Hanoi. (www.adb.org/Documents/Events/2009/Poverty-Social-Development/papers.asp).

UNAIDS (Joint United Nations Programme on HIV/AIDS). 2009. "25th Meeting of the UNAIDS Programme Coordinating Board." Geneva (December 8–10).

Wagstaff, A., and M. Claeson. 2004. *Rising to the Challenges: The Millennium Development Goals for Health.* Washington, DC: World Bank.

Wodon, Q., and H. Zaman. 2010. "Higher Food Prices in Sub-Saharan Africa: Poverty Impact and Policy Responses." *World Bank Research Observer* 25 (1): 157–76.

World Bank. 2006. *Global Economic Prospects: Economic Implications of Remittances and Migration.* Washington, DC: World Bank.

———. Forthcoming. "El Salvador Public Expenditure Review." World Bank, Washington, DC.

———. Various years. *World Development Indicators.* Washington, DC: World Bank.

World Food Programme. 2009. "Households Go Hungry As Financial Crisis Bites." Rome (June 11).

3

Growth Outlook and Macroeconomic Challenges in Emerging Economies and Developing Countries

The recovery of the global economy has been more robust than expected. Driven by strong internal demand in many emerging economies and the recovery of global trade, GDP growth in emerging and developing countries is projected to accelerate to 6.3 percent in 2010, from 2.4 percent in 2009. Supporting the economic recovery are expansionary macroeconomic and, especially, fiscal policies. Fiscal deficits in emerging and developing countries, up by almost 3 percent of GDP in 2009, are projected to remain high in 2010. More than in previous crises, many countries sustained spending plans and raised social spending to mitigate the effects of the downturn on the poorest people, although the differences among countries are wide. While financial market conditions for emerging and developing countries are improving and capital flows are returning, international bank financing and foreign direct investment are projected to remain weak in 2010.

Although the short- and medium-term growth prospects for most emerging and developing countries are positive, the question arises: to what extent does the current shock have longer-run implications that could knock countries off their track of solid growth? The question is especially important for low-income countries because poverty is so much more pressing there than in countries with higher incomes. History does not suggest that low-income countries can uniformly escape global shocks without absorbing long-lasting damage to both growth and welfare. In past crises, it has often taken several years for low-income countries to bring growth rates back into positive territory. Even so, the turnaround in low-income countries this time is projected to be faster than in previous crises, thanks to countercyclical fiscal policies and better macroeconomic fundamentals in place at the beginning of the crisis. Commodity exporters are helped by the fairly quick recovery of commodity prices. And financial systems in low-income countries have been less affected by turmoil than those in advanced economies.

The recovery is still vulnerable, however, and the rapid expansion of fiscal deficits and the greater reliance on domestic sources of financing in many countries may not be sustainable. External debt ratios in low-income countries, deteriorating in the short run, should be watched.

Optimal exit policies from policy support should depend on country circumstances.

- *Countries where private demand is still weak should continue supporting activity if policy space is available.*
- *Some countries, however, are facing financing constraints—they cannot delay adjustment. Donors should assist them by following up on commitments to increase aid.*
- *All countries should adopt credible medium-term fiscal adjustment plans to bolster confidence in macroeconomic policies and undertake policy reforms to secure long-term growth.*

The economic recovery

Global economic activity is recovering from the deepest recession since the Second World War, albeit at a moderate pace. According to the International Monetary Fund's (IMF) *World Economic Outlook,* growth of global output will increase to 4.2 percent in 2010, from a decline of 0.6 percent in 2009 (table 3.1). The recovery, supported by improving financial conditions and rising world trade (figure 3.1), is led by emerging economies in Asia, where growth rates now exceed precrisis levels. The prospects for developing countries, including the poorest, are improving as well, although growth rates have not yet recovered to the levels seen in the years before the crisis.[1]

The underlying factors driving the expansion differ from country to country. While economies in Asia and Latin America are bolstered by a recovery of private consump-

tion and investment, private demand growth in emerging Europe is expected to remain sluggish, and several countries remain dependent on exceptional policy stimulus. Commodity exporters are benefiting from firmer global demand for raw materials and higher commodity prices. Even so, the recovery remains vulnerable, most notably in advanced countries and the economies of Eastern Europe, where high unemployment, moderate income growth, and weaker household balances are dampening consumption growth, posing risks for the global outlook. In addition, in the medium–term, growth rates in some groups of countries, especially low-income countries, are not expected to reach the high levels recorded before 2008.

Because the recovery is in an early stage and unemployment rates are still elevated, global inflation has remained low, although some economies, especially in Asia, are showing the first signs of price pressures. Inflation risks are rising in Latin America as well, where output gaps in some countries are closing rapidly.

Commodity prices are recovering

Following the sharp drop in commodity prices in late 2008, prices for most commodities rebounded sharply in 2009 and are continuing their upward trend in 2010 as the global recovery gains momentum (figure 3.2). The increases are helping to mitigate the impact of the crisis on commodity exporters. Food prices are the exception, because good harvests in Sub-Saharan Africa and elsewhere have given an opportunity to rebuild stocks. But food

TABLE 3.1   **Global output**
percent change

Region	2007	2008	2009	Projection	
				2010	2011–13
World output	**5.2**	**3.0**	**−0.6**	**4.2**	**4.4**
Advanced economies	2.8	0.5	−3.2	2.3	2.4
Emerging and developing economies	8.3	6.1	2.4	6.3	6.6
Central and Eastern Europe	5.5	3.0	−3.7	2.8	3.8
Commonwealth of Independent States	8.6	5.5	−6.6	4.0	4.1
Developing Asia	10.6	7.9	6.6	8.7	8.6
Middle East and North Africa	5.6	5.1	2.4	4.5	4.8
Sub-Saharan Africa	6.9	5.5	2.1	4.7	5.7
Western Hemisphere	5.8	4.3	−1.8	4.0	4.2

Source: World Economic Outlook.

FIGURE 3.1   **Short-term indicators of production and trade are recovering**

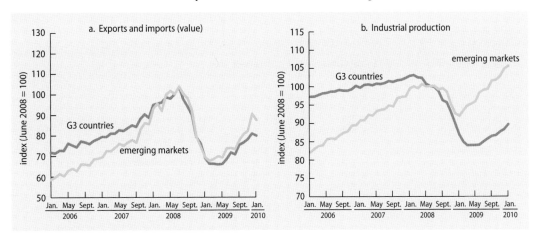

Source: IMF International Financial Statistics; Bloomberg; Haver Analytics; central banks.
Note: Data are weighted by PPP-GDP, 2006.

FIGURE 3.2   **Commodity price indexes rebounded strongly in 2009**

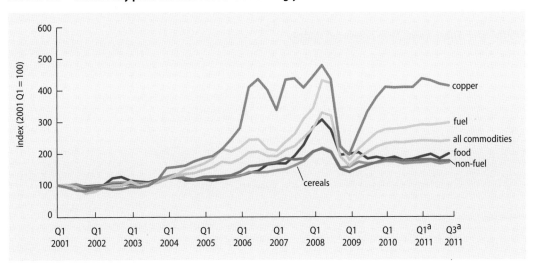

Source: IMF.
Note: Indexes are in U.S. dollars.
a. Projected

and commodity prices, relatively high by historical standards, are projected to remain so, given the prospects for further medium-term demand growth and continuing supply constraints in many sectors.

Financial conditions are improving, but financial flows remain below precrisis levels

Financial market conditions for emerging and developing countries have improved consider-

ably since the onset of the crisis. Bond spreads have declined, stock markets in both emerging and developing countries have recovered sharply, and exchange rate volatility has come down considerably (figures 3.3–3.5). Some borrowers—sovereigns and prime corporations in particular—quickly regained market access following a brief interruption at the end of 2008. Financial market access for subinvestment-grade borrowers in emerging and developing countries has also improved. But access to international bank financing remains

FIGURE 3.3   Bond spreads have declined in emerging markets and developing countries

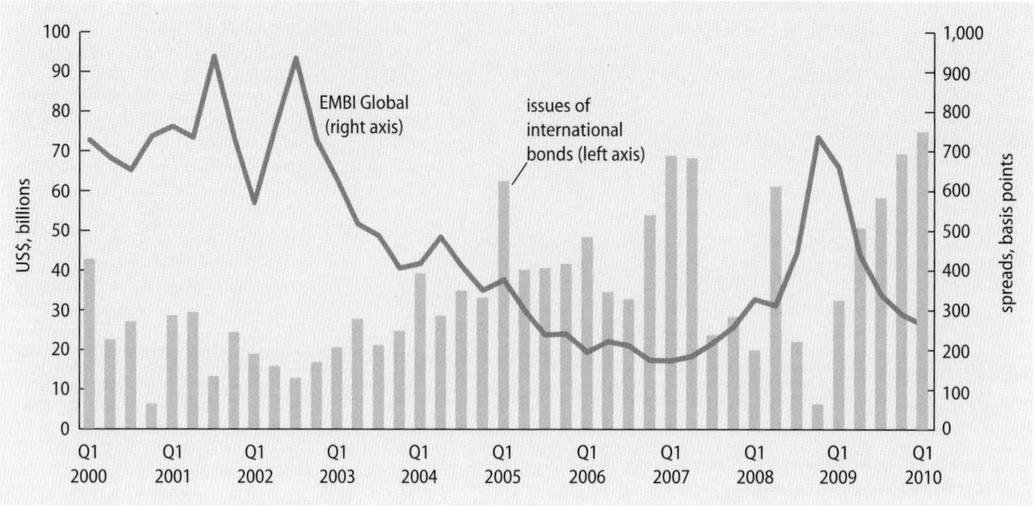

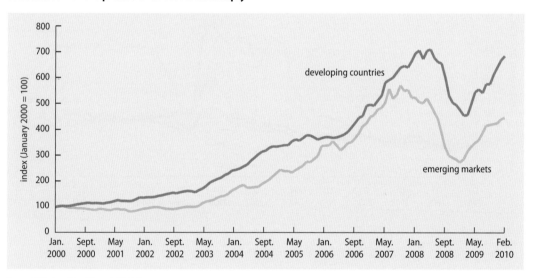

Source: Dealogic; Bloomberg.
Note: Bond issues and spreads as of end-March 2010..

FIGURE 3.4   Share prices have recovered sharply

Source: IMF International Financial Statistics.
Note: Prices are in the local currency.

limited as banks in advanced economies continue deleveraging.

Financial policies, such as improved financial sector regulation and crisis measures, have contributed to avoidance of widespread banking crises in emerging and developing countries. The public response to the financial crisis has been broad, covering several instruments, such as liquidity support, deposit insurance, bank interventions, and recapitalizations. Banking sectors in many emerging economies have also benefited from higher financial market resilience, including less volatility in exchange and interest rates,[2] and therefore have avoided negative dynamics from balance sheet effects.

FIGURE 3.5   **Exchange rates have been less volatile: Daily spot exchange rates**

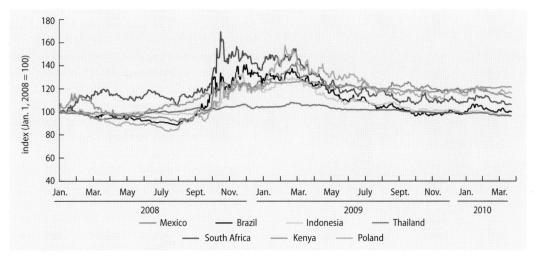

Source: Bloomberg.
Note: Exchange rates are in national currency per U.S. dollars.

FIGURE 3.6   **The cost of external debt financing has come down**

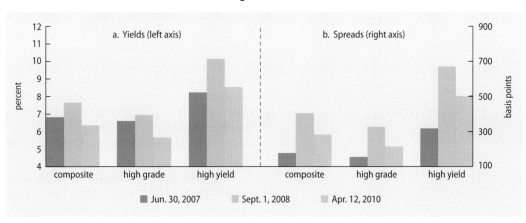

Source: Bloomberg.

Even so, concerns about systemic risks to the solvency of banks and corporations linger. The cost of external debt financing remains elevated in some emerging and developing countries, where spreads on high-yield external corporate bonds are still substantially above those before the collapse of Lehman Brothers in September 2008 (figure 3.6). In addition, some countries in Eastern Europe and the Commonwealth of Independent States (CIS) continue to face uncertainties as a result of high external debt refinancing needs and private sector foreign currency debt. The fallout from the crisis

has also affected bank loan portfolios in many countries, as evidenced by the rising shares of nonperforming loans (figure 3.7).

Despite the general improvement in market conditions, financial flows to emerging and developing countries have not recovered to those seen in the years preceding the financial crisis (table 3.2). In emerging economies, net inflows of foreign financial resources (capital flows and transfers) are not expected to exceed 8.2 percent of GDP this year, down from an average of about 12 percent in 2007–08, mainly because of the sharp drop in bank

FIGURE 3.7 **The share of nonperforming loans to total loans has been rising**

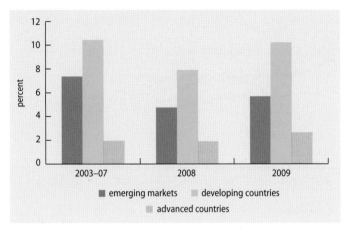

Source: IMF 2009b.

TABLE 3.2 **Net financial flows**

percent of GDP

Flows	2007	2008	2009	2010
Emerging market economies	12.6	11.4	8.7	8.2
Private capital flows, net	8.0	7.0	3.2	3.1
of which: private direct investment	5.4	5.1	3.3	3.3
Private portfolio flows	0.8	−0.5	−0.3	0.1
Private current transfers	4.1	3.7	3.8	3.6
Official capital flows and transfers, net	0.4	0.7	1.7	1.6
Memorandum item:				
Reserve assets	−3.9	−1.6	−2.5	−1.9
Developing countries	14.0	17.7	13.9	13.9
Private capital flows, net	6.6	7.7	5.2	5.3
of which private direct investment	6.6	6.2	4.8	4.7
Private portfolio flows	−0.7	−0.6	−0.4	−0.2
Private current transfers	5.6	5.8	5.2	5.1
Official capital flows and transfers, net	1.8	4.2	3.6	3.5
Memorandum item:				
Reserve assets	−4.0	−2.3	−1.6	−1.0

Source: World Economic Outlook.
Note: Equally weighted.

financing (figure 3.8), especially in Asia and Latin America, and foreign direct investment. Developing countries are facing weak foreign direct investment activity as well, because overcapacity in extractive industries remains considerable despite rising global demand for commodities. Overall, net financial flows are projected to decline to 13.9 percent of GDP in 2010, from 15.9 percent in 2007–08.

The drop in foreign direct investment in developing countries is partly offset by the

recovery of workers' remittances (table 3.3). Although remittances to countries in Latin America, North Africa, and the Middle East were weaker than expected in 2009, they appear to have reached a bottom toward the end of the year. At the same time, remittance flows to South and East Asia, largely originating in the Gulf countries, surprised on the upside in 2009, with particularly strong increases in Bangladesh and Pakistan. Overall, remittances to emerging and developing countries are projected to increase by 2 percent in 2010, following a 6 percent decline in 2009.

Current account imbalances in emerging and developing countries have been shifting in recent years, mainly as the result of the sharp swings in world trade and terms of trade since late 2008 (figure 3.9). Fuel-exporting countries have been most hit by fluctuations in the external accounts, a reflection of the high volatility of oil prices and insufficient export diversification. Nonfuel primary product exporters face strong fluctuations as well, but less so than fuel-exporting countries. Despite these fluctuations, there have been reductions in external imbalances in the past two years within the group of emerging and developing countries. The number of emerging economies with high balance of payments deficits and the number of high surplus emerging economies and developing countries declined in 2009 (figure 3.10).

Even with the large differences in external conditions among emerging and developing countries, there has been a remarkable similarity in international reserve developments across groups of countries and regions. Helped by the recovery in international trade and capital flows, and the allocation of IMF special drawing rights, almost all countries rebuilt international reserves (as measured by reserve coverage in months of imports) in 2009, after a decline in 2008 (figure 3.11). At the end of 2009, 80 percent of emerging markets and 75 percent of developing countries had reserves that could be considered adequate (equivalent to three months of imports of goods and services). For emerging economies, reserves as a share of short-term debt also increased, and at the end of 2009 about 70 percent of emerg-

FIGURE 3.8   Bank financing to emerging markets dropped sharply in 2009

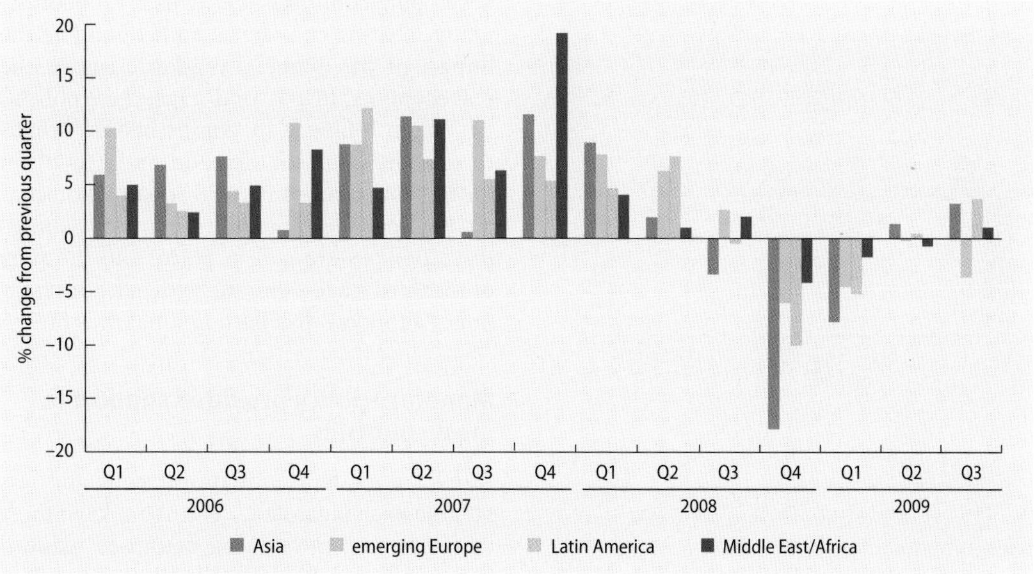

Source: Bank for International Settlements (BIS).
Note: Adjusted for exchange rate changes. Changes are calculated as flow adjusted for exchange rate changes as a share of the stock in the previous quarter.

TABLE 3.3   Inflows of international remittances
US$billions

	Annual average 1992–2002	Annual average 2003–07	2008	2009[a]	2010[b]	2011[c]
Emerging market economies	58.9	177.2	283.3	266.0	271.7	279.1
Developing countries	8.4	26.1	47.1	46.4	47.5	48.8
Fragile states	2.2	5.1	9.7	8.6	8.8	9.1

Source: World Bank remittances data.
a. Remittances include workers' remittances, compensation of employees, and migrant transfers.
b. Estimate.
c. Forecast base case scenario.

ing economies had reserves that exceeded the stock of short-term debt.[3]

Thanks to good policies, the recovery is stronger than in past crises

Overall, emerging and developing countries weathered this global crisis better than past ones. Their financial markets and exchange rates have not shown the sharp fluctuations of past crises, and the rebound in economic activity is stronger than expected. Healthier fiscal accounts, reduced debt, better debt maturity structures, low inflation, and higher international reserves gave many countries room for countercyclical policies that were

often not an option in previous crises. Further, stronger balance sheets and continued access to financing, especially for prime borrowers, helped private corporations in emerging and developing countries to deal better with adverse conditions than they had in the past. Local bond markets have also benefited some of these countries, with larger enterprises in Asia and Latin America able to rely on local markets for their refinancing needs.

Nonetheless, the crisis has depressed disposable incomes in many countries

The crisis and the pace of recovery have deeply affected disposable incomes in many coun-

FIGURE 3.9   **Changes in terms of trade have swung sharply since 2008**

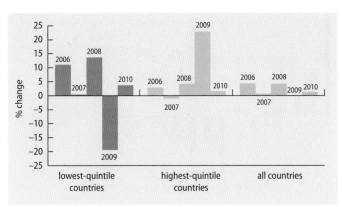

Source: IMF staff calculations.
Note: Quintile groups are based on the average of terms-of-trade changes in 2008–09 and 2009–10.

have differed. In general, most emerging and developing countries first focused on addressing weakening confidence and containing the impact of the financial market crisis on the real economy. In a second stage, these policies have been followed by comprehensive efforts to support domestic demand and growth in the medium term—mainly through expansionary macroeconomic policies. In most countries these policies are still in place, and the start of the third stage—exiting from extraordinary policy support—has been gradual thus far.

Monetary policy provided support in most countries

Aided by moderate inflation trends and less volatile exchange rates, central banks in most emerging and developing countries reduced policy interest rates in 2009. About 70 percent of emerging economies and close to 60 percent of developing countries followed a path toward lower rates last year. In some countries, higher policy interest rates were initially needed to preserve market confidence. These increases were more modest than in previous crises, however, and in many cases were quickly reversed. In most countries, lower interest rates were associated with depreciations of nominal effective exchange rates. As a result, monetary conditions in most emerging and developing countries—as measured by a simple summary indicator incorporating nominal interest rates and nominal effective exchange rates[4]—ap-

tries, where a contraction in real activity was sometimes reinforced by a deterioration in the terms of trade (figure 3.12). In 2008–10, about a third of emerging and developing countries were experiencing declines in disposable incomes, with potentially serious adverse effects on poverty. Central and Eastern Europe has been particularly hard hit, with nine countries facing cumulative income declines, in total averaging more than 8 percent.

Macroeconomic policy trends

Reflecting cross-country differences in initial conditions and the international transmission of the crisis, macroeconomic policy responses

FIGURE 3.10   **External imbalances have come down in emerging and developing countries**

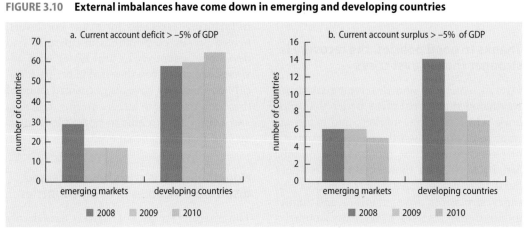

Source: World Economic Outlook.

FIGURE 3.11   **Almost all countries rebuilt their international reserves in 2009**

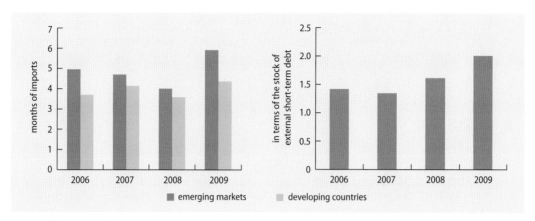

Source: World Economic Outlook.
Note: The median ratio is shown. "Stock of the external short-term debt" = outstanding (on remaining maturity basis) plus amortization scheduled on medium- and long-term debt.

pear to have become more accommodating in 2009 (figure 3.13).[5]

The financial crisis resulted in a sharp decline in money growth in emerging and developing countries (figure 3.14). The decline was largest in countries that had seen the strongest growth in the precrisis years. But as a result of the even stronger decline in nominal GDP growth rates, measures of excess liquidity, such as the nominal money gap, increased. This suggests that despite the fall in money growth, additional liquidity remained available to support corporations and households during the crisis period.

Expansionary fiscal policies support the recovery

Measured by the median general government balance, fiscal deficits in emerging and developing countries expanded by almost 3 percent of GDP in 2009 (figure 3.15) and are projected to increase further in 2010 in more than one-third of the countries, despite some decline in the median balance. Some countries, especially emerging economies, have put stimulus plans in place. But in most countries the widening deficit is the result of weakening revenue, including the disproportionate impact of the crisis on trade—and thus on revenues from import tariffs—and on consumption taxes. Some countries have also lost

FIGURE 3.12   **Deteriorating terms of trade sometimes reinforce contraction in economic activity**

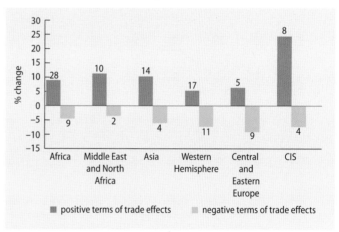

Source: IMF Staff calculations.
Note: The figure shows, by region, average real per capita GDP growth rates adjusted for the per capita value of net terms-of-trade changes. The numbers above and below the bars show the number of countries.

corporate tax revenue as the contribution of key sectors in the economy (such as natural resources and other export sectors) declined. Moreover, tax administrations may be facing bigger enforcement challenges during the crisis and its aftermath as tax planning becomes more aggressive. Many countries are more exposed to such challenges because of their weak administrative capacity, large informal sectors, and the constrained cash positions of taxpayers.

FIGURE 3.13   **Monetary policy conditions became more accommodating in 2009**

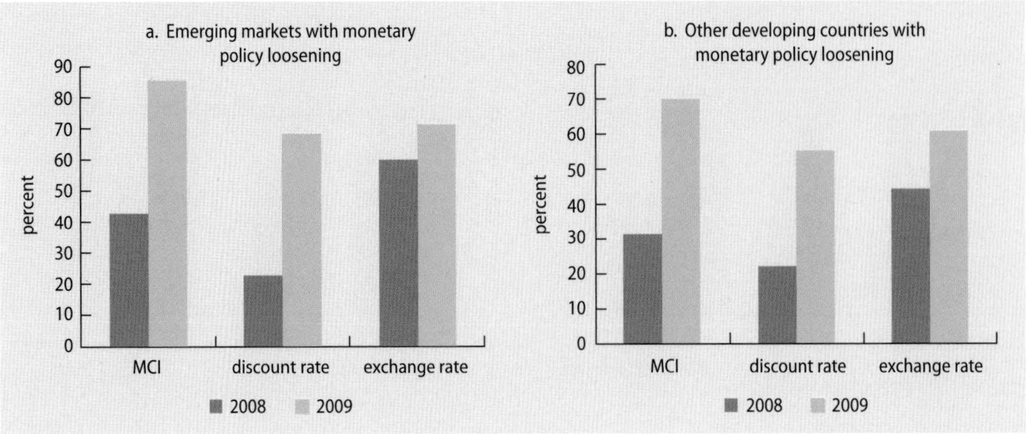

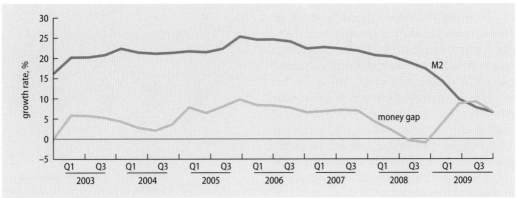

Source: IMF International Financial Statistics.
Note: Monetary policy loosening is based on Monetary Conditions Index (MCI) calculations.

FIGURE 3.14   **Average year-on-year growth in money and the money gap in emerging markets**

Source: IMF International Financial Statistics; Haver Analytics.
Note: The money gap is the difference between year-on-year growth rates of the M2 money supply and nominal GDP. The sample includes emerging-market countries that have data on both for the whole sample period shown.

Despite falling revenues, emerging and developing countries as a group have allowed automatic stabilizers to work and have maintained previous spending plans during the financial crisis. To some extent they have increased social spending related to the crisis, supporting domestic demand and sustaining the recovery. But the overall numbers on spending conceal wide differences in policy stances and conditions. About half of emerging and developing countries cut spending in 2009 in reaction to the crisis, a pattern likely to be repeated to some extent in 2010 (figure 3.16). The steepest spending cuts were in fuel-

exporting countries that faced sharp terms-of-trade deteriorations after the collapse of oil prices in the second half of 2008. Expenditures were less affected in other emerging and developing countries, especially nonfuel commodity exporters. Thanks to higher oil prices, many fuel-exporting countries will be able to reverse these policies in 2010.

But many countries are not on a sustainable fiscal path

Widening government deficits pose financing challenges for many countries, especially

FIGURE 3.15   Fiscal deficits expanded in 2009

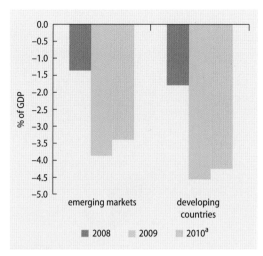

Source: World Economic Outlook.
a. Projected.

those with limited access to capital markets. Emerging markets rapidly regained access to sovereign debt markets following the collapse of Lehman Brothers in September 2008, but developing countries with limited or no market access are more constrained in their options. A country-by-country analysis of budget financing shows that most countries in this group were able to finance rising deficits with increased domestic and foreign financing. On average, budget financing needs of developing countries increased by about 3 percentage points of GDP in 2009, about half from domestic sources (mainly domestic bank loans and the drawing down of government deposits in the banking system) and the rest from foreign sources (mainly aid). In some countries, however, governments could not mobilize significant additional foreign resources despite

FIGURE 3.16   Growth in real primary spending, 2010 projections

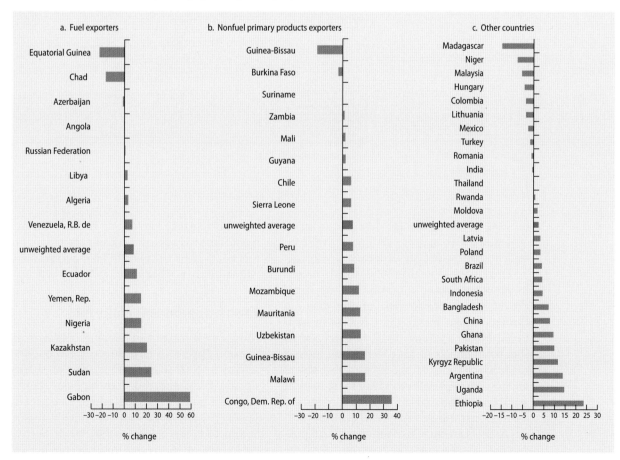

Source: World Economic Outlook.

MAP 3.1   How the crisis undermined GDP growth in 2009

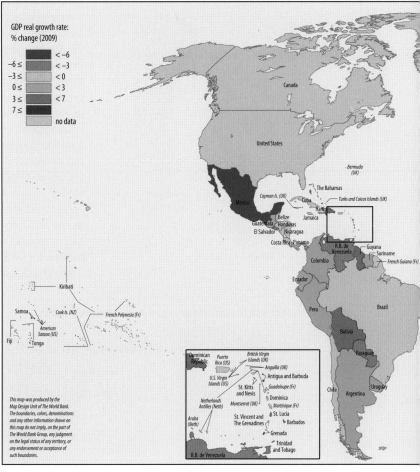

Source: World Economic Outlook.

pressing needs. As budget deficits remain elevated in 2010, many governments will continue to borrow heavily in domestic markets.

This is not sustainable. While fiscal stimulus in many developing countries has supported the recovery, there are risks of crowding out through higher interest rates. Recent International Monetary Fund (IMF) research shows significant effects of fiscal deficits on interest rates, which could dampen private investment and force governments to spend more on debt service payments and less on social programs.[6] These effects will be stronger when initial deficits or debts are high. Expansionary fiscal policies may also become counterproductive if the positive demand effects are more than offset by higher private saving or reduced investment. That may occur if consumers and investors adapt their behavior to take into account higher future tax liabilities.

The macroeconomic policy mix

Most emerging and developing countries as a group appear to have supported economic activity in 2009 with a combination of expansionary fiscal and monetary policies (figure 3.17 and box 3.1). In some countries, expansionary fiscal policies were combined with less accommodating monetary conditions. Such a policy mix is not necessarily incoherent. In fact, it may be useful in countries facing large capital

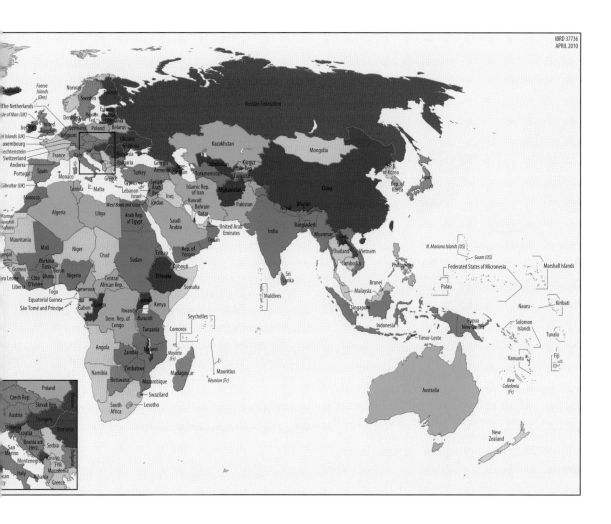

outflows and pressures on the exchange rate. In such a situation, rising interest rates may be appropriate to avoid excessive exchange rate volatility and ensure that sufficient external financing remains available for the economy. On average, growth in countries with this policy mix in 2009 was not weaker than in countries that had expansionary policies on both the monetary and fiscal front.

Adapting monetary and fiscal policies to changing circumstances

As the recovery in emerging and developing countries takes hold, questions arise about the best approach to exit from policy stimulus.[7] The appropriate timing and nature of exit policies depend on individual country circumstances. In many countries, where private demand components are still cyclically weak and sufficient policy space is available, monetary and fiscal policy should remain geared toward supporting activity. Governments in these countries should lay out a credible exit strategy to maintain confidence in the authorities' commitment to macroeconomic stability. Monetary and fiscal support should be gradually removed when private demand is sufficiently strong to sustain growth. In addition, to support fiscal consolidation, reforms to strengthen fiscal institutions could be initiated now.

FIGURE 3.17   Most countries responded with expansionary fiscal and monetary policy

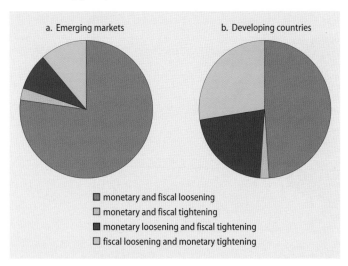

Source: IMF International Financial Statistics.
Note: Fiscal conditions are defined based on the change in government balance as a percent of GDP in 2008–09. Monetary conditions are based on the change in the MCI from 2008Q4 to 2009Q3.

A number of countries, however, are not in a position to delay adjustment and should act in 2010 to reduce fiscal deficits. In some cases, this reduction should be accompanied by a gradual tightening of the monetary policy stance. Three broad groups of countries can be distinguished.

Most developing countries financed widening budget deficits in 2009 by increasing reliance on domestic sources of financing. This financing policy, while appropriate when the global economy was facing the risks of a further sharp downturn, cannot be continued for very long, especially in countries with weak external payments positions, low reserves, or rapidly rising debt. Without higher aid inflows, financing constraints and the need to maintain fiscal sustainability will compel many countries to move to more prudent policies in 2010.

Some developing economies with fiscal sustainability problems may still be able to finance deficits in the current environment. But they could rapidly face external financing pressures if the perception takes hold that fiscal discipline is not a priority. If there are no signs of rising inflation, accommodating monetary policies can be maintained for some time to support domestic demand, unless

strong downward pressures on the exchange rate (flexible regime) or reserves (fixed regime) emerge.

Several countries, mainly emerging economies, face high or rising rates of inflation. The economic dynamics underlying these phenomena differ from country to country. In several countries, the first signs of rising inflationary expectations are becoming visible in the context of exceptional macroeconomic policy support. In some other countries, inflation rates remained stubbornly high in 2009, notwithstanding depressed demand conditions, usually reflecting a lack of confidence in monetary policy. In both categories of countries, a move toward a more restrictive monetary and fiscal policy stance would be warranted.

Maintaining confidence in macroeconomic stability remains a priority for all countries. Credible medium-term fiscal adjustment plans are important to manage expectations by reducing the risks of crowding out and unsustainable debt dynamics. To maintain the ability of fiscal policy to respond to future crises, a preferable strategy would aim to reduce debt ratios to their precrisis levels in the medium term. In addition to phasing out temporary stimulus measures, this approach will require some emerging economies to make improvements in their structural primary balance.[8] To enhance confidence that future fiscal adjustment will not lead to an appreciable increase in the tax burden, the medium-term adjustment plans could emphasize the following elements.

- *Phasing out temporary stimulus measures while strengthening well-targeted social safety nets.* A large number of emerging and developing countries are supporting domestic activity with ad hoc measures, such as increased spending on public works or reductions in tax rates. Medium-term fiscal consolidation plans should envisage public investment at levels consistent with fiscal sustainability and available financing, and phase out tax reductions presented as temporary stimulus measures. At the same time, temporary social programs should be

BOX 3.1   Quality of macroeconomic policies in low-income countries

As in previous years, IMF staff conducted surveys among mission chiefs to gauge their assessments of the quality of macroeconomic policies in low-income countries. In 2009 low-income countries made good progress in the quality of monetary policies, a reflec-tion of the rapid response to the global crisis in many countries and governance in the public sector. At the same time, governance in monetary and financial institutions showed deterioration, while little change was recorded in other areas.

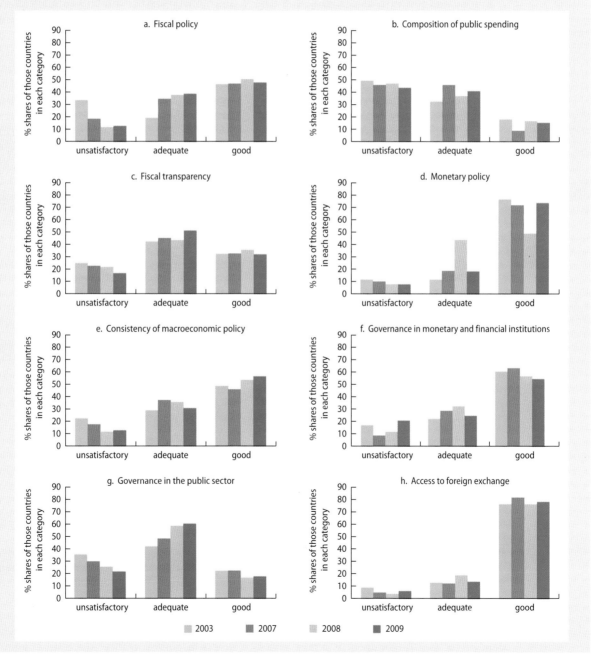

replaced with cost-effective, well-targeted, permanent social safety nets.

- *Structural cuts in nonpriority spending.* Governments should continue their efforts to reduce nonpriority spending, through further improvements in public financial management and by eliminating expenditure categories such as badly targeted fuel and food subsidies. Although the decline in food and fuel prices since mid-2008 has allowed some countries to reduce spending on inefficient general subsidies, further progress could be made in replacing general subsidies with programs better targeted to the poor.
- *Improving revenue performance.* Many emerging and developing countries have room for further improvements in tax systems and revenue administration, including measures aimed at widening the tax base to include informal sectors, further shifts away from trade taxes to domestic taxes, and addressing governance problems. Well-functioning revenue administrations, in combination with tax systems that minimize distortions, lay the basis for better revenue performance and create a more stable investment climate (box 3.2).

Countries with strong fiscal policies in the period leading to the global crisis have been better able to deal with its effects than countries with weak policies. They regained faster access to international financing on more favorable terms—and were better able to offset the effects of falling world demand with countercyclical fiscal policies in 2009 and 2010. This experience argues in favor of a countercyclical, medium-term fiscal rule that aims to generate savings during good years and create room for countercyclical policies during crisis periods. Although almost 60 emerging and developing countries have had some type of fiscal rule since the 1990s,[9] helping to maintain fiscal discipline, only some of these are designed to smooth out the effects of fluctuations in commodity export prices and other external shocks. Chile and Nigeria are countries where a countercyclical fiscal rule on the basis of prudent projections of commodity export prices

has helped to stabilize the macroeconomic effects of the crisis (box 3.3).

Strengthening international policy cooperation

The global crisis of confidence that eventually caused the collapse in world trade in 2008 required a global response: a simultaneous fiscal and monetary policy stimulus in countries with sufficient room to maneuver for such policies. The prospects of sustaining the current economic recovery will be enhanced if advanced, emerging, and developing countries continue to cooperate in the implementation of exit strategies and policies aimed at increasing growth. The agreement among the Group of Twenty (G-20) leaders at Pittsburgh to create a new process for mutual policy assessments is an important step in the right direction, but policy cooperation cannot be limited to those countries. Enhanced policy cooperation will be necessary in the following areas.

Avoiding protectionism. Restrictions on international trade and services, government subsidies for domestic industries, distortions to foreign direct investment, informal pressures on banks to give preference to domestic borrowers—all constitute serious threats to the economic recovery. Political pressures to maintain financial support to domestic industries indefinitely and to take more far-reaching protective measures could rise if unemployment remains relatively high in the coming years, in line with current expectations. Governments should eschew such protectionist policies and make strong efforts to reinvigorate the Doha Round. An ambitious Doha Round would constitute a major step toward a higher growth path for the world economy: a recent study puts potential annual GDP gains from multilateral trade liberalization at $300 billion to $700 billion.[10]

Increasing aid levels and aid effectiveness. Insufficient progress has been made in enhancing aid effectiveness, and aid still falls well short of the 2005 Gleneagles commitments, in particular for Africa. In addition, many donor countries have reduced their aid budgets, while others face pressures to reduce aid in light of

BOX 3.2　Mobilizing additional revenue in developing countries: Key issues for tax policy and revenue administration

The international financial crisis and its consequences for economic activity have put additional pressure on an already fragile revenue situation in many developing countries. Although the revenue situation in most countries is expected to improve as the effects of the crisis dissipate and temporary stimulus measures are phased out, some policy changes made in response to the crisis, and during the precrisis period that saw substantial increases in food and fuel prices, may have longer-term effects on revenues. An example is the proposed change to the value added tax (VAT) directive of the West African Economic and Monetary Union to allow for broader exemptions and a second (lower) rate on selected items. In addition, taxpayer compliance may have declined in many countries, posing challenges for revenue administration.

The policy tools that developing countries can mobilize to deal with the potential revenue loss stemming from the crisis and other ongoing challenges may be more limited today than in the 1980s and 1990s, and those that are left may involve stronger political commitments. The vast majority of countries have already implemented broad-based consumption taxes (typically VATs) at rates that are not particularly low in general and with bases that are generally narrow. Moreover, corporate tax rates have fallen dramatically since the early 1990s (by about one-quarter on average), and countries have intensified the use of tax incentives, further narrowing the tax base.

Country experiences in addressing these challenges differ, sometimes significantly, but common areas for reform exist.

Tax policy

Tax bases can be broadened, especially for VAT and profit taxes. This is not an issue of improving tax administration to better handle the informal sector (which is a separate and ongoing challenge); it primarily means rationalizing the use of income tax incentives (such as tax holidays) and reducing significantly the reliance on VAT exemptions as a (costly and largely ineffective) social policy tool.

The taxation of individuals is, in many countries, limited to the taxation of wages of the public sector and large enterprises. The taxation of unincorporated small and midsize enterprises remains largely elusive—both for technical and for political economy

reasons. Addressing these issues is key to improving the equity of tax systems.

Some tax sources remain underexploited in many countries—excise taxes on alcohol and tobacco, and environmental taxes (fuel and car taxes, for example) are important examples.

The institutional framework for policy making, including coordination at the country level between the various government entities with responsibility for tax policy, is deficient in many developing countries and often leads to fragmentation of policy decisions with negative consequences for revenues— for example, between trade and tax policy, industrial and tax policy, and central and local taxation. Countries should better integrate tax policy making into macroeconomic management, and strengthen the coordination mechanisms across government entities.

Taxes on real property have historically yielded very little revenue for a number of reasons, including the lack of a proper framework for sharing taxation powers between central and regional levels of government. This revenue source remains underexploited in many developing countries.

Revenue administration

Tax agencies should also develop a strategy to enhance revenue administration. The primary objective of the strategy should be to contain the rise in noncompliance often observed during periods of crisis. If left unchecked, rising noncompliance could lead to substantial forgone revenue and provide unfair competitive advantages to noncompliant businesses.

To achieve this objective, the following four sets of measures could be considered.

- Assistance to taxpayers could be expanded by adjusting advance payments, accelerating tax refunds, and making greater use of payment extensions.
- Communication with the taxpayer population could be improved. An effective communication program for taxpayers and other key stakeholders in the tax system should aim at clearly conveying to stakeholders and the public the various elements of the tax agency's compliance strategy.
- Legislative reforms that facilitate revenue administration could be enacted. Needed reforms vary from country to country; they could include mea-

continued

BOX 3.2 **(continued)**

sures such as the strengthening of transfer-pricing rules or the introduction of default assessments and indirect audit methods.

Enforcement could be strengthened, including the reassessment of controls over the largest taxpayers, the intensification of arrears collection, securing tax withholding, giving greater attention to loss-reporting businesses, and enhancing the scrutiny of cross-border transactions and offshore evasion.

Early warning for shifts in taxpayer compliance is crucial for prevention. The sooner a tax agency can identify an increase in noncompliance, the faster it can respond. Few tax agencies, however, have the capacity to estimate the precise level of the overall tax gap. In this situation, tax agencies should identify and track compliance indicators that can be more easily measured, such as increases in late filing of tax returns and growth in tax arrears.

Government support for tax administration is critical. Like all government agencies, tax agencies face the prospect of declining budget allocations in an economic downturn as governments seek to create fiscal room for high-priority social expenditures. However, it should be recognized that the task of tax administration becomes more demanding during difficult economic times. In this situation, substantial cuts in tax agencies' budgets are likely to reduce the effectiveness of tax collection and further aggravate a decline in revenue.

Tax agencies should align their near-term compliance strategies and medium-term modernization plans. Sustaining revenue collection over the medium term will require tax agencies to address their most fundamental weaknesses (such as poor organizational and staffing arrangements, weak taxpayer services and enforcement programs, and outdated information systems). By their nature, such problems can be addressed only over the medium term, but in developing a compliance strategy for the economic crisis, tax agencies should not neglect their medium-term goals.

tighter domestic fiscal constraints. These pressures must be resisted. A substantial increase in aid, at least in line with existing international commitments, is essential to allow developing countries, especially those in vulnerable debt situations and with limited alternative sources of finance, to generate resources for higher growth, improve social protection for the most vulnerable, and enhance food security.

The medium- and long-term economic effects of the crisis in low-income countries

Over the past few decades, a low-income country's growth rate in one decade has generally been a poor predictor of its growth rate in the next decade, while many policies and country characteristics are more stable. An emerging and vibrant empirical literature points to growth nonlinearities—accelerations (periods of high growth) and growth decelerations (periods of abrupt and severe growth slowdowns)—as an important development fact that until recently has not been in the spotlight.[11] Moreover, an extensive theoretical literature explores the possibility of low-income countries falling into prolonged periods of underdevelopment, commonly known as poverty traps.[12] Finally, crises can result in sharp declines in investment in education and health, declines that potentially can have long-lasting effects.[13]

Past growth

This section thus puts the current crisis in historical perspective and examines the prospects for growth in the medium to long run. Although the uncertainties are enormous, and the light that recent history can shed is limited, some preliminary and conditional answers are possible.

Transmission mechanisms from the global crisis seem to vary considerably across countries. While advanced economies have primarily suffered a financial and banking crisis, most developing countries primarily were hit by an external demand effect, although some, nota-

BOX 3.3   A fiscal rule for commodity exporters: The cases of Chile and Nigeria

Several commodity exporters have in recent years adopted medium-term frameworks for fiscal policy aimed at reducing the impact of commodity price fluctuations on the domestic economy. These frameworks allowed countries to build up sizable reserves during the commodity price boom of 2007–08, helped to stabilize expenditures, and created additional space for countercyclical policies in 2009. Chile and Nigeria illustrate the benefits of such a fiscal rule.

Since the beginning of the decade, fiscal policies in Chile have been based on a structural fiscal surplus rule aimed at mitigating the effects of fluctuations in prices for copper and molybdenum, the country's main commodity exports. Each year, the authorities make a calculation of structural revenue, consistent with potential GDP and long-term projections of copper and molybdenum prices. The annual spending budget is set on the basis of total structural tax and nontax (mainly mining) revenue minus a structural surplus. Fiscal surpluses are used to feed two sovereign wealth funds established under the 2006 Fiscal Responsibility Law: the Pension Reserve Fund to cover the government's long-term pension liabilities; and the Economic and Social Stabilization Fund, established to smooth fiscal expenditure and finance regular or extraordinary public debt amortization. The consistent implementation of the fiscal rule, which has received broad public support, and the sovereign wealth funds have served Chile well in recent years. Rising copper prices since the middle of the decade have allowed Chile to accumulate substantial reserves in the Economic and Social Stabili-

zation Fund, creating a comfortable buffer to offset the sharp revenue declines in 2009.

Nigeria introduced an oil-price-based fiscal rule in 2004 as a framework for the annual budget process, which was subsequently formalized in the 2007 Fiscal Responsibility Act. In the annual Medium-Term Fiscal Strategy presented to parliament, expenditures are set on the basis of relatively prudent projections for oil prices and production. If actual oil revenues exceed the budgeted levels, the surpluses are transferred to accounts held by the federal, state, and local governments at the central bank according to a preset intergovernmental sharing formula. Balances accumulated in the accounts can be used as a source of budget financing at the various levels of government if the actual oil price falls below the reference price for three consecutive months.

The fiscal rule is supported by a limit on the federal government's fiscal deficit of 3 percent of GDP, enshrined in the Fiscal Responsibility Act. The fiscal rule helped Nigeria stabilize expenditures and accumulate sizable reserves during the oil price boom of 2007–08. Although the political backing for the new approach does not seem to be as strong as in Chile, and lower levels of government are not bound by the Fiscal Responsibility Act, the fiscal rule has served Nigeria well thus far. Notwithstanding extraordinary distributions from the central bank accounts in response to political pressures during the oil price boom, Nigeria accumulated sufficient resources to avoid a contraction of public spending in 2009, reducing the effects of the global economic downturn.

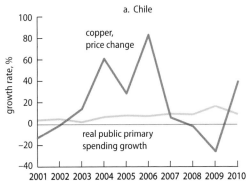

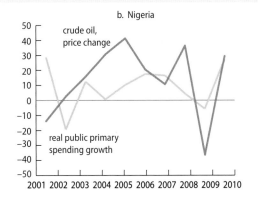

Source: World Economic Outlook.

MAP 3.2   Across the world, 884 million people lack access to safe water—84 percent of them in rural areas

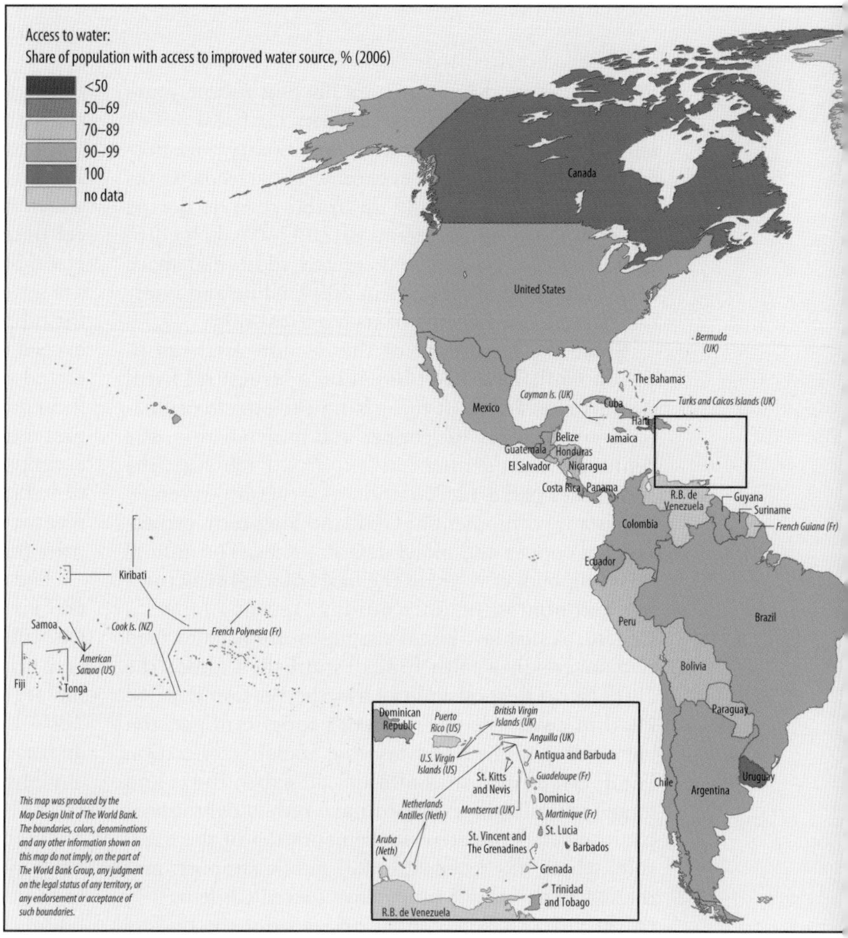

Access to water:
Share of population with access to improved water source, % (2006)

- <50
- 50–69
- 70–89
- 90–99
- 100
- no data

This map was produced by the Map Design Unit of The World Bank. The boundaries, colors, denominations and any other information shown on this map do not imply, on the part of The World Bank Group, any judgment on the legal status of any territory, or any endorsement or acceptance of such boundaries.

Source: World Economic Indicators.

bly fuel exporters, were also hit by a terms-of-trade and, perhaps to a lesser extent, a capital flows effect. From a methodological point of view, this difference is quite important because these types of external shocks are more familiar to low-income countries than the financial shock is to advanced countries, therefore permitting a more credible historical analysis of the effects in low-income countries.

The historical analysis that follows focuses on external demand, terms of trade, and capital flows as the three main transmission mechanisms of the crisis affecting low-income countries.[14] The analysis consists of four exercises, each tackling the importance of external shocks from a slightly different angle. The first is a simple event study that illustrates the growth paths of past crises and compares these to the current crisis. The second and third exercises focus on the medium-run effects of the crisis. Specifically, an impulse response analysis (a time-series analysis) is employed to estimate the effects over time, complemented with five-year growth panel regressions. The last exercise is concerned with the longer-run implications of the crisis using recently devel-

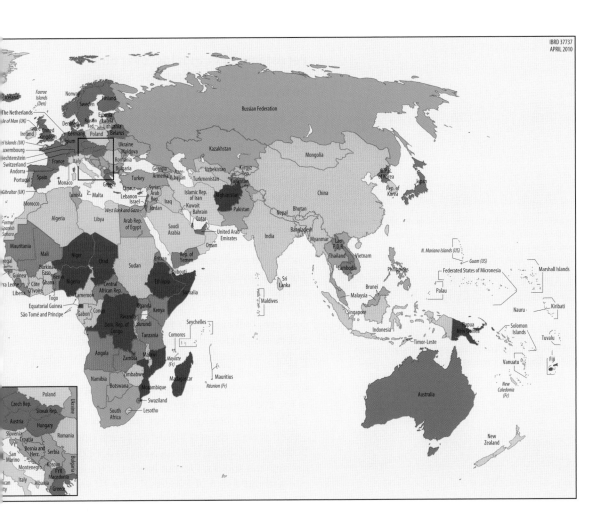

oped methods to capture possible sharp and very persistent drops in growth rates.

Global shocks

In past global crises, growth declined sharply leading toward the crisis year, but low-income countries experienced the worst of the crises about a year after the global low point was reached (figure 3.18). In addition, recovery seemed to be faster in the world economy than in low-income countries. More precisely, while recovery in the world began almost im-

mediately after the crisis year, it took about three years for a turnaround to take place in low-income countries in previous global crises. The good news is that low-income countries have tended to recover fully in the sense that they have reached or surpassed their precrisis growth rate after about five years.

The current crisis is distinguished by more synchronization between low-income countries and global cyclical growth movement. Also, IMF forecasts imply a more rapid V-shape recovery path out of the recession than in previous crises.

FIGURE 3.18   After previous crises, low-income countries recovered more slowly than the world economy

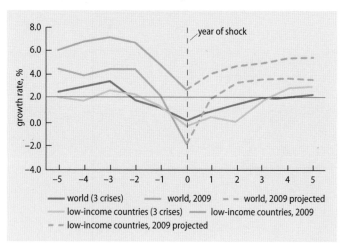

Source: IMF staff calculations.
Note: The figure plots the average per capita GDP growth in the world and in low-income countries five years before and five years after the global crises (centered at zero on the horizontal axis) of 1975, 1982, and 1991, and the current crisis. Also shown in dashed lines are IMF projections until 2013.

FIGURE 3.19   Growth of terms of trade and external demand in low-income countries in past and current crises

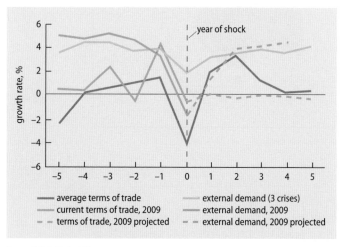

Source: IMF staff calculations.
Note: The figure plots the terms of trade and external demand growth in low-income countries five years before and five years after the global crises (centered at zero on the horizontal axis) of 1975, 1982, and 1991, and the current crisis. Also shown in dashed lines are IMF projections until 2013.

Unlike previous crises in which terms-of-trade growth suffered a sharp downturn relative to external demand growth, the current crisis is characterized by a sharp decline in export demand, with terms-of-trade growth

on average moving around historical averages (figure 3.19).[15]

Persistence of output loss over time using time series or impulse response analysis

An impulse response function analysis, as in Cerra and Saxena (2008), examines whether terms of trade and external demand have historically been associated with severe output losses and whether such output losses have been permanent in low-income countries.[16] Figure 3.20 presents impulse responses of output losses, measured as the percentage change from a linear growth trend to a terms-of-trade shock and an external demand shock, respectively.[17] The solid orange line is the mean of output loss, and the dashed lines reflect one standard deviation from the mean. A key assumption is that countries will eventually return to the growth rate existing before the shock. This assumption is quite reasonable because most of the low-income countries considered in these exercises tend to revert to their preexisting growth trend in the five years following the shock.

The main message is that the impact on output is negative and highly persistent under both types of shock, but especially under external demand shocks. Output losses continue to rise without a sign of a reversal even 10 years after an external demand shock, mounting to a cumulative loss of over 6 percent of GDP. This result may stem from interactions of external demand shocks with private and public investment decisions or policy responses. The output loss path eventually becomes flat as growth reaches its precrisis rate. But after a decade, lower growth and a substantial loss of output is likely to have detrimental effects on tax revenues, income, and certainly welfare.

The impulse response analysis is replicated for Sub-Saharan Africa (figure 3.21). One notable difference is that terms-of-trade shocks seem to have had a larger and more persistent effect than external demand shocks in the rest of low-income countries. Many Sub-Saharan countries are commodity exporters, particularly fuel exporters, and are thus more prone to

FIGURE 3.20   **Output losses are highly persistent, especially under external demand shocks**

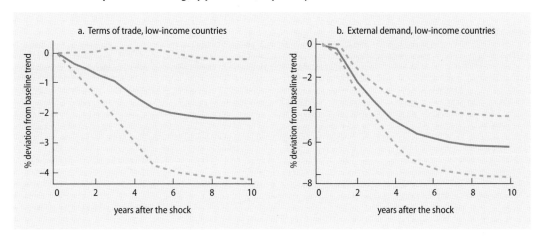

Source: IMF staff calculations.
Note: Impulse response of output loss in low-income countries to terms-of-trade and external demand shocks. Dashed lines are 1 standard deviation from the mean output loss.

FIGURE 3.21   **In Sub-Saharan Africa terms-of-trade shocks have larger and more persistent effects**

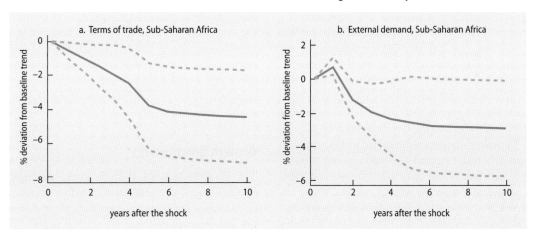

Source: IMF staff calculations.
Note: Impulse response of output loss in Sub-Saharan Africa countries to terms-of-trade and external demand shocks. Dashed lines are 1 standard deviation from the mean output loss.

terms-of-trade shocks. This issue is explained further below regarding growth downbreak.

Regression analysis

A third exercise employs five-year panel growth regressions as an alternative approach to investigating the impact of terms-of-trade, external demand, and foreign direct investment (FDI) shocks on medium-term per capita GDP growth.[18] In particular, the estimation re-

sults are based on panel regressions that combine time-series and cross-country information,[19] and the sample is restricted to nonfuel exporters. Fuel exporters are excluded from the baseline sample because these countries' growth experience has been heavily influenced by external demand for fuel. In the baseline specification, per capita growth is regressed on lagged per capita GDP growth, and the three shock variables (growth in terms of trade and external demand and the lag of the difference

TABLE 3.4   Growth regression results

Variables	Entire time period			Before 1989			After 1989		
	(1) All	(2) Low-income countries, non-fuel	(3) Other countries, non-fuel	(4) All	(5) Low-income countries, non-fuel	(6) Other countries, non-fuel	(7) All	(8) Low-income countries, non-fuel	(9) Other countries, non-fuel
Lagged growth	−0.209***	−0.167**	−0.237**	−0.577***	−0.487***	−0.662***	−0.292***	−0.287***	−0.261***
	(0.066)	(0.077)	(0.095)	(0.092)	(0.096)	(0.110)	(0.063)	(0.080)	(0.083)
Growth in terms of trade	0.123***	0.115*	0.111**	0.031	0.030	0.023	0.156**	0.131*	0.182***
	(0.047)	(0.064)	(0.053)	(0.028)	(0.046)	(0.028)	(0.063)	(0.077)	(0.066)
Growth in external demand	2.603***	1.960***	3.419***	1.332**	0.617	2.599**	1.727***	1.665*	1.769**
	(0.606)	(0.736)	(0.786)	(0.609)	(0.599)	(1.135)	(0.666)	(0.938)	(0.706)
Lagged change in (FDI / GDP)	0.631***	0.221	1.010***	0.599	−0.404	1.773***	0.783***	0.517*	0.953***
	(0.187)	(0.222)	(0.270)	(0.633)	(0.732)	(0.528)	(0.243)	(0.305)	(0.319)
Observations	529	281	248	181	92	89	348	189	159
Number of countries	88	48	40	86	47	39	88	48	40

Source: IMF staff calculations
Robust standard errors in parentheses
*** $p < 0.01$; ** $p < 0.05$; * $p < 0.1$.

in FDI-to-GDP ratio) are all measured in five-year averages.[20] Columns 1–3 in table 3.4 present results for "All" nonadvanced nonfuel countries, nonfuel low-income countries, and nonfuel non-low-income countries. The comparison between low-income countries and non-low-income countries is intended to provide some insights into the differential effects of these shocks to the two income groups.

For low-income countries, terms-of-trade growth and external demand growth obtain positive and significant coefficient estimates, indicating a positive impact on medium-term growth (column 2 of table 3.4). While the coefficient estimate on FDI for low-income countries using the entire time period in the sample is insignificant, it is highly significant for "All" and non-low-income countries along with the coefficient estimates for terms of trade and external demand (columns 1 and 3, respectively). Columns (4–9) present results from splitting the sample in the periods before and after 1989 (the median year in the sample). Coincidentally, "after 1989" is the period when growth increased dramatically in most low-income countries. Note that most of the effect of terms-of-trade and external demand growth for low-income countries has been driven by variation in the period after 1989 (columns 5 and 8). Even more notable is that in the post-1989 sample the FDI coef-

ficient becomes positive and significant. That may not be surprising given that FDI in low-income countries has been plentiful only in the past decade or so.[21] The broad message of this exercise is that regression results seem to reinforce the impulse response findings showing economically significant effects of the shocks in the medium run.

Growth downbreaks

The analysis shows that external demand shocks, such as those faced by low-income countries in 2009, cause growth to slow down not just immediately but for several years. An even greater concern, though, is the risk that the global crisis may cause an essentially permanent decline in growth in many low-income countries—that is, a growth "downbreak." Many low-income countries have enjoyed relatively strong growth over the past 10–15 years, when a favorable external environment prevailed. The concern is that, with the global shock, this could change. Underlying this concern is the observation that, whereas output paths in the advanced countries tend to be reasonably steady, in developing countries they are often characterized by "mountains, cliffs, and plains."[22] This exercise employs the methodology by Berg, Ostry, and Zettelmeyer (2008) to obtain growth downbreaks (sus-

FIGURE 3.22   In low-income countries, growth downbreaks are more associated with terms-of-trade shocks, giving hope for smoother recovery

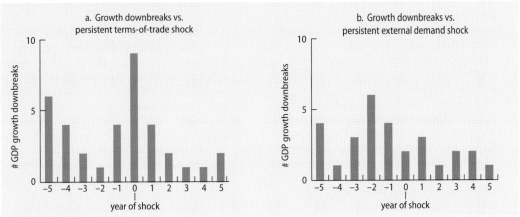

Source: Berg and others forthcoming.
Note: The left panel plots the number of GDP growth downbreaks in a large sample of low-income countries during the periods leading up to and following a large persistent terms-of-trade shock (year 0 on the horizontal axis). A large persistent terms-of-trade shock is defined as the worst 10 percent of the distribution of all terms-of-trade shocks, measured as the difference of the average three-year terms-of-trade growth before and after a year of shock. The right panel is the same, except that the shock is to external demand, measured as partner-country real growth weighted by export shares.

tained declines in the rate of growth) in low-income countries and to explore whether terms-of-trade and external demand shocks are correlated with such "cliffs."

One pattern emerging from figure 3.22 is that persistent negative terms-of-trade shocks have often coincided with growth downbreaks in the past. However, persistent negative partner-country demand shocks have shown no association with growth downbreaks. This phenomenon may be related to the fact that terms-of-trade changes are usually strongest in commodity sectors, and that these sectors often find it more difficult to adjust to the new environment than do, for instance, industrial sectors. The supply factors that produce the commodities in question cannot easily switch to other uses, such as satisfying domestic demand or finding other export markets. The resulting decline in foreign income could squeeze imports and activity persistently, thus impeding productive activities throughout the economy.

This remarkable observation suggests that if indeed the current crisis has affected primarily low-income countries through external demand and not through terms of trade, there may be more reason for hope for a smoother recovery.[23]

Notes

1. In this chapter, the group of developing countries includes mainly low-income countries and some middle-income countries that are not considered emerging economies. High-income oil-exporting countries are excluded from this category.
2. IMF 2009g, box 1.2; IMF 2009d.
3. The adequacy of reserves depends on many factors, including the volatility of exports and imports, fluctuations in the terms of trade, the level and maturity structure of external debt, and the vulnerability to sudden shifts in international capital movements. While reserve adequacy should be assessed country by country, a level equivalent to three months of imports is often used as a rule of thumb, especially for low-income countries. For a discussion on optimal reserve determination, with a focus on low-income countries, see Drummond and Dhasmana (2008).
4. The evolution of monetary policy stance is approximated by the Monetary Conditions Index (MCI), a summary indicator of the impact of policy rates and exchange rates on domestic demand. The MCI combines nominal short-term interest rates and the nominal effective exchange rate (with a one-third weight for the latter) in a single index. The change in the indicator is calculated up to 2009Q3, except for

Vietnam and Rwanda, which have data only until 2009Q1. The MCI is a useful indicator of direction in the monetary policy stance: it is simple to calculate and based on data readily available. However, it also suffers from various caveats (including, for example, the use of common weights across diverse countries), so detailed country results need to be interpreted with some caution.

5. In many countries that reduced rates in 2009, inflation came down faster than nominal rates, propping up real interest rates. Temporary factors, such as commodity price movements, may have contributed to the fall in inflation, however, mitigating the impact of higher real rates on spending and investment decisions.

6. See IMF 2009e and Baldacci and Kumar, forthcoming. An increase in fiscal deficits of 1 percent of GDP is found to increase 10-year nominal bond yields by about 20 basis points in the medium term, and an increase in the debt-to-GDP ratio of 1 percent increases rates by approximately 5 basis points. Although the econometric analysis is based on a sample of advanced and emerging economies, it is plausible that low-income countries show similar relations between deficits, debt, and interest rates.

7. For a detailed discussion of exit strategies see IMF 2010a.

8. IMF 2010b.

9. IMF 2009a.

10. This represents approximately 0.5–1.2 percent of 2008 world GDP. See Adler and others (2009).

11. Hausmann, Pritchett, and Rodrik 2005; and Berg, Ostry, and Zettelmeyer 2008.

12. See the literature review in Azariadis and Stachurski (2007) and more specifically the debt trap model in Kehoe and Levine (1993).

13. Benhabib and Spiegel 1994; Krueger and Lindahl 2001.

14. Data are from IMF. External demand is partner-country real GDP growth, 2000 = 100, weighted by trade exports to all partner countries (APR 2009 Global Economic Environment). Terms of trade are for goods (World Economic Outlook [WEO] latest update). Capital flows are proxied by direct investment in reporting economy in billions of U.S. dollars.

15. Data on foreign direct investment were not available to produce a similar plot. This observation is also shown in more formal growth regression analysis in Berg and others (work in progress).

16. Daniel Leigh very helpfully provided his Stata code and invaluable input. For methodological details, see Cerra and Saxena (2008) and IMF 2009g, ch. 4.

17. The shock dummy variable for both terms of trade and external demand was constructed as follows: A restricted sample was constructed in which values below and above the 1st and 99th percentiles were excluded to mitigate the effects from extreme values. The crisis periods belong to the left tail of the moving-average growth (based in two periods) distribution, where the left tail is based on one standard deviation of the restricted sample defined above. Results are qualitatively similar to two alternative shock definitions considered.

18. A similar estimation methodology was followed in Drummond and Ramirez (2009).

19. Using a statistical estimation method called generalized method of moments (GMM).

20. An alternative growth regression specification would be the Barro-Solow type regression. This alternative was not considered, because it suffers from the well-documented endogeneity and omitted variable problems, which the specification used here is less subject to.

21. The robustness of these results to alternative specifications and subsamples has been checked.

22. Pritchett 2000.

23. The definitions of "persistent" and "large" can be found in the note to figure 3.22. It turns out that large negative external demand shocks such as those experienced by many countries in 2009 are not unprecedented for many low-income countries. In the sample used for figure 3.22, there were 68 instances in which countries faced external demand shocks larger than they faced in 2009 (assuming IMF projections for the out-years).

References

Adler, M., C. Brunel, J. C. Hufbauer, and J. J. Schott. 2009. "What's on the Table? The Doha Round as of August 2009." Working Paper 09-6. Peterson Institute for International Economics. Washington, DC.

Azariadis, C., and J. Stachurski. 2007. "Poverty Traps." In *Handbook of Economic Growth*, Vol. 1, Ch. 5, edited by P. Aghion and S. N. Durlauf. Amsterdam: Elsevier Science.

Baldacci, E., and M. Kumar. Forthcoming. "Deficits, Debt, and Interest Rates." IMF working paper. Washington, DC.

Benhabib, J., and M. Spiegel. 1994. "The Role of Human Capital in Economic Development: Evidence from Cross-Country Data." *Journal of Monetary Economics* 34: 143–73.

Berg, A., J. D. Ostry, and J. Zettelmeyer. 2008. "What Makes Growth Sustained." Working Paper 08/59. International Monetary Fund, Washington, DC.

Berg, A., C. A. M Pattillo, H. Weisfeld, C. Papageorgiou, N. Spatafora, and S. P. Tokarick. Forthcoming. "The Short-Run Effects of the Crisis in Low-Income Countries." International Monetary Fund, Washington, DC.

Cerra, V., and S. C. Saxena. 2008. "Growth Dynamics: The Myth of Economic Recovery." *American Economic Review* 98: 439–57.

Drummond P., and A. Dhasmana. 2008. "Foreign Reserve Adequacy in Sub-Saharan Africa." Working Paper WP/08/150. International Monetary Fund, Washington, DC.

Drummond P., and G. Ramirez. 2009. "Spillovers from the Rest of the World into Sub-Saharan African Countries." Working Paper WP/09/155. International Monetary Fund, Washington, DC.

Erickson and others 2004<<Please complete or delete cite>>

Hausmann, R., L. Prichett, and D. Rodrik. 2005. "Growth Accelerations." *Journal of Economic Growth* 10: 303–29.

IMF (International Monetary Fund). 2009a. "Fiscal Rules: Anchoring Expectations for Sustainable Public Finances." Washington, DC (*www.imf.org/external/np/pp/eng/2009/121609.pdf*).

———. 2009b. "Global Financial Stability Report." Washington, DC (October).

———. 2009c. "Regional Economic Outlook-Sub-Sahara Africa." Washington, DC (Fall).

———. 2009d. "Review of Recent Crisis Programs." Washington, DC (September 14).

———. 2009e. "The State of Public Finances Cross Country." IMF Staff Position Note, SPN/09/25. Washington, DC (November).

———. 2009f. *World Economic Outlook.* Washington, DC (Spring).

———. 2009g. *World Economic Outlook.* Washington, DC (October).

———. 2010a. "Exiting from Crisis Intervention Policies and Fiscal Consolidation in the Post-Crisis World." Washington, DC (February).

———. 2010b "Strategies for Fiscal Consolidation in the Post-Crisis World." Washington, DC (February).

Kehoe, T., and D. Levine. 1993. "Debt-Constrained Asset Markets." *Review of Economic Studies* 60: 865–88.

Krueger, A. B., and M. Lindahl. 2001. "Education for Growth: Why and for Whom?" *Journal of Economic Literature* 39 (4): 1101–36.

Pritchett, L. 2000. "Understanding Patterns of Economic Growth: Searching for Hills among Plateaus, Mountains, and Plains." *World Bank Economic Review* 14: 221–25.

4

Outlook for the Millennium Development Goals

How will the global economic crisis alter precrisis trends in the Millennium Development Goals (MDGs)? With only five years left until the target date of 2015, it is obvious that several of the MDGs will not be attained, globally or by a majority of countries. Many of the goals are too high for low-income countries, given their low starting points. Many countries, including low-income ones, have seen substantial gains in recent years, however, and entered the current crisis in a stronger position than in past crises (chapters 1 and 2). Important questions are whether the gains will be preserved, and what happens if the fragile recovery slips into a prolonged stagnation.

The crisis is likely to have a lasting impact on human development indicators that will not overcome even a robust economic recovery. Although growth in emerging and developing countries is currently accelerating, should growth slow or deteriorate, progress toward the MDGs will suffer even more. A decline in growth would have a significant impact on poverty and undernourishment. The impact of a growth slowdown on some of the other MDG indicators analyzed is more muted, although the cost in absolute numbers—additional children dying or uneducated, additional people left without clean water—could be large because of the size of the population underlying each rate. Countries can achieve better development outcomes through improved policies, most notably shifts in expenditures, increases in domestic revenue, and better service delivery. Stronger policies are unlikely to compensate fully for the deterioration in human development indicators that result from slower growth, however. In the current context, better development outcomes will thus depend on the speed at which the global economic recovery supports increases in developing countries' export revenues and external finance.

This chapter looks at these issues in two ways. It first presents alternative scenarios for progress on some key human development–related MDGs based solely on different forecasts of GDP growth, with the results aggregated by regions. This relatively limited approach provides a general sense of the impact of the crisis and the potential envelope for the MDGs looking ahead over the next five to ten years. The second part of the chapter then takes into account a broader set of determinants of progress in the MDGs, including fiscal policy (public expenditures and their composition plus revenue efforts), export revenues, terms of trade, aid flows, remittances, and foreign borrowing. This richer analysis allows a much more robust view of how the external economic environment and developing-country policies will affect progress toward the MDGs. The scope of the analysis, however, and the variables involved, make it extremely difficult to provide comprehensive forecasts of human development indicators for developing countries. Instead, this section illuminates the channels that influence MDG outcomes through the lens of two types of low-income developing-country structure based on natural endowments—those that are resource poor and those that are resource rich.[1]

Forward analysis of the MDGs

The original analytical framework underpinning the assessment of policies as developed by the World Bank and the International Monetary Fund (IMF) in the first *Global Monitoring Report* in 2004 remains very valid today for organizing this policy assessment (figure 4.1). The two key pillars for achieving the development outcomes are economic growth and delivery of services to the poor—the very two factors likely to be most affected by global economic crisis. That is why the lessons of history regarding the effects of growth decelerations on various human development indicators are examined in chapter 2. Although not the only driver, growth will likewise be a key factor in projecting the postcrisis trends for the MDGs. The other key factor, effective service delivery, is difficult to assess even in the best of circumstances.[2]

The current crisis has resulted in a deterioration in human development indicators that will have important future effects even with a robust economic recovery. If growth were to stagnate or slow, the impact on human welfare in developing countries would be severe. Projecting the aggregate outlook for the MDGs is fraught with difficulties (box 4.1).[3] Nevertheless, it is essential to assess where things stand in the aftermath of the crisis, as developing countries enter a new and less favorable external environment.

The alternative scenarios of progress toward the MDGs presented here are based on a simplified reduced-form analysis linking economic growth—the key variable of the crisis and the recovery scenarios—to the MDG indicators.[4] The simulations are based

FIGURE 4.1   Framework linking policies and actions with development outcomes

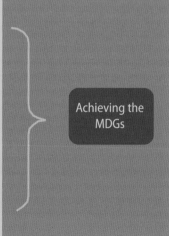

Source: World Bank 2004a.

BOX 4.1   **Uncertainty and risk in projecting attainment of the MDGs**

There are many uncertainties and risks in projecting development outcomes. One is the strength and timing of the economic recovery. Another is the complexity of the relationships between the MDGs and their determinants, which are still poorly understood. Among the MDGs the impact of economic performance on poverty is better established, although the elasticity of poverty to growth can vary with country circumstances and initial conditions. Furthermore, human development outcomes are influenced by a wide range of factors, including the evolution of household incomes and public resources, as well as the consequences of supply and demand for policies, institutional actions, and microlevel services. Given the complexity and differing assumptions about the recovery, assessments of human development outcomes can be wide ranging.

Another important uncertainty in forecasting progress toward the MDGs is fiscal adjustment—public expenditures and their composition are key determinants of human development indicators in low-income countries. A deterioration in the macroeconomic environment may reduce government income, thus endangering public expenditures essential for progress toward the MDGs. However, aid, external borrowing, and international reserves may provide the fiscal space needed to protect social spending, while remittances may help to support private expenditures. Hence, fiscal adjustment and thus the implications of slower growth for the MDGs will vary from country to country depending on circumstances and conditions entering the crisis.

Several studies point to other problems in accounting for all of the influences on human development indicators. An increase in public expenditures does not necessarily improve education and health outcomes; nor does economic growth alone. Links between public expenditures and social sector outcomes are weak. Supply-side factors associated with effective service delivery are preconditions for improving basic service provision—school facilities, books, health clinics, vaccination programs, qualified teachers and health staff, and the like. Client demand for services and various other factors at the local level—household incomes, distance and opportunity costs, voice and participation of clients, educational attainment of mothers, corruption, and cultural and religious norms—also matter and may vary by community. The empirical regularity of these potential determinants can become difficult to establish at the country, regional, and global levels.

Source: Dinh, Adugna, and Myers 2002; Adams and Bevan 2000; Filmer, Hammer, and Pritchett 2000, 2002; Devarajan and Reinikka 2004; World Bank 2004.

---

on GDP growth because it is a major determinant of progress toward the MDGs, and it is the only determinant that is projected for a large group of countries and that is anchored by the short-, medium-, and long-term economic outlook in the International Monetary Fund's (IMF) *World Economic Outlook* and the long-term growth projections that underpin the World Bank's *Global Economic Prospects*. Because of the many uncertainties described in box 4.1, these projections relating progress in the MDGs to alternative scenarios for GDP growth are necessarily subject to large margins of error and should be taken as illustrative.

The estimated relationship between poverty and growth is based on household surveys in more than 100 countries and assumes that the underlying income or expenditure distribution is relatively stable during changes in economic growth.[5] The poverty analysis brings 31 new household surveys to the 2010 *Global Monitoring Report* and new projections of per capita income growth in the aftermath of the crisis. The analysis also considers four other MDGs—primary education completion, infant mortality, gender equality in education, and access to clean water—for which aggregate quantitative analysis is currently feasible (future reports will expand the analysis to other MDGs). The relationship between GDP growth and each indicator is estimated for each country.

MAP 4.1   **In 2007, 72 million children worldwide were denied access to education**

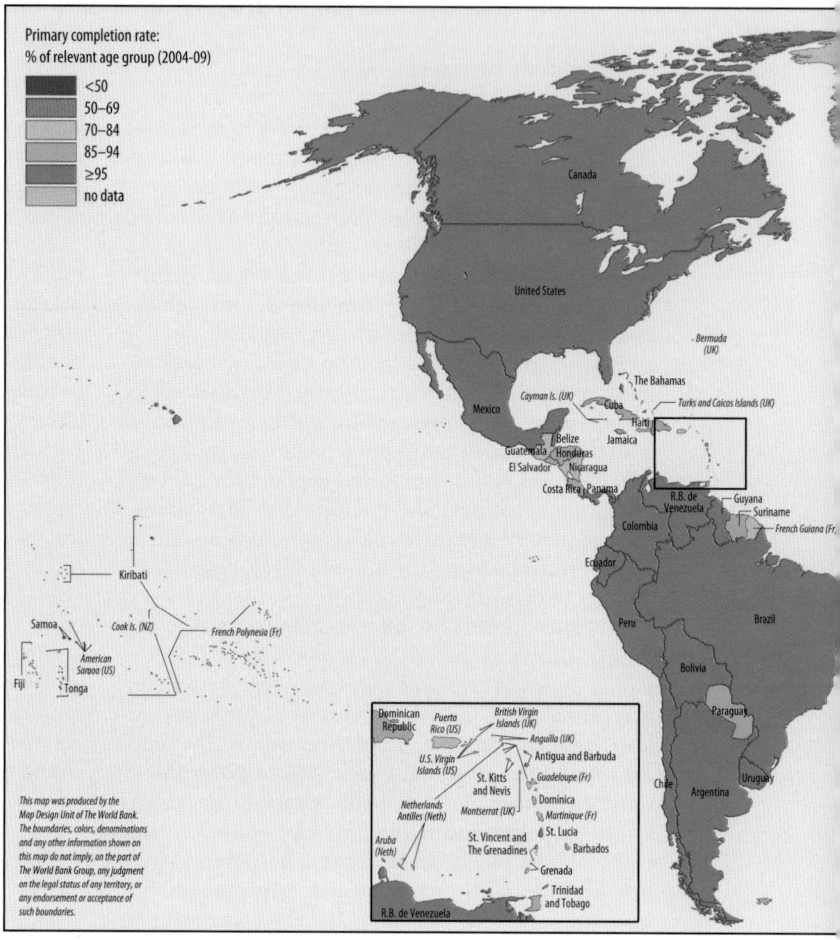

Source: World Development Indicators.

The results show that growth generally was significantly related to progress in the human development indicators. However, confirming all the caveats mentioned above, the estimations using growth alone accounted for only 30–40 percent of past variations of the MDG indicators across countries and time. These coefficients were then used to forecast each MDG indicator for each country, based on alternative scenarios for GDP growth. Although it is certainly possible to include other determinants of the MDG indicators in the estimation, it is not practical to forecast these other indicators on a country-by-country basis (box 4.2).

Three global scenarios for progress on human development–related MDGs

Three global scenarios for GDP growth address the risks of the current global economic crisis: a postcrisis trend; a high-growth or precrisis trend; and a low-growth scenario.

The postcrisis trend assumes a relatively rapid economic recovery in 2010, with strong growth continuing into the future, as described in chapter 2.[6] This is essentially the base case forecast for growth in developing countries after the crisis.

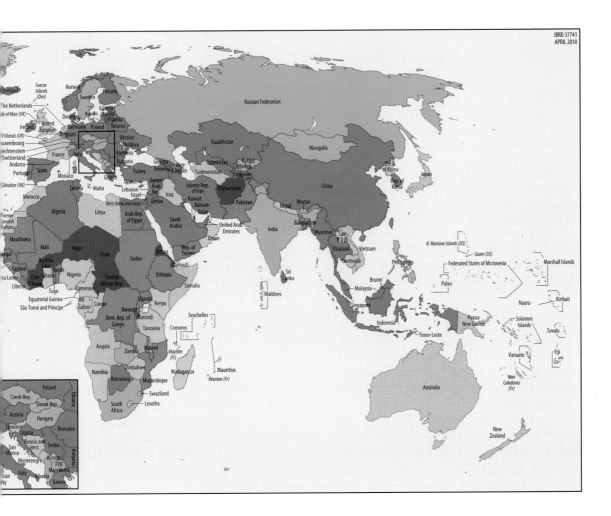

The precrisis trend gives the forecast path for the MDGs if developing countries had continued their impressive growth performance during 2000–07, the period just before the global economic crisis. The impact of the crisis on the MDGs can thus be measured by comparing the postcrisis trend with this one.

The low-growth scenario assumes that the recovery projected for the postcrisis trend will not take place in the medium run. The scenario assumes little or no growth for about five years, when it begins to slowly recover. This scenario follows the pattern of past responses to severe external shocks in developing countries.

The impact on the very poor

Recent economic shocks have taken a toll on the poor. The crisis left an estimated 50 million more people in extreme poverty in 2009, and some 64 million more will fall into that category by the end of 2010 relative to a precrisis trend.[7] New estimates suggest that the large global spike in food prices in 2008 may have led the incidence of undernourishment to rise by around 63 million people, while

BOX 4.2   Estimating the impact of growth on human development indicators

The relationship between GDP growth and the MDGs was estimated taking into account a policy index reflecting the country's level of policy and institutions plus a set of initial conditions (for example, adult female literacy rate, urbanization, ethnic fractionalization, level of income, and location by geographical region).[a] Several policy indexes had a significant relationship with the MDG indicators. Among these, the World Bank's Country Policy and Institutional Assessment (CPIA) rating was selected because it is a broader measure than one based solely on governance indexes. It covers economic management, structural policies, policies for social inclusion and equity, and public sector management and institutions. The explanatory power of the equations

jumps from 30–40 percent using growth as the sole explanatory variable to 80 percent when the index of policy and initial conditions are taken into account. These estimations help to refine the understanding of the relationship between growth and the human development indicators. However, it did not prove possible to use the policy index or the initial conditions in the alternative scenarios for future progress in the MDG indicators, given the difficulties involved in forecasting these variables in many countries.

a. The use of the policy index is similar to the empirical works of Wagstaff and Claeson (2004), Rajkumar and Swaroop (2002), and Filmer and Pritchett (1999). The CPIA is available in the *World Development Indicators*.

the crisis itself may have led to an additional 41.3 million undernourished people, or 4.4 percent more undernourished people in 2009 than would have been the case without the economic crisis.[8]

A rapid economic recovery (the postcrisis trend) would improve the situation for many of the extremely poor and lead to substantial

reductions in the poverty rate, to 15 percent in 2015, well below the MDG target of 20.4 percent (table 4.1). Nevertheless, the crisis has imposed a lasting cost on poverty reduction. Had the crisis not interrupted the rapid economic progress made by developing countries through 2007 (the precrisis trend), the poverty rate at $1.25 a day would have fallen to

TABLE 4.1   Poverty in developing countries, alternative scenarios, 1990–2020

Region and scenario	1990	2005	2015	2020
Global level				
Percentage of the population living on less than $1.25 a day				
Postcrisis	41.7	25.2	15.0	12.8
Precrisis	41.7	25.2	14.1	11.7
Low-growth	41.7	25.2	18.5	16.3
Number of people living on less than $1.25 a day (millions)				
Postcrisis	1,817	1,371	918	826
Precrisis	1,817	1,371	865	755
Low-growth	1,817	1,371	1132	1053
Sub-Saharan Africa				
Percentage of the population living on less than $1.25 a day				
Postcrisis	57.6	50.9	38.0	32.8
Precrisis	57.6	50.9	35.9	29.9
Low-growth	57.6	50.9	43.8	39.9
Number of people living on less than $1.25 a day (millions)				
Postcrisis	296	387	366	352
Precrisis	296	387	346	321
Low-growth	296	387	421	428

Source: World Bank staff calculations using the PovcalNet database.

about 14 percent by 2015, implying that an additional 53 million people would have been lifted out of extreme poverty. Things could be worse than the postcrisis trend, however. If the economic outlook deteriorates to the low-growth scenario, the poverty rate could fall only to 18.5 percent, with an additional 214 million people living in absolute poverty by 2015 (relative to the postcrisis trend).

On current or postcrisis growth trends, poverty in Sub-Saharan Africa is projected to drop to 38 percent by 2015—more than 9 percentage points short of its target. Before the crisis the region had been on a path to reach a poverty rate of 35.9 percent, which would have lifted another 20 million people out of poverty by 2015. If growth stagnates into the low-growth scenario, the trend gap could more than double, implying an additional 55 million people remaining in extreme poverty by 2015.

The long-term nature of the cumulative effects becomes clearer when global projections are extended 10 years forward. The postcrisis trend suggests that by 2020, 826 million people (12.8 percent) in developing countries will be living on less than $1.25 a day, implying that 71 million more people will be living in absolute poverty in 2020 as a result of the crisis. The low-growth scenario would result in a rise of 227 million living in absolute poverty compared with the postcrisis trend. The corresponding increases in poverty for Sub-Saharan Africa in 2020 are 31 million more people in poverty for the postcrisis trend and 76 million more for the low-growth scenario. The five additional years would leave Sub-Saharan Africa still short of halving poverty, the MDG target for 2015.

Poverty rates vary considerably among the other regions (annex tables 4A.1 and 4A.2). Even in the low-growth scenario, the East Asia and Pacific region more than meets its poverty target, in large part because of China's success in reducing poverty. South Asia, on the strength of India's achievement, meets the poverty target in the postcrisis trend but not in the low-growth scenario. Middle-income countries in Europe and Central Asia

are projected to miss the poverty reduction MDG at poverty lines of both $1.25 and $2 a day. However, the poverty rates in these countries are very low to start with (about 4 percent at $1.25 a day and about 9 percent at $2 a day in 2005), so a higher poverty line of $4 to $5 a day is more meaningful for this group of countries.

Overall, the projection for the $2 a day poverty threshold is less promising. In the postcrisis trend, 2 billion people, or one-third of the population of developing countries—more than half of the 1990s level—remain in poverty at $2 a day.

Impact on selected human development indicators

The crisis will have serious and lasting costs and gaps for other human development indicators as well (figure 4.2 and table 4.2). According to the projections for 2015, as a result of the crisis:

- The number of infants dying would increase by 55,000. Without the crisis, 260,000 additional children under the age of five could have been prevented from dying in 2015. The cumulative total from 2009 to 2015 could reach 265,000 and 1.2 million, respectively. The consequences for infant mortality in Africa are grave, with some 30,000–50,000 additional infant deaths in 2009, virtually all of them girls.[9] The tragedy is not just these added deaths— more than 3 million infants die in Africa every year, a number that could be reduced through better policies and interventions.
- Some 350,000 more students will fail to complete primary school.
- Some 100 million more people will lose access to safe drinking water.

The impact on gender equality in education and on access to safe water is muted in these scenarios (although even small changes in these indicators can translate into large numbers of people affected) because these indicators are influenced by forces that change only slowly. For example, the

FIGURE 4.2   The long-run effect of slower growth on selected MDGs is worrisome

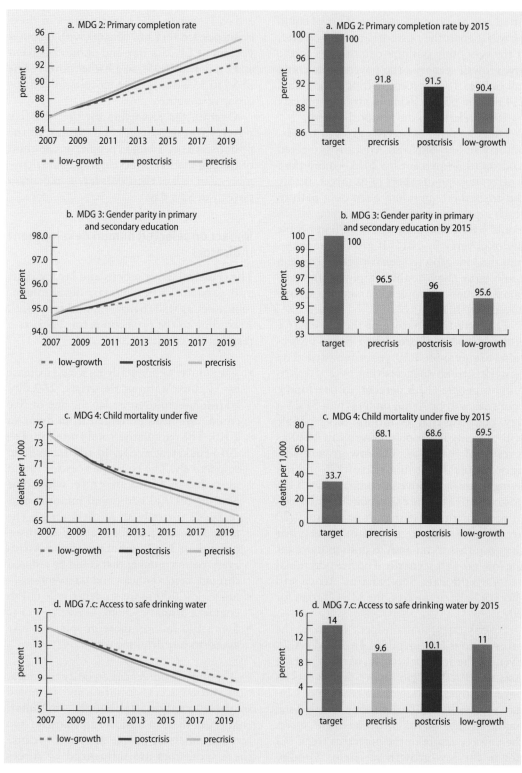

Source: World Bank staff calculations.

TABLE 4.2 Trends for other MDG human development indicators by region and alternative economic scenarios

MDG and region	Target	1991	2007	2015 Postcrisis	2015 Precrisis	2015 Low-growth
MDG 2: Primary completion rate (%)						
East Asia and Pacific	100	101	98	100	100	99.3
Europe and Central Asia	100	93	98	99.9	100	99.9
Latin America and the Caribbean	100	84	100	97.9	100	97.7
Middle East and North Africa	100	78	90	94.9	95.6	93.6
South Asia	100	62	80	82.4	91.7	81.9
Sub-Saharan Africa	100	51	60	67.3	67.6	66.7
All developing countries	100	78	85	91.5	91.8	90.4
MDG 3: Ratio of girls to boys in primary and secondary education (%)	Target	1991	2007			
East Asia and Pacific	100	89	99	100	100	100
Europe and Central Asia	100	100	102	99.4	100	97.8
Latin America and the Caribbean	100	98	103	100	100	100
Middle East and North Africa	100	78	96	95.6	98.2	94.7
South Asia	100	70	89	92.7	94.4	92.1
Sub-Saharan Africa	100	79	86	89.7	89.9	89.1
All developing countries	100	83	95	96.0	96.5	95.6
MDG 4: Child mortality under five (per 1,000)	Target	1990	2007			
East Asia and Pacific	19	56	27	24.6	18.6	24.9
Europe and Central Asia	17	50	23	18.8	15.4	21.7
Latin America and the Caribbean	18	55	26	23.7	19.7	25.4
Middle East and North Africa	26	78	38	36.7	29.2	37.3
South Asia	42	125	78	76.0	62.7	76.6
Sub-Saharan Africa	61	183	146	139.5	138.7	141.0
All developing countries	34	101	74	68.6	68.1	69.5
MDG 7.c: Access to improved water source (% population w/access)	Target	1990	2006			
East Asia and Pacific	16	32	13	3.3	0.6	4.1
Europe and Central Asia	5	10	5	0	0	1.8
Latin America and the Caribbean	8	16	9	5.4	4.5	7.1
Middle East and North Africa	6	11	12	8.3	7.4	10.0
South Asia	13	27	13	9.3	5.1	10.2
Sub-Saharan Africa	26	51	42	39.1	38.8	39.8
All developing countries	12	24	14	10.1	9.6	11

Source: World Bank staff estimates.

participation by girls in school reflects in part the educational level of the mother, and access to safe water is affected by the degree of urbanization. The impact of slower growth on the MDGs increases, however, as the time horizon is extended further into the future (for example, fewer girls being educated now means that eventually women of childbearing age will have less education).

In general, the impact of the low-growth scenario on development outcomes will be cumulative and long term (figure 4.3).

• If the baseline scenario (the postcrisis trend) holds up, human development indicators will continue to improve albeit less rapidly owing to the extended impact of the crisis. By 2015 the differences between the gains

FIGURE 4.3   The long-run effect of slower growth is especially worrisome in Sub-Saharan Africa

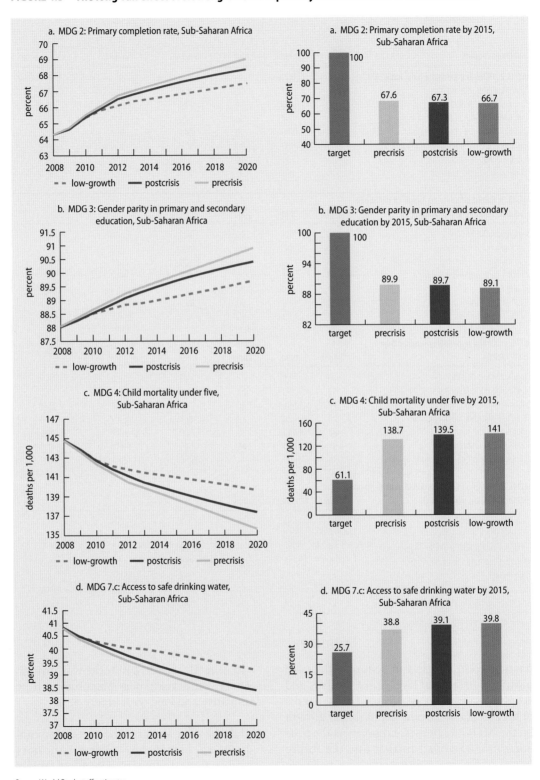

Source: World Bank staff estimates.
Note: The precrisis period is 2000–07.

projected in the postcrisis trend and those for the precrisis trend will become discernible, especially for human development outcomes such as primary school completion and infant mortality.

- Like the compounding effects of interest rates, these gaps will intensify from 2015 to 2020. A look at the long-term impact reveals that the projected slide in human development outcomes will become damaging and irreversible unless action is taken now.

- The world needs to avoid economic stagnation. If the growth trend in developing countries becomes sluggish for a long time, as in the low-growth scenario, development outcomes will deteriorate or stall, as happened in many low-income countries in Sub-Saharan Africa during the 1970s and 1980s.

Spending strategies under less favorable circumstances

What can developing countries do if the external economic environment remains unfavorable, and what impacts might their policy and spending strategies have on development outcomes? The three global growth scenarios provided a broad picture of the likely impact of the crisis on poverty. But these scenarios cannot be used to explore the scope for mitigating the effects of external shocks on poverty through appropriate policy adjustments. For this purpose, the broad country coverage achieved in the scenarios given above is set aside in favor of a richer analysis of the impact of policies.

To begin, low-income countries are divided into two groups—those that are resource rich and those that are resource poor.[10] A representative economy of each type is then constructed based on the average indicators for all of the low-income countries in that group (tables 4A.1 and 4A.2 in the annex summarize the social and economic indicators that characterize each country archetype; for the most part they correspond to the latest median statistics from the World Bank's World Development Indicators database. The assumptions and data used in constructing

each of the two representative economies are given in box 4.3.

These simulations use the World Bank's Maquette for MDG Simulations (MAMS), a model that analyzes the implications of strategic choices for economic outcomes, including changes in human development indicators (see box 4A.1 in the annex for more discussion).[11] MAMS' main contribution is its integration of government services and their impact on the economy, including on the MDGs and the labor market, within a standard recursive dynamic computable general equilibrium framework. Several MAMS features are useful for assessing the impact of alternative scenarios on MDGs. The model incorporates a formal representation of the production of government services (education, health, and infrastructure) that takes into account demand, supply, and efficiency. It allows for complementarity or synergy effects across the MDGs—for example, better access to clean water may improve health, which may boost school attendance, labor productivity, and economic growth. It shows the economywide repercussions of scaling up (or down) human development services, including the impact on economic growth, relative prices, the exchange rate, and the allocation of resources between government and nongovernment sectors. And it makes possible the consideration of sequencing and time-related trade-offs through a recursive treatment of dynamics that tracks indicators over time.

The low-income, resource-poor country

The analysis for the low-income, resource-poor archetype (LIRP) considers four cases (the reference year for the analysis is 2009, and the simulation period is 2010–20):

- The *base case* is relatively optimistic. It assumes that GDP growth recovers by 2011 to the growth rate in 2008. The annual growth rate in 2012–20 is slightly higher than in 2011 (see figure 4.4 for GDP growth under different LIRP cases). Growth in foreign aid is slower after 2010

BOX 4.3   Assumptions for the archetype countries

The low-income, resource-rich (LIRR) archetype has a natural resource that it exports. The government receives 70 percent of the income, and foreign investors get the rest. In 2009 government income from the natural resource was 8.4 percent of GDP. All output of the natural resource commodity is exported and accounts for 56 percent of the value of total exports. Government borrowing is 2.6 percent of GDP, and foreign debt is 49 percent of GDP. The country receives no debt relief during the simulation period.

The low-income, resource-poor (LIRP) archetype is more dependent than the LIRR on foreign aid, which equals about 6.5 percent of GDP, and its foreign debt is higher, at 65 percent of GDP. Like the LIRR, it receives no debt relief during the analysis period.

The poverty headcount rate at $1.25 a day (the indicator for MDG 1) is 49.6 percent for the LIRP

archetype and 61.8 percent for the LIRR—the median values for the countries in each group. The poorest statistics for the LIRR result partly from the "natural resource curse" associated with past conflicts and corruption; see, for example, Collier and Goderis (2007). Median GDP per capita is $598 for the LIRP and $482 for the LIRR. Similarly, both the LIRP and the LIRR are assumed to have the median value of their group for share of the population with access to clean water (MDG 7); the under-five mortality rate (MDG 4); and selected education indicators, including the gross completion rate for primary school (MDG 2) and gross enrollment rates at all three levels (primary, secondary, and tertiary). The analysis looks especially at the evolution of MDGs 1, 2, 4, and 7.

Government and nongovernment payments and foreign debt of archetype countries, 2009
percent of GDP

Payment	Low-income, resource-poor countries	Low-income, resource-rich countries
Income from natural resource	n.a.	8.4
Foreign aid	6.5	1.2
Taxes	20.2	16.0
Private borrowing	0.5	0.4
Foreign borrowing	4.0	2.6
Foreign debt	65.0	48.8
Foreign direct investment	1.9	1.7
Remittances	1.3	1.2

Source: Go and others, forthcoming.
Note: n.a. = not applicable.

than in the previous decade, reflecting a decline in GDP growth in donor countries.[12] Remittance growth and foreign direct investment (FDI) fall relative to the previous decade, also reflecting a decline in GDP growth in the countries from which the payments flow. By 2015 world prices have recovered to 2008 precrisis levels.

• The *low-aid case* represents an extreme, negative case with a weak recovery in GDP growth (to just 40 percent of real GDP growth in the base case), driven by a deteriorating external environment and a decline

in productivity growth. World prices, FDI, and foreign aid all grow at slower rates than in the base case (25 percent of base case rates). The growth slowdown for foreign aid and other government receipts leads to reduced development spending (defined as spending on education, health, water and sanitation, and infrastructure), as the government fails to reduce spending in other areas. Remittances are assumed to grow at the same annual rate as in the base case because these payments are based on personal connections, and there is little reason to expect them to respond negatively to slower growth in the developing countries.

- In the *low-aid internal 1 case* the government makes internal adjustments to offset the effects on the MDGs of a weak recovery in GDP and reduced growth in foreign inflows. The government reduces growth in nondevelopment spending (to 90 percent of such spending in the base case), increases receipts from domestic taxes (by half a percentage point of GDP over the base case), and uses the resulting fiscal space to expand development spending.

- In the *low-aid internal 2 case,* the government further improves policies and service delivery relative to the low-aid internal 1 case, resulting in a moderately higher GDP growth (55 percent of the base-case rate).[13]

Slow growth in the low-income, resource-poor country results in a severe deterioration in human development indicators. All four of the MDGs covered by the analysis (poverty, primary school gross completion rate, under-five mortality rate, and share of population with access to safe water) decline in the low-aid simulation relative to the base case (figure 4.5). By 2020 the poverty rate is more than 20 percentage points higher, the under-five mortality rate 15 points higher, and the share of the population with access to safe water 4 percentage points lower in the low-aid case than in the base case. The gross primary school completion rate improves in all scenarios, as students enrolled in lower grades (reflecting recent strong expansion in primary enrollment) proceed through the primary level. Because of a natural decline in the intake of out-of-cohort students, progress tends to level off.[14]

With better expenditure management and internal effort in the low-aid internal 1 case, including a government shift in expenditures to protect development spending and increased domestic tax collection, all the MDGs (except poverty reduction) do better than under the low-aid case. The poverty rate in the low-aid internal 1 case is marginally higher than in the low-aid case, because

FIGURE 4.4   Annual GDP growth for LIRP under four cases

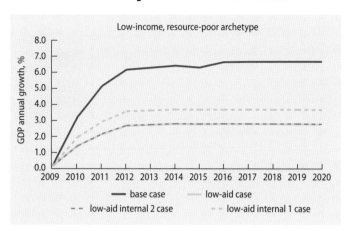

Source: Go and others, forthcoming.

the increase in taxes (predominantly indirect taxes in low-income countries) reduces expenditures or incomes of the poor.

Under the low-aid internal 2 case, a more substantial improvement in MDG indicators can be accomplished by combining improved fiscal policies with policies that improve overall productivity. Progress toward the MDGs improves relative to the low-aid internal 1 and the low-aid cases, although not enough to catch up with the base case.

Thus policy adjustments to support development spending and improve overall economic productivity are critical to limiting the impact on human development indicators of an externally induced decline in GDP growth (for example, the current crisis). However, to the extent that policies cannot maintain trend growth in the face of an external shock, then a deterioration in human development indicators is inevitable. This fact highlights the importance of a global response to the crisis that focuses on ensuring strong flows of aid, limiting the deterioration in developing countries' access to external finance, and maintaining open export markets to permit trade expansion at more attractive world prices.

The low-income, resource-rich country

The pattern of results for the low-income, resource-rich archetype (LIRR) is similar to

MAP 4.2   Tuberculosis kills around 1.3 million people a year, or 3,500 a day

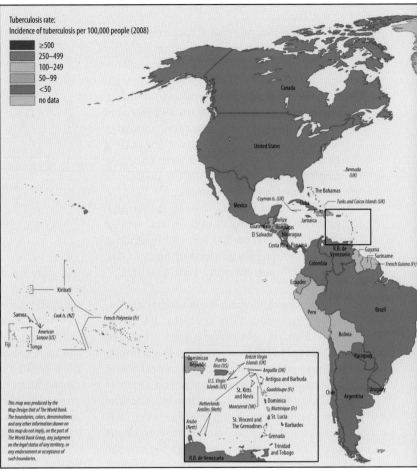

Source: World Development Indicators.

that of the LIRP, including GDP growth rates in figure 4.4. Under the optimistic base case, which, unlike the other scenarios, includes a strong recovery in the world price of the natural resource export, all MDG indicators continue to improve. Internal adjustment (that is, the government reduces growth in nondevelopment spending, increases domestic taxes, and uses the resulting fiscal space to expand spending on education, health, water and sanitation, and infrastructure) in the context of stagnant export prices for the natural resource improves progress toward the MDGs but is not sufficient to bring the country up to the path of the base case (figure 4.6). A resource-rich country has the ability to draw down reserves accumulated from its resource exports or to increase government foreign borrowing, in both cases creating a capital inflow, captured by the government. This option, incorporated into the low-aid internal 2 simulation, can move progress on the MDGs closer to the base path. [15] But at the level reported, the LIRR country cannot make up for the impact of the financial crisis on MDGs through internal adjustment alone.

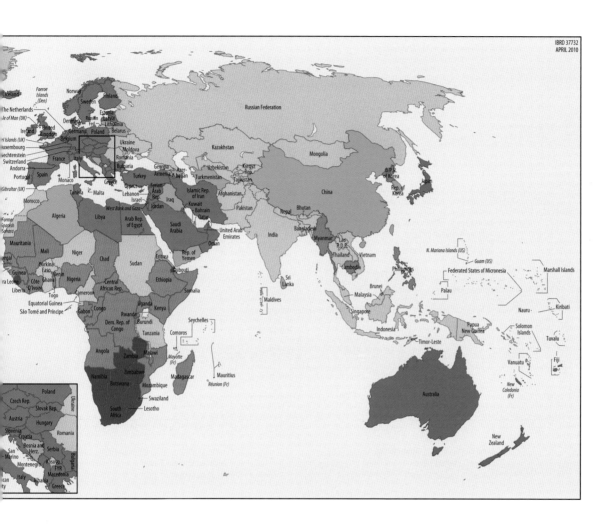

Summary and conclusions

This chapter presented forecasts of MDG outcomes at the global level and for Sub-Saharan Africa based solely on alternative assumptions for growth in developing countries. It also explored the scope for policy improvements to mitigate the impact of slower growth on progress toward the MDGs through simulations using two archetypical low-income countries, one representing those that are resource rich and the other those that are resource poor. While understanding the prospects for progress toward the MDGs is of crucial importance as the world looks forward to 2015 and beyond, it should be recognized that such analysis inevitably is fraught with difficulties given data gaps and still-limited knowledge about the processes that determine these outcomes.

The projections given here indicate that the economic crisis will lead to a deterioration across all MDGs, extending beyond 2015. In all the growth scenarios, the world

FIGURE 4.5   **Simulated MDG outcomes for the LIRP archetype under alternative cases**

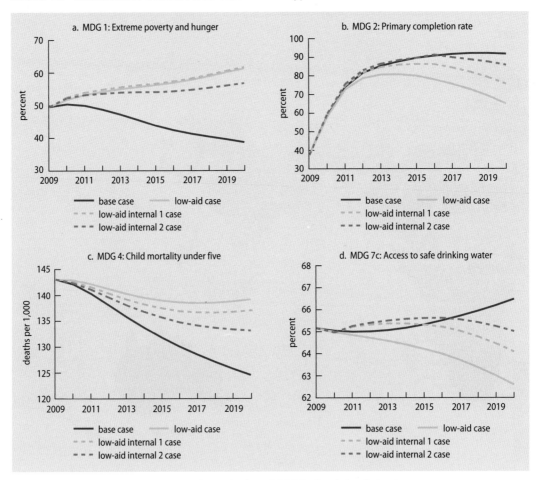

Source: World Bank staff calculations using the Maquette for MDG Simulations (MAMS). See Go and others, forthcoming.

will meet the MDG of halving its headcount poverty rate using a poverty line of $1.25 a day. However, the poverty rate in 2015 is considerably higher in the low-growth scenario (18.5 percent) than in the postcrisis trend (15 percent), which assumes a rapid recovery from the crisis. The rough magnitude of the projected effects on hunger is similar. Underlying these figures are considerable regional variations. Sub-Saharan Africa poses the greatest challenge—it has the highest poverty

rates and will have the most difficulty achieving its regional poverty reduction targets.

The projected impact of alternative scenarios for growth on the other MDGs analyzed here—completion of primary school, under-five mortality rate, gender equality in education, and access to safe water—is more limited, although small changes in these percentages may involve large numbers of people. This muted effect reflects the presence of significant lags, perhaps most obviously

FIGURE 4.6   Simulated MDG outcomes for the LIRR archetype under alternative cases

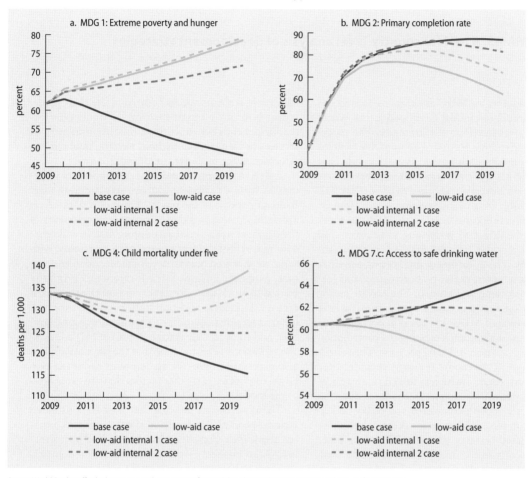

Source: World Bank staff calculations using the Maquette for MDG Simulations (MAMS). See Go and others, forthcoming.

in education. The negative effects of slower growth will make themselves more strongly felt in the long run, however.

Country-level simulations for the two low-income archetypes indicate that, if the global economic environment and domestic GDP growth recover rapidly, continued progress will take place across the MDGs that are covered here (poverty, primary completion, under-five mortality, and access to safe water). If the global recovery is weak, internal efforts (including spending switches toward

development and tax increases) lead to some improvement in the MDGs compared with a scenario with no improvement in policies. However, the improvement from internal efforts alone falls far short of that required to achieve the base-case levels of the MDG indicators. Thus, while policy matters, better development outcomes hinge critically on a rapid global recovery that improves export conditions, terms of trade, and capital flows for low-income countries. Chapter 5 turns to this subject.

Annex: Forecast, Tools, and Data

BOX 4A.1   MAMS: A tool for country-level analysis of development strategies

MAMS (Maquette for MDG Simulations) is an economywide simulation model developed at the World Bank to analyze development strategies. The model integrates a dynamic recursive computable general equilibrium model with an additional module that links specific MDG or poverty-related interventions to progress on poverty and other MDGs. This link is made possible by a disaggregation of government activities into functions related to MDG services (education, health, and water and sanitation) and infrastructure as well as a residual for other government activity. The government finances its activities from domestic taxes, domestic borrowing, and foreign aid (borrowing and grants). The private sector disaggregation varies between applications; where private provision of MDG services is important, such services are included, complementing the contribution of government services to MDG progress. The factors of production in the model typically include three types of labor, each of which is linked to an education cycle: those with incomplete secondary education (unskilled), those with completed secondary education but incomplete tertiary (semi-skilled), and those with completed tertiary (skilled). The labor force variable depends on the functioning of the education system in the model. The other factors of production include public capital stocks by government activity and a private capital stock. Growth in the stock of government infrastructure capital contributes to overall growth by adding to the productivity of other production activities.

MAMS covers MDGs in the areas of poverty, education, health, and water and sanitation. For poverty, a log-normal distribution is assumed; other applications have used microsimulations. For other MDGs, a set of functions links the level of each indicator to a set of determinants. The determinants include the delivery of relevant services and other indicators, also allowing for the recognition that achievements in one MDG can have an impact on other MDGs. Other than education, service delivery for other MDGs is expressed relative to the size of the population. In education, students successfully complete their grade, repeat it, or drop out of their cycle. Student performance depends on educational quality (quantity of services per student), household welfare, public infrastructure, wage incentives, and health status.

A MAMS country database is a synthesis of information from a variety of sources, structured to meet the requirements of the model. The model parameters are defined using this data. The main components of the database are a social accounting matrix and other data that reflect the functioning of the economy, with some emphasis on human development and infrastructure. More specifically, the information is primarily related to stock data (for labor and other production factors, students, and population) and elasticities (related to substitutability in production, consumption, and trade as well as to responses in MDG indicators to various determinants). For the simulations, it is also necessary to provide assumptions about the evolution of policies and other factors that are exogenous to the model.

The government policies that may be considered include spending—its level and allocation across different areas, including education, health, and infrastructure—and financing—policies for taxation, domestic and foreign borrowing, and foreign aid. Economic performance is measured by the evolution of:

- poverty and other MDG targets
- macro-indicators, including GDP (split into private and government consumption and investment, exports, and imports); the composition of the government budget, the balance of payments, and the savings-investment balance; total factor productivity; and domestic and foreign debt stocks
- sectoral structure of production, employment, incomes, and trade
- the labor market, including unemployment and the educational composition of the labor force

Note: For more information about MAMS, see www.worldbank.org/mams.

TABLE 4A.1   Alternate scenarios for poverty reduction, based on a poverty line of $1.25 a day, by region

Scenario	Region or country	1990	2005	2015	2020	1990	2005	2015	2020
Postcrisis		Percentage of the population living on less than $1.25 a day				Number of people living on less than $1.25 a day (millions)			
	East Asia and Pacific	54.7	16.8	5.9	4.0	873	317	120	83
	China	60.2	15.9	5.1	4.0	683	208	70	56
	Europe and Central Asia	2.0	3.7	1.7	1.2	9	16	7	5
	Latin America and the Caribbean	11.3	8.2	5.0	4.3	50	45	30	27
	Middle East and North Africa	4.3	3.6	1.8	1.5	10	11	6	6
	South Asia	51.7	40.3	22.8	19.4	579	595	388	352
	India	51.3	41.6	23.6	20.3	435	456	295	268
	Sub-Saharan Africa	57.6	50.9	38.0	32.8	296	387	366	352
	Total	41.7	25.2	15.0	12.8	1,817	1,371	918	826
Precrisis		Percentage of the population living on less than $1.25 (2005 PPP) a day				Number of people living on less than $1.25 (2005 PPP) a day (millions)			
	East Asia and Pacific	54.7	16.8	5.5	3.5	873	317	111	73
	China	60.2	15.9	5.0	3.9	683	208	69	55
	Europe and Central Asia	2.0	3.7	1.5	1.1	9	16	7	5
	Latin America and the Caribbean	11.3	8.2	4.6	3.9	50	45	28	25
	Middle East and North Africa	4.3	3.6	1.7	1.4	10	11	6	6
	South Asia	51.7	40.3	21.5	17.9	579	595	367	326
	India	51.3	41.6	22.7	19.6	435	456	283	259
	Sub-Saharan Africa	57.6	50.9	35.9	29.9	296	387	346	321
	Total	41.7	25.2	14.1	11.7	1,817	1,371	865	755
Low-growth		Percentage of the population living on less than $1.25 (2005 PPP) a day				Number of people living on less than $1.25 (2005 PPP) a day (millions)			
	East Asia and Pacific	54.7	16.8	7.8	5.8	873	317	159	122
	China	60.2	15.9	6.0	4.7	683	208	82	67
	Europe and Central Asia	2.0	3.7	2.5	2.2	9	16	11	10
	Latin America and the Caribbean	11.3	8.2	6.5	5.7	50	45	39	36
	Middle East and North Africa	4.3	3.6	3.3	2.7	10	11	12	11
	South Asia	51.7	40.3	28.6	24.6	579	595	489	447
	India	51.3	41.6	29.4	25.2	435	456	367	333
	Sub-Saharan Africa	57.6	50.9	43.8	39.9	296	387	421	428
	Total	41.7	25.2	18.5	16.3	1,817	1,371	1,132	1,053

Source: World Bank staff calculations, using PovcalNet.

TABLE 4A.2 **Alternate scenarios for poverty reduction, based on a poverty line of $2.00 a day, by region**

Scenario	Region or country	1990	2005	2015	2020	1990	2005	2015	2020
Postcrisis		Percentage of the population living on less than $2.00 a day				Number of people living on less than $2.00 a day (millions)			
	East Asia and Pacific	79.8	38.7	19.4	14.3	1,274	730	394	299
	China	84.6	36.3	16.0	12.0	961	473	220	168
	Europe and Central Asia	6.9	8.9	5.0	4.1	32	39	22	18
	Latin America and the Caribbean	19.7	16.6	11.1	9.7	86	91	67	62
	Middle East and North Africa	19.7	16.9	8.3	6.6	44	52	30	26
	South Asia	82.7	73.9	57.0	51.0	926	1,091	973	926
	India	82.6	75.6	58.3	51.9	702	828	728	686
	Sub-Saharan Africa	76.2	73.0	59.6	55.4	391	555	574	595
	Total	63.2	47.0	33.7	29.8	2,754	2,557	2,060	1,926
Precrisis		Percentage of the population living on less than $2.00 (2005 PPP) a day				Number of people living on less than $2.00 (2005 PPP) a day (millions)			
	East Asia and Pacific	79.8	38.7	18.6	13.4	1,274	730	379	280
	China	84.6	36.3	15.7	11.8	961	473	216	166
	Europe and Central Asia	6.9	8.9	4.5	3.7	32	39	20	16
	Latin America and the Caribbean	19.7	16.6	10.3	8.8	86	91	62	56
	Middle East and North Africa	19.7	16.9	8.0	6.1	44	52	29	24
	South Asia	82.7	73.9	55.5	49.0	926	1,091	946	890
	India	82.6	75.6	57.2	50.9	702	828	715	674
	Sub-Saharan Africa	76.2	73.0	57.6	52.4	391	555	555	563
	Total	63.2	47.0	32.6	28.4	2,754	2,557	1,991	1,830
Low-growth		Percentage of the population living on less than $2.00 (2005 PPP) a day				Number of people living on less than $2.00 (2005 PPP) a day (millions)			
	East Asia and Pacific	79.8	38.7	22.2	18.1	1,274	730	451	379
	China	84.6	36.3	16.9	13.6	961	473	233	191
	Europe and Central Asia	6.9	8.9	7.1	6.2	32	39	31	27
	Latin America and the Caribbean	19.7	16.6	14.5	12.9	86	91	88	82
	Middle East and North Africa	19.7	16.9	14.1	11.4	44	52	52	45
	South Asia	82.7	73.9	63.9	57.8	926	1,091	1,089	1,049
	India	82.6	75.6	64.6	57.9	702	828	808	766
	Sub-Saharan Africa	76.2	73.0	65.1	62.5	391	555	627	671
	Total	63.2	47.0	38.2	34.9	2,754	2,557	2,338	2,254

Source: World Bank staff calculations, using PovcalNet.

TABLE 4A.3   **Detailed data for archetypes**
Median values by archetype, selected variables

Variable	Low-income, resource-poor (LIRP)	Low-income, resource-rich (LIRR)
Poverty headcount ratio at $1.25 a day (% of population)	49.6	61.8
Poverty headcount ratio at $2.00 a day (% of population)	76.7	80.5
Elasticity of poverty to income	−1.01	−1.01
Poverty headcount ratio at national poverty line (% of population)	44.2	45.4
Primary school completion rate, total (% gross)	55.8	59.9
Primary school enrollment (% gross)	95.9	95.2
Secondary school enrollment (% gross)	31.6	35.5
Tertiary school enrollment (% gross)	3.2	4.7
Under-five mortality rate (per 1,000)	115.2	141.6
Maternal mortality ratio, modeled estimate (per 100,000 live births)	720.0	825.0
Maternal mortality ratio, national estimate (per 100,000 live births)	478.0	613.0
Improved water source (% of population with access)	65.0	60.0
Improved sanitation facilities (% of population with access)	30.0	31.5
Foreign direct investment, net inflows (% of GDP)	2.7	6.5
Foreign direct investment, net outflows (% of GDP)	0.0	0.0
Foreign direct investment inflow outflows (% of GDP)	2.7	6.5
Net current transfers, remittances (% of GDP)	8.9	4.5
Official current transfers, receipts, foreign aid (% of GDP)	2.5	1.7
External debt stocks (% GNI)	29.9	49.5
External debt stocks private (% GNI)	0.0	0.0
External debt stocks public (% GNI)	29.9	49.5
External debt stocks public, median (% GDP)	28.0	48.6
Gross fixed capital formation (% of GDP)	20.8	18.3
Gross fixed capital formation, private (% of GDP)	10.7	11.3
Labor force participation rate (% of total population ages 15–64)	74.3	71.4
Resource exports (% of GDP)	0.4	19.0
Resource exports (% of merchandise exports)	3.4	67.9
Mining value added (% of GDP)	0.7	3.3
Interest payment on private external debt (% of GDP)	0.0	0.0
Interest payment on public external debt (% of GDP)	0.3	0.5

Source: World Bank 2009b.

Notes

1. Resource intensity is an important factor in the performance of low-income countries and has been used to classify developing countries in several studies; see Collier and O'Connell (2006); IMF (2006); Ndulu and others (2007); and Arbache, Go, and Page (2008).
2. World Bank 2004b.
3. Even short-term assessments are necessarily projections because of the infrequency of the underlying data. Household surveys of incomes and expenditures are generally undertaken only every five or more years in many developing countries.
4. The estimation uses a logistic function, similar to Clemens, Kenny, and Moss (2007) but with per capita income as a key determinant instead of a time trend. Income rather than social spending is used as the independent variable because of data and other difficulties with fiscal adjustment and public expenditures. The logistic curve was used for the projections because it has a smoother transition across income levels, although the elasticity form (double-log regressions) by income level or region yielded similar results.
5. World Bank PovcalNet database.
6. See also IMF (2010); World Bank (2010b).
7. World Bank 2003, p. 41. These calculations update estimates found in Ravallion (2009) and World Bank (2009a).
8. Tiwari and Zaman 2010; World Bank 2010a.
9. Friedman and Schady 2009.
10. The low-income countries are disaggregated into resource rich and resource poor using data on exports of fuel ore and minerals as a share of merchandise exports. See table 4A.3 in the annex for more details.
11. See Bourguignon, Diaz-Bonilla, and Lofgren (2008) and Lofgren and Diaz-Bonilla (2010) as well as www.worldbank.org/mams.
12. The growth rate is set at 3 percent, the assumed annual GDP growth in developed countries from 2010 onward.
13. This is 15 percent higher than the annual GDP growth in the pessimistic scenario with internal adjustment (low-aid internal 1 case).
14. The primary gross completion rate (MDG 2) is defined as the total number of primary school graduates (regardless of age) as a share of the total population of the theoretical graduation age. If MDG 2 were measured by the net completion rate (the number of graduates of the theoretical right age as a share of the total population of the same age), the tendency for the indicator to level off would be weaker, especially for the base case.
15. In the model this is done by increasing foreign borrowing, which reduces the net asset position of the country relative to the rest of the world and is equivalent to drawing down foreign exchange reserves or liquidating foreign investment financed by the natural resource in the past. Here, the annual growth rates in foreign borrowing are assumed to be twice the annual growth rates in the base. As a result, the foreign debt stock in foreign currency is 30 percent higher in 2020 for the low-aid internal 2 case than for the other scenarios. Relative to GDP, the foreign debt stock is around 10 percentage points higher in 2020 for the low-aid internal 2 case than for the low-aid internal 1 case (which has a slightly slower rate of GDP growth and similar evolution for the exchange rate). References

References

Adams, C. S., and D. Bevan. 2000. "The Cash Budget as Restraint: The Experience of Zambia." In *Investment and Risk in Africa,* ed. P. Collier and C. Patillo. New York: St. Martin's Press.

Arbache, J., D. Go, and J. Page. 2008. "Is Africa's Economy at a Turning Point?" In *Africa at a Turning Point?* ed. D. Go and J. Page, pp. 13–85. Washington, DC: World Bank.

Bourguignon, François, Carolina Diaz-Bonilla, and Hans Lofgren. 2008. "Aid, Service Delivery and the Millennium Development Goals in an Economywide Framework." In *The Impact of Macroeconomic Policies on Poverty and Income Distribution: Macro-Micro Evaluation Techniques and Tools,* ed. François Bourguignon, Maurizio Bussolo, and Luiz A. Pereira da Silva, pp. 283–315. Washington, DC: World Bank.

Clemens, M. A., C. J. Kenny, and T. J. Moss. 2007. "The Trouble with the MDGs: Confronting Expectations of Aid and Development Success." *World Development* 35 (5): 735–51.

Collier, P., and S. O'Connell. 2006. "Opportunities and Choices." *Explaining African Economic Growth,* ch. 2 of synthesis vol. Nairobi: African Economic Research Consortium.

Collier, P., and B. Goderis. 2007. "Commodity Prices, Growth, and the Natural Resource Curse: Reconciling a Conundrum." Oxford University, Centre for the Study of African Economies, Oxford, U.K.

Devarajan S., and R. Reinikka. 2004. "Making Services Work for the Poor." *Journal of African Economies* 13 (Supp. 1): i142–66.

Dinh, H., A. Adugna, and B. Myers. 2002. "The Impact of Cash Budgets on Poverty Reduction in Zambia: A Case Study of the Conflict between Well-Intentioned Macroeconomic Policy and Service Delivery to the Poor." Policy Research Working Paper 2914. World Bank, Washington, DC.

Filmer, D., J. Hammer, and L. Pritchett. 2000. "Weak Links in the Chain: A Diagnosis of Health Policy in Poor Countries." *World Bank Research Observer* 15 (2): 188–224.

———. 2002. "Weak Links in the Chain II: A Prescription for Health Policy in Poor Countries." *World Bank Research Observer* 17 (1): 47–66.

Filmer, D., and L. Pritchett. 1999. "The Impact of Public Spending on Health: Does Money Matter?" *Social Science and Medicine* 49 (10): 1309–23.

Friedman, J., and N. Schady. 2009. "How Many More Infants Are Likely to Die in Africa as a Result of the Global Financial Crisis?" Policy Research Working Paper 5023. World Bank, Washington, DC.

Go, D., H. Lofgren, S. Robinson, and K. Thierfelder. Forthcoming. "The Impact of the Global Economic Crisis on MDGs in Archetypical Developing Countries." World Bank, Washington, DC.

IMF (International Monetary Fund). 2006. *Regional Economic Outlook: Sub-Saharan Africa*. Washington, DC.

———. 2010. *World Economic Outlook*. Washington, DC (January).

Lofgren, H., and C. Diaz-Bonilla. 2010. "MAMS: An Economywide Model for Development Strategy Analysis." World Bank, Washington, DC.

Ndulu, B. J., L. Chakroborti, L. Lijane, V. Ramachandran, and J. Wolgin. 2007. *Challenges of Africa Growth: Opportunities, Constraints, and Strategic Directions*. Washington, DC: World Bank.

Rajkumar, A., and V. Swaroop. 2008. "Public Spending and Outcomes: Does Governance Matter?" *Journal of Development Economics* 86 (1): 96–111.

Ravallion, M. 2009. "The Crisis and the World's Poorest." *Development Outreach*, World Bank, Washington, DC (December).

Tiwari, S., and H. Zaman 2010. "The Impact of Economic Shocks on Global Undernourishment" Policy Research Working Paper 5215. World Bank, Washington, DC.

Wagstaff, A., and M. Claeson. 2004. *Rising to the Challenges: The Millennium Development Goals for Health*. Washington, DC: World Bank.

World Bank. 2004a. *Global Monitoring Report 2004: Policies and Actions for Achieving the Millennium Development Goals and Related Outcomes*. Washington, DC: World Bank.

———. 2004b. *World Development Report 2004: Making Services Work for Poor People*. Washington, D.C.: World Bank.

———. 2009a. "Protecting Progress: The Challenge Facing Low-Income Countries in the Global Recession." Background paper prepared for the G-20 Leaders' Meeting, Pittsburgh, PA, September 24–25.

———. 2009b. *World Development Indicators*. Washington, DC: World Bank.

———2010a. "Food Price Watch." Washington, DC (February).

———. 2010b. *Global Economic Prospects 2010*. Washington, DC: World Bank.

5

The International Community and Development: Trade, Aid, and the International Financial Institutions

The global economic crisis severely reduced developing-country external resources by drastically curtailing their export revenues and their access to private capital flows. As elaborated in previous chapters, the resulting decline in economic activity sharply increased poverty and impaired public services to the poor. To a degree, the international system worked effectively to support developing-country access to external resources and limit the rise in poverty. Despite initial fears, increased trade restrictions in reaction to the crisis affected only a small part of international trade. Bilateral donors increased aid (at least through 2008), and the international financial institutions (IFIs) dramatically increased their lending. As the global recovery has taken hold, developing-country export revenues have begun to recover, and their access to external finance to improve, although both remain well below precrisis levels.

Despite these positive signs, the global recovery remains fragile, and continuing efforts of the global community to support development are essential. Although aid has hit record levels, aid flows remain well below those envisioned in donor promises, and the more constrained fiscal environment is a serious threat to future aid efforts. Further progress is required to strengthen aid effectiveness and improve aid allocation. Reaching agreement on the Doha Round would support an open trading environment and generate substantial increases in market access for developing countries. And the crisis has raised new development challenges, including questions about the sustainability of the IFIs' policy responses and their policies and structure for dealing with the challenges in the future—questions that now need to be resolved.

Recovering from the crisis through trade

World trade contracted by about 12 percent in 2009, and all regions experienced deep declines in imports (figure 5.1). Although demand for exports declined significantly in most developing countries, countries dependent on durable goods exports felt the sharpest decline. Demand was more resilient for nondurable consumer goods (such as clothing and food) and services (except the more volatile tourism sector). And continued growth in China meant countries in East Asia faced smaller drops in export demand than elsewhere. Developing countries also had sharp

FIGURE 5.1   Trade has bottomed out and started to recover

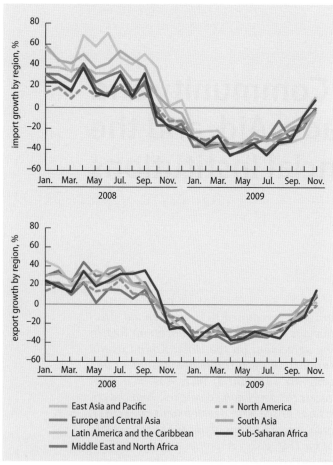

Source: World Bank Development Economics Trade and International Integration, Trade Watch, January 2010 (www.wordlbank.org/research/trade).
Note: Trade volume is the 3-month over 3-month growth rate (rolling, seasonally adjusted 3-month moving average).

declines in external finance: net private capital flows to developing countries in 2009 are estimated to have fallen almost 70 percent from their 2007 peak. Remittances, as much as 20 percent of GDP in some countries, have been more stable than capital flows and merchandise trade but nevertheless declined by an estimated 6.1 percent in 2009. All in all, by mid-2009, the collapse in developing-country external resources necessitated a sharp contraction in import demand, which fell to 25 percent below precrisis levels.

Almost a year into the trade recovery, especially in East Asia and the Pacific and Latin America, the dollar value of global trade remains around 20 percent lower than its precrisis level and 40 percent lower than it would have been had world trade continued to grow at its 2002–08 trend. A number of advanced indicators of trade developments underscore the fragility of the recovery. For instance, the Baltic Dry Index and air freight traffic point to a fragile rebound. The index, a measure of the cost of shipping bulk cargo by sea, picked up in February 2009 after a seven-month drop but has been hovering since then (figure 5.2). Given the uncertain recovery and still-depressed investment activity, world trade is projected to expand by only 4.3 percent in 2010 and by 6.2 percent in 2011.[1] While a strong recovery in developing countries' exports will depend on global macroeconomic developments, policies in both rich and poor

FIGURE 5.2   Baltic Dry Index points to a fragile rebound in shipping by sea

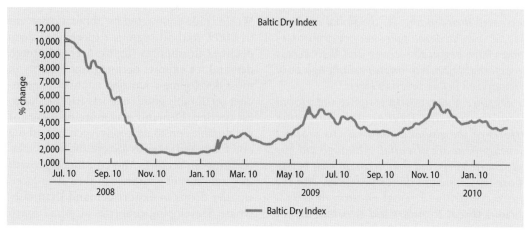

Source: Baltic Exchange Information Services Ltd 2010.

countries can play an important role. In particular, expanding developing-country access to foreign exchange through supporting trade finance, aid for trade, and maintaining an open trading environment will continue to play a critical role. These issues are taken in turn in the rest of this section.

Trade finance remains weak but shows signs of recovery

While the decline in developing-country exports was largely driven by the collapse in global demand, there is some evidence that the global credit crunch and sharp contraction in trade credit also contributed to the trade decline. For example, although surveys found that demand has been the major driving factor behind the contraction in trade credit, many respondents acknowledged that the reduced availability of trade finance instruments in their institutions contributed to the fall in trade finance volumes.[2] As the financial crisis deepened, trade finance tightened because of higher lending costs and risk premiums resulting from rising liquidity pressures, capital scarcity, and heightened risk aversion among trade finance providers for counterparty and country risks. The drying up of the secondary market for short-term exposure exacerbated the problem, as banks and other financial institutions deleveraged and such key players as Lehman Brothers exited the market. In an environment of global recession, banks may also have felt additional pressure to hold back on trade finance following implementation of the Basel II Accord on banking laws and regulations, which increased the risk sensitivity of capital requirements.

To mitigate the effects of these trade finance constraints, governments and multilateral development institutions responded with a range of trade finance programs, including a pledge by the Group of 20 (G-20) leaders at their April 2009 London Summit to ensure $250 billion in support for trade. The World Bank Group provided additional guarantees as well as liquidity for trade finance through the International Finance Corporation's (IFC) Global Trade Finance Program and Global Trade Liquidity Program. Recent data on export insurance and guarantees suggest that export credit agencies prevented a complete drying up of trade finance markets during the crisis.[3]

Lessons from past crises suggest that effective public actions in support of trade finance should be guided by several key principles, including the avoidance of moral hazard and the crowding out of commercial banks by setting clear time limits and exit strategies for intervention programs and by sharing, rather than fully underwriting, risk.[4] The substantial resources committed by G-20 leaders and multilateral institutions to support trade finance during the crisis underscore the critical importance of establishing a systematic and reliable mechanism to collect data on trade finance to monitor the market. Such a system could be used not only to assess how current interventions are influencing credit supply but also to provide an early warning of stress in trade credit provision.

Recent trade finance data indicate slight signs of improvement. According to a September 2009 report of the International Chamber of Commerce, banks' ability to provide trade credit has improved, reflecting enhanced capacity and liquidity in the banking sector and efforts by the international community to support trade finance instruments.[5] Data from the Society for Worldwide Interbank Financial Telecommunication document that short-term trade finance messages sent between banks for letters of credit, guarantees, and documentary collections collapsed in January 2009 and have gradually recovered since then, returning to positive territories in January 2010 (figure 5.3). Yet the number of trade messages during January-February 2010 remained more than 10 percent below the number registered during the same period in 2007 or 2008.

Maintaining an open trading environment is critical

World leaders acknowledged early on the systemic risks stemming from protectionist policy responses such as those used during the Great Depression. The G-20 communiqués at the Washington, London, and Pittsburgh Summits in 2009 provided assurances that

FIGURE 5.3   Short-term trade finance messages increased steadily from Jan. 2009 to Feb. 2010

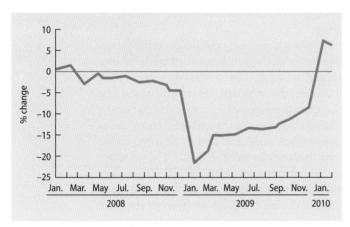

Source: SWIFTNET (www.swift.com).

FIGURE 5.4   Tariff rates fell except in upper-middle-income countries, 2008–09

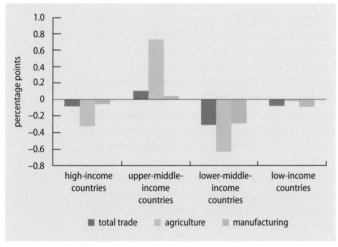

Source: World Bank staff calculations.

governments would refrain from discriminatory trade measures. Since the onset of the crisis, many countries have adopted policies that favored domestic over foreign products.[6] In particular, all G-20 countries have imposed measures restricting trade since the November 2008 summit.[7] The Global Anti-dumping Database records a 19.7 percent rise in industry requests for trade barriers in 2009 over 2008, when requests were already 35.0

percent higher than in 2007. According to the World Trade Organization's (WTO) quarterly monitoring report, some 350 trade-restrictive measures had been put in place as of December 2009, although some of them have since been removed. Protectionist measures have included tariff increases (although tariff rates fell in many countries—figure 5.4—and generally remained below bounded limits set in multilateral trade agreements), various quantitative restrictions, trade remedies (antidumping) and subsidies, and domestic purchase requirements in stimulus packages.[8] The fourth report of the Global Trade Alert, published in February 2010, confirms that "low fever" protectionism continues, with several of the largest economies taking discriminatory measures.[9]

Meanwhile, some countries have reacted to the crisis by reducing trade barriers—about 77 trade-liberalizing measures have been taken since the onset of the crisis—in an effort to reduce costs for industries and households (figure 5.5).[10] Furthermore, the newly adopted trade restrictions have been applied mainly to specific sectors (such as agriculture and iron and steel, followed at some distance by consumer electronics and textiles, clothing, and footwear). The affected products account for only about 0.5 percent of world trade (although the backlog of ongoing investigations of requests for trade remedies may imply some increase in 2010). Also, many policies aimed at stimulating domestic demand and economic activity may have benefited trading partners when applied on a nondiscriminatory basis.

While protectionist measures taken during the crisis undoubtedly curtailed trade flows, they have affected a relatively small share of global trade, and their effect on international trade has been secondary to the lack of aggregate demand and the global credit crunch. So, while some countries and industries have seen their exports depressed by protectionist measures, the global trading system has largely weathered the threat of beggar-thy-neighbor policies that loomed large at the outset of the crisis. Perhaps helping to moderate a resort to protectionist measures is the interdependence of countries in global supply and production chains. Domestic producers rely on imported parts, and exporters rely on foreign end-user markets—and vice versa. The average trade-to-GDP ratio today is about 60 percent, up from 27 percent in 1970, and trade in parts and components, an indicator of the internationalization of supply chains, has more than doubled as a share of trade in manufactures. WTO rules and disciplines have also helped, as have the monitoring, surveillance, and information exchange under its auspices.

The danger of more protectionist responses during the global recovery—especially if it continues to be jobless—underlines the importance of maintaining an open trading environment. In particular, keeping trade open will be key to counter the effects of the withdrawal of expansionary fiscal and monetary policies and to support the global economic recovery.

Keeping up with the Doha Development Agenda

The global economic crisis has confirmed that trade rules matter and that WTO rules constrain protectionism. Indeed, it is worth noting that countries have been less able to resist protectionist pressures in areas not covered by multilateral disciplines or with limited coverage. Examples include export subsidies by the European Union and the United States, national bailout packages that call for preferential treatment for domestic firms, more restrictive policies on workers providing cross-border services, and discriminatory procurement.

Concluding the Doha Round remains an important milestone. As the global economy gradually recovers, governments must ensure that the long-run benefits of an open and transparent multilateral trading system are not compromised by short-run pressures to protect domestic markets. Concluding the Doha Round would not only improve market access. It would also strengthen the international trading system, constrain future increases in

FIGURE 5.5   **About 350 trade-restrictive measures and 80 trade-liberalizing measures have been implemented or initiated since the onset of the crisis, but some have already been removed**

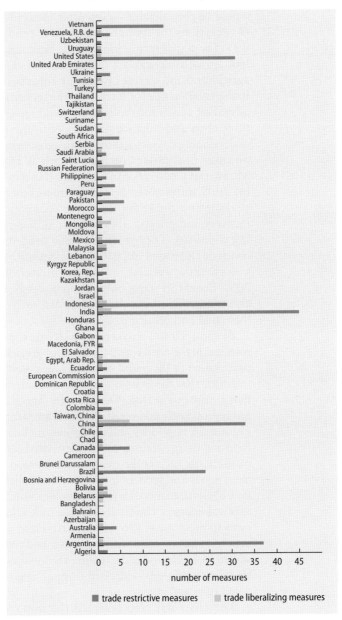

Source: World Bank calculations based on WTO (2009).

tariffs and subsidies, help governments resist protectionist pressures as they unwind current expansionary policies, and provide a much needed boost to keep markets open.

So what is on the table at the negotiations in Geneva matters. Based on current proposals, the Doha Round would do as much as any previous round, if not more to open trade.[11] The gains in market access would be considerable—even after factoring in exceptions for special and sensitive products. The round would lower tariff bindings, ban agricultural export subsidies, and cap agricultural and marine production subsidies. It also offers scope for increasing the security of market access for services. It would lower trade costs and enhance the competitiveness of developing countries through an agreement on trade facilitation. At the Seventh WTO Ministerial Conference in Geneva in November 2009, ministers reiterated the importance of trade and the Doha Round to economic recovery and poverty alleviation in developing countries. They reaffirmed the need to conclude the round in 2010 and to engage in a stocktaking exercise in the first quarter of 2010. But at this stage, only strong leadership and engagement by world leaders can revive the round and bring it to closure.

Beyond Doha, government actions in response to the crisis reveal the need for greater cooperation in the multilateral trading system to ensure that the cross-border policy matters that are not on the Doha Development Agenda are appropriately addressed. Potential areas for negotiating new rules and disciplines include food and energy security and trade-related climate change such as the treatment of environment goods and services to increase the global flow of clean, energy-efficient technologies and renewal energy. The limited guidelines and rules in these areas allow for discriminatory actions to be imposed with impunity, and the stalled Doha Round is preventing these issues from being properly addressed through negotiated rules and norms.

The crisis has also revealed the importance of strengthening monitoring and public reporting of government measures to improve transparency in the trading system so that WTO-compatible policies can be readily distinguished from discriminatory policies. Transparency is critical in maintaining a predictable and open trading system. Free-flowing information on policies affecting trade is essential for cooperation among countries seeking to manage the crisis. Comprehensive and timely notification of trade contingency measures (public procurement, subsidies, and other nontariff measures) to WTO bodies is needed to ensure proper monitoring.

Expanding aid for trade

Aid for trade has become more urgent with the global economic crisis. As the world economy recovers, developing countries will rely on international markets as a source of demand to revitalize economic growth. Enhancing the competitiveness of firms in developing countries by lowering trade costs through better trade policies and regulations, institutional support for trade, trade-related infrastructure, and trade-related adjustment is particularly important. Improving trade logistics is a priority for development (box 5.1). Sustaining efforts to deliver on the commitments made at the 2005 WTO Ministerial Meeting (in Hong Kong, China) to expand aid for trade should continue to be a priority.

The second global review of aid for trade, held in Geneva in July 2009, found that developing countries are setting priorities for trade in national development strategies; that donors are offering more and better aid for trade; and that new partners are engaging in cooperation among developing countries. Allocations to aid for trade have increased without reducing resources to other development priorities.[12] Improving the effectiveness of aid for trade requires strengthening its regional dimension and the contribution of the private sector, better evaluating its impact, and mobilizing resources beyond 2010.

World Bank Group concessional aid-for-trade lending has increased. Its concessional lending to low-income countries rose from $2.3 billion annually in 2002–05 to $3.9 billion in 2007–08 (table 5.1). The IFC investments in building new productive capacity and infrastructure in low-income countries have added another $3.4 billion in private investments. The aid-for-trade program of the World Bank Group, as with other donors,

---

BOX 5.1   Facilitating trade through logistics reforms

Efficient logistics contribute to trade and development. Evidence from the 2007 and 2010 World Bank Logistics Performance Index (LPI) indicates that, for countries at the same level of per capita income, those with the best logistics performance do better: they can expect 1 percent additional growth in GDP and 2 percent additional growth in trade.[a] Efficient trade logistics systems support trade diversification and attract foreign direct investment.

The 2010 LPI points to modest but positive trends in customs use of information technologies for trade and investment in private services. It finds that logistics overperformers—countries with a higher LPI score than income would predict—have consistently invested in reforms. Encouraging trends are emerging in infrastructure, reflecting successful trade facilitation projects. In port management, separation of commercial activities from the regulatory missions of the port authority is now the norm in developing countries, and there are many examples of successful private participation in container terminal operations. Automation of customs procedures is also common, with only a few countries lacking some form of automated customs system. But logistics professionals also confirmed that the quantity and performance of infrastructure, especially roads and ports, remain significant bottlenecks in most low-income countries—and, in relative terms, even more so in middle-income countries.

Transport reform has become a key development priority. Traditional efforts to facilitate trade have focused on supporting trade infrastructure investment and modernizing customs. Looking forward, the focus will be extended to new areas, such as the market for logistics services, coordination of border processes, and joint cross-border initiatives, especially for landlocked countries (World Bank 2006). Some of these reforms can be implemented at the country level. Others require bilateral and regional cooperation, such as border and transit trade for landlocked countries.

Taking a more comprehensive approach to the clearance of goods is a key element in the new trade facilitation agenda. It requires better collaboration among all border management agencies—including standards, sanitary, phytosanitary, transport, and veterinary agencies—and modern approaches to regulatory compliance. It matters little that customs agencies employ high levels of automation and examines goods selectively if other government agencies are not automated and continue to routinely inspect all imported goods regardless of the risk they pose.

a. The LPI summarizes the performance of countries in six areas: efficiency of the customs clearance process, quality of trade and transport-related infrastructure, ease of arranging competitively priced shipments, competence and quality of logistics services, ability to track and trace consignments, and frequency with which shipments reach the consignee within the scheduled or expected time (Arvis and others 2010). The LPI is based on more than 5,000 country assessments by more than 1,000 international freight forwarders. It provides trade profiles for 155 countries.

---

goes beyond concessional lending commitments to low-income countries—the conventional definition used by the Organisation for Economic Co-operation and Development (OECD) and the WTO—and includes nonconcessional trade–related lending to middle-income countries. Promoting trade-led growth in middle-income countries generates market opportunities for neighboring low-income countries and has positive spin-offs for the world economy.

The World Bank Group—working with other organizations such as the WTO, United Nations Conference on Trade and Development, United Nations Development Programme, and the International Trade Center—has provided technical assistance and financing for trade capacity-building projects. The significant progress in integrating trade into development strategies reflects a collective effort by governments and donors and by the trade and development communities. One measure of this integration is that two-thirds of country assistance strategies, which partner governments and the World Bank forge, identify trade as a priority.

TABLE 5.1 World Bank Group trade-related activities, 2007 and 2008
commitments, US$ millions

Year, income group, activity	Public sector (loans and grants)	Private sector (IFC)	Total
2007			
Low-income countries (IDA)	**4,267**	**3,514**	**7,782**
Country programs	3,313	3,020	6,332
Regional activities	954	495	1,449
Middle-income countries (IBRD)	**4,905**	**6,302**	**11,206**
Total 2007	*9,172*	*9,816*	*18,988*
2008			
Low-income countries (IDA)	**3,520**	**3,304**	**6,824**
Country programs	3,245	2,770	6,016
Regional activities	275	533	808
Middle-income countries (IBRD)	**8,263**	**5,772**	**14,035**
Total 2008	*11,782*	*9,076*	*20,858*

Source: World Bank staff calculations.
Note: This table uses the OECD-WTO definition of sectoral coverage for aid for trade. IDA = International Development Association; IBRD = International Bank for Reconstruction and Development.

Bringing aid flows back on track

Global aid has risen, and donors are so far holding to their commitments to increase aid. But it remains only 80 percent of the 2010 level implied by donor promises, and the shortfall is particularly large for aid to Africa. Increasing aid must remain a political priority to prevent the crisis from seriously damaging development prospects and to keep alive the hope of halving poverty by 2015.

Aid volumes rose in real terms during the crisis years, 2008–09, but greater efforts are still needed

Following an 11.7 percent increase in 2008, total net official development assistance (ODA) from the OECD's Development Assistance Committee (DAC) countries rose slightly by 0.7 percent in real terms in 2009. (But in current U.S. dollars, it actually fell from $122.3 billion in 2008 to $119.6 billion in 2009.) The 2009 figure represents 0.31 percent of members' combined gross national income (GNI). ODA from the United States, the largest donor, rose 5.4 percent in real terms to $29 billion—0.20 percent of GNI, up from 0.19 percent in 2008 (figure 5.6). Aid from the United Kingdom rose to $11.5 billion, 0.52 percent of GNI. Combined ODA from the 15 European Union members of the

DAC fell back slightly to 10 percent in real terms to $67 billion (44 percent of all DAC ODA).

Other donors recording a sharp increase in aid in real terms were Greece (up 28.7 percent), Portugal (22.3 percent), and Spain (22.6 percent). The four largest donors in 2008, measured as a share of GNI, were Sweden (0.98 percent), Luxembourg (0.97 percent), Norway (0.88 percent), and the Netherlands (0.80 percent). Non-DAC aid continues to grow in importance, rising 63 percent in real terms in 2008 to $9.5 billion (for non-DAC donors reporting to DAC). Arab donors, led by Saudi Arabia, were the largest and fastest-growing component: their aid rose to $5.9 billion, a real increase of 115 percent over 2007.

The rise in aid is encouraging, but there is no room for complacency. DAC members have reaffirmed their aid commitments and agreed to maintain aid flows in line with these commitments. But in the current economic climate, donor countries have difficult budgetary choices to make and foreign aid could be at risk. Following the early 1990s recession, official development assistance from DAC donors fell from 0.33 percent of their combined GNI in 1992 to 0.22 percent in 1997. And the 2010 targets are slipping away. At the 2005 Group of Eight Summit in Gleneagles, Scotland, donors aimed to raise official development assistance by $50 billion in 2010 over the level in 2004 (2004

FIGURE 5.6   Net official development assistance rose in real terms in 2008 and 2009

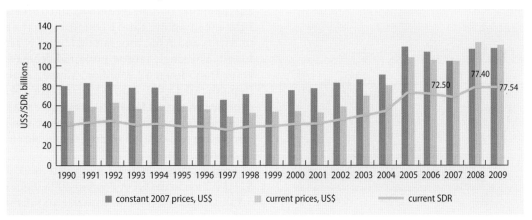

Source: OECD DAC.
Note: SDR = special drawing rights.

prices and exchange rates). And they pledged to increase official development assistance to Sub-Saharan Africa by $25 billion by 2010, more than double the 2004 level. Achieving the global aid target implies an increase of more than $20 billion in real terms from the 2008 level. The most recent OECD survey of donors' forward-spending plans indicates that after factoring in the aid increases already programmed, donors need to provide an additional $14 billion to meet the 2010 target. Nor is the outlook for 2011 more encouraging. Aid is programmed to increase only 3 percent in real terms in 2011 over that programmed for 2010.

Meeting the pledge to Sub-Saharan Africa will require an even greater effort. Aid to the region has risen considerably since the start of the decade, growing at 5 percent a year. In 2008 the region received 37 percent of global official development assistance—up from 30 percent in 1999–2000—with a much higher share as grants. But much of the increase has been in the form of debt relief and emergency and humanitarian assistance (figure 5.7).[13] At the 2002 Monterrey Conference on Financing for Development, donors pledged that debt relief would not displace other components of official development assistance. Meeting the Gleneagles target would require an increase of $20 billion over 2008, equivalent to a rise in net official development assistance of 25 percent annually for 2009 and 2010. Donors' forward-spending plans are for an additional

FIGURE 5.7   Significant amounts of official development assistance are in debt relief and humanitarian assistance

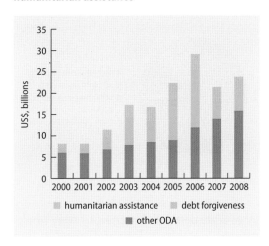

Source: OECD DAC.
Note: ODA = official development assistance.

$2 billion allocation for Sub-Saharan Africa, leaving a gap of $18 billion.

Programmable aid in support of core development programs is critical to achieving the MDGs, because it can be incorporated into developing-country budgets.[14] Although the share of programmable aid has risen, nonprogrammable categories still commanded a large share of aid flows in 2008 (figure 5.8). Nonprogrammable aid made up 35 percent of gross official development assistance flows from bilateral donors in 2008. That was down from a peak of 47 percent in 2005–06, when

FIGURE 5.8   **Trends in gross official development aid from bilateral donors, by type, 2000–08**

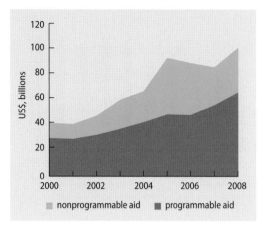

Source: OECD DAC.

FIGURE 5.9   **Gross official development aid from bilateral donors, 2008**

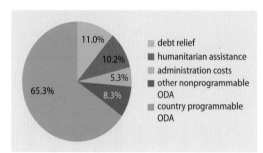

Source: OECD DAC.

large-scale debt relief operations were implemented (notably in Iraq and Nigeria), but was still well above the 28 percent recorded in 2000. Debt relief and humanitarian assistance combined accounted for 21 percent of gross bilateral flows in 2008 (figure 5.9).

The outlook for country programmable aid is mixed. Based on information that donors provide to OECD-DAC, 102 countries are expected to benefit from a $10.3 billion increase in country programmable aid by 2010 (over 2005). Most likely to realize large increases are the priority aid partners for several DAC members, countries where the scaling up is firmly rooted in donor country strategies. An increase of more than $100 million is programmed for 33 countries, including Ethiopia, Kenya, Tanzania, and Vietnam,

as well as for such middle-income countries as Colombia, Indonesia, Serbia, and Turkey. Less encouraging: for 51 countries, mainly in Africa and Asia, programmable aid is set to fall. The single largest projected decrease is for Iraq, down $2.5 billion. China, Arab Republic of Egypt, and Thailand are also expected to see aid fall in 2010 by more than $200 million each from 2005. But there is no discernible reallocation of programmable aid to poorer countries.

Fragile states combined received a total of $21.3 billion in net ODA flows in 2008 (figure 5.10). Despite their weak capacity and institutions, the share of total net ODA flows that goes to fragile states rose from 14 percent in 2001 to 16.5 percent in 2008. However, this aid is heavily concentrated in four recipients that account for more than 54 percent of the total. Almost one-quarter went to Afghanistan in 2008. If the flows going to Afghanistan are excluded, the share of total ODA going to fragile states has actually declined slightly, from 13.3 percent in 2001 to 12.7 percent in 2008. Additionally a large share of ODA to these countries has been in the form of emergency assistance or debt relief.

Making aid more effective

The Accra Agenda for Action, prepared by participants in the Third High Level Forum on Aid Effectiveness in Accra September 2008, is a roadmap for making aid more effective.[15] It builds on the aid business model of the Paris Declaration on Aid Effectiveness, agreed in March 2005, and signals profound changes for donors and developing countries. The agenda aims to strengthen country ownership of the development process and align donor priorities with those of the country by building effective and inclusive partnerships. To achieve these goals, it calls for donors to make aid more predictable, rationalize the division of labor among donors, untie aid from the provision of goods and services in the donor country, allocate aid according to need and merit, and address the problem of countries that receive too little aid. Efforts by donors to meet their commitments for increased aid must also be matched by better

FIGURE 5.10   **Fragile states received $21.3 billion net official development assistance in 2008**

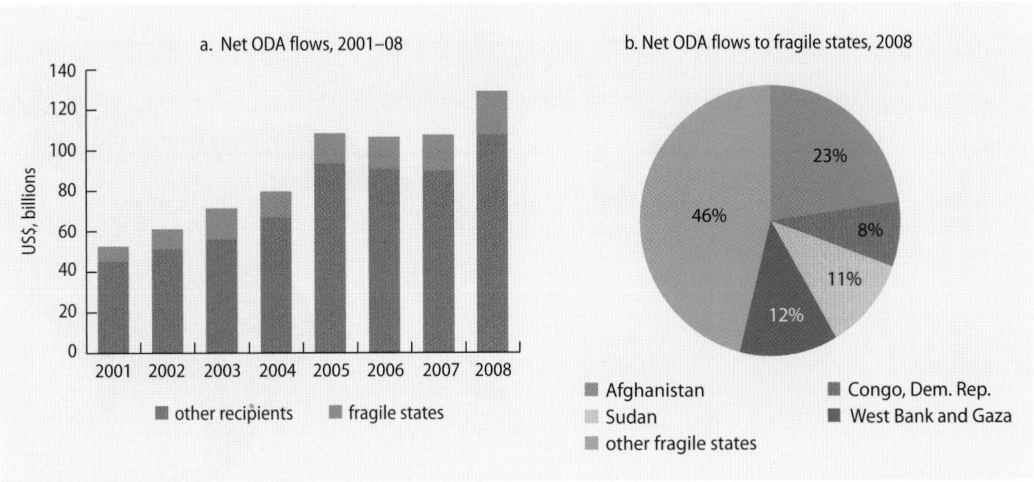

a. Net ODA flows, 2001–08

b. Net ODA flows to fragile states, 2008

Legend:
- Afghanistan
- Sudan
- other fragile states
- Congo, Dem. Rep.
- West Bank and Gaza

(other recipients / fragile states)

Source: OECD DAC.

policies in developing countries to absorb and use aid more efficiently.

Predictable aid is fundamental to its effectiveness. To smooth shortfalls from aid surprises, aid-dependent countries must rely on their limited scope for domestic borrowing, which can increase inflation and crowd out private investment. Without good information on the resources that will be available, aid recipients cannot plan their own expenditures or participate meaningfully in determining how aid is allocated and used. However, recipients also need to improve their own budget planning and programming to be able to use the forward-looking information from donors.

DAC donors have committed to making aid more predictable so that developing countries can plan for long-term sustainable growth. But in many cases donors do not reveal their aid spending plans early enough for countries to factor them into their medium- and long-term planning, or they fail to stick to their commitments. Although the OECD does publish annual information on donors' forward-spending plans, these data are of limited use for developing countries: for reasons of confidentiality, the reports do not show country breakdowns, do not represent firm aid commitments, and for some countries are incomplete. Donors need to agree on an acceptable way of making their planning assumptions

accessible to developing-country policy makers to reduce information gaps. One option would be a forum for presenting and discussing trends in future allocations in detail. Under the recent International Aid Transparency Initiative, a group of development partners, partner countries, and nongovernmental organizations (NGOs) will prepare a common set of standards for all donors and countries to report on aid, including forward-looking aid plans.

Reducing fragmentation and strengthening aid coordination is essential to enhancing aid effectiveness. When aid comes in too many small slices from too many donors, transaction costs go up and recipient countries have difficulty managing their own development agenda. In 2006, 38 recipient countries each received assistance from 25 or more DAC and multilateral donors. In 24 of these countries, 15 or more donors collectively provided less than 10 percent of that country's total aid. The number of aid agencies has also grown enormously, with about 225 bilateral and 242 multilateral agencies funding more than 35,000 activities each year. A recent OECD survey revealed that in 2007 there were 15,229 donor missions to 54 countries—more than 800 to Vietnam alone. The scope for reducing the number of donors operating in some countries without jeopardizing diversification or overall aid levels is thus considerable.

MAP 5.1   **Each year of a girl's education reduces, by 10 percent, the risk of her children dying before age five**

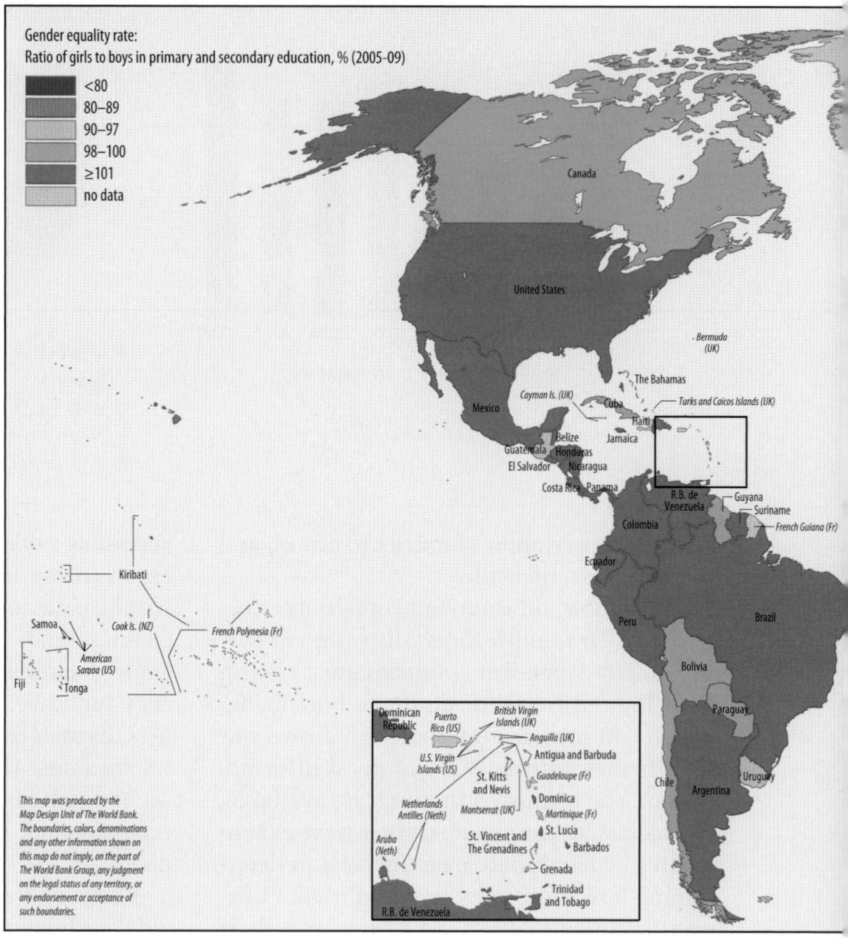

Gender equality rate:
Ratio of girls to boys in primary and secondary education, % (2005–09)

- <80
- 80–89
- 90–97
- 98–100
- ≥101
- no data

Canada

United States

Bermuda (UK)

The Bahamas

Cayman Is. (UK)   Cuba   Turks and Caicos Islands (UK)

Mexico   Haiti

Belize   Jamaica

Guatemala   Honduras

El Salvador   Nicaragua

Costa Rica   Panama

R.B. de Venezuela   Guyana

Suriname

Colombia   French Guiana (Fr)

Ecuador

Kiribati

Peru   Brazil

Samoa   Cook Is. (NZ)   French Polynesia (Fr)

American Samoa (US)

Bolivia

Fiji   Tonga

Paraguay

Dominican Republic   Puerto Rico (US)   British Virgin Islands (UK)

Anguilla (UK)

U.S. Virgin Islands (US)   Antigua and Barbuda

St. Kitts and Nevis   Guadeloupe (Fr)

Netherlands Antilles (Neth)   Dominica

Montserrat (UK)   Martinique (Fr)

Aruba (Neth)   St. Lucia

St. Vincent and The Grenadines   Barbados

Chile   Argentina

Uruguay

Grenada

Trinidad and Tobago

R.B. de Venezuela

This map was produced by the Map Design Unit of The World Bank. The boundaries, colors, denominations and any other information shown on this map do not imply, on the part of The World Bank Group, any judgment on the legal status of any territory, or any endorsement or acceptance of such boundaries.

Source: World Development Indicators.

There is broad agreement on the need for a coherent division of labor among donors, and the Accra Agenda for Action urges donors to concentrate on fewer countries and sectors. Doing so would require coordinated allocation principles and aid monitoring across the whole donor community. But this is a sensitive topic, touching on comparative advantage, specialization, and delegation. Some progress has been achieved with broader use of program-based approaches, and elaboration of principles, including the 2007 European Union Code of Conduct on Complementarity and Division of Labor. Donors have started

working together to reduce the number of diagnostic reviews and duplicative missions. It is critical that recipient countries take a strong leadership role in coordinating donor activities.

The full benefit of untying aid remains unrealized. Untying aid and allowing developing countries to make their own procurement decisions are key to making aid more effective. Untied aid procured through open international competition offers the best prospect of good value for money and, when coupled with sound procurement systems, supports

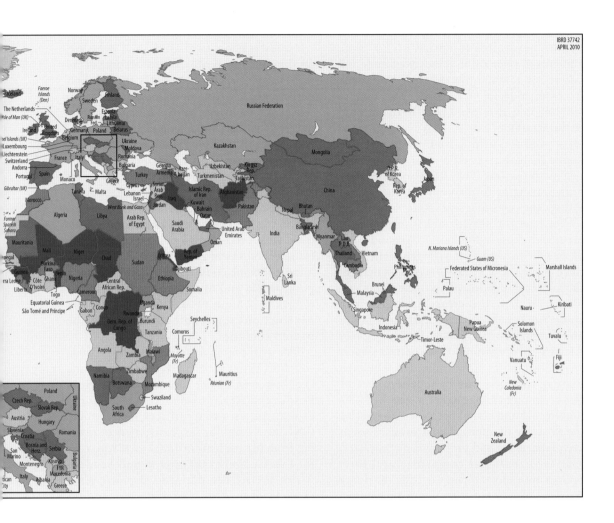

developing-country ownership of aid. Numerous studies confirm that goods, works, and services procured under tied aid regimes that restrict procurement to suppliers from the donor country cost 15–25 percent more on average and are more influenced by supplier interests and capacities.

Since the landmark agreement by DAC donors in 2001 to untie financial aid to the least developed countries, there has been good progress. DAC donor countries have formally untied more than four-fifths of their ODA to the least developed countries, and a wider process of untying aid is under way. As of

2007, 79 percent of ODA was untied, 17 percent was still tied, and the status of 4 percent was not reported. Donors have recommended several changes, such as removing the thresholds below which untying is not required and including highly indebted poor countries not classified as least developed countries. Other provisions invite non-DAC donors to untie their aid as much as possible and to respect internationally agreed principles of environmental sustainability and corporate social responsibility.

Donors have committed to untying aid in categories traditionally regarded as difficult to untie and outside the scope of the 2001 agreement, such as food aid, technical cooperation, and consultant costs. Several DAC donors have already untied all or large amounts of their aid in these categories, and others are moving toward this. Under the Accra Agenda for Action, all DAC donors will elaborate their plans in 2010 to untie aid to the maximum extent. They have agreed to resist pressures arising from the global economic crisis to retie aid or to introduce new tied aid programs. They are also committed to improving performance in advance notifications and reporting on contract awards.

The case for untying aid is unequivocal on effectiveness and efficiency grounds. But despite the marked shift to largely untied aid, there is very little evidence-based analysis of the impact of untying on recipient countries. Does it reduce or increase administrative costs? Are benefits realized in the absence of an efficiently managed public finance regime? And why do opportunities for contract awards to local suppliers remain limited? The high share of contracts won by suppliers in some donor countries highlights a gap between untying aid and actual outcomes, suggesting the existence of informal constraints, such as prequalification and procurement processes, that favor national companies and limit opportunities for suppliers outside the donor country. DAC donors that report on contract awards indicated that in 2007 two-thirds of contracts (in number and value) were awarded to suppliers in OECD countries, the majority to suppliers in the donor country.

Many aid allocations are still driven by factors other than need and merit. Aid allocation practices differ widely. Multilateral development agencies have largely adopted aid allocation formulas aimed at ensuring efficient and transparent allocation, but most bilateral donors still allocate aid not on need and merit but on geopolitical ties and self-interest. A recent study using DAC data finds that almost half the predicted value of aid is still determined by donor-specific factors, one-third by need, a sixth by self-interest, and 2 percent by performance.[16] But research

also suggests that donor aid allocation has changed greatly over the past three decades, with the influence of colonial ties, trade relationships, political allies, and debt levels diminishing as allocations become more responsive to recipient country income and performance.[17] Aid allocation patterns also reflect greater attention to countries recovering from conflict and facing external shocks. Aid from private sources, up in recent years, also affects overall aid allocation (box 5.2).

Considerable scope remains for a more rational, results-oriented, and needs-driven aid allocation mechanism. A substantial share of aid goes to middle-income countries, which received 46 percent of net ODA from all sources in 2008 (figure 5.11). While middle-income countries are home to many poor people and may need to step up their efforts to achieve the MDGs, they usually have options for funding not open to the poorest countries.

The distribution of aid among low-income countries varies widely. Over the past decade India received $1 per capita in aid, whereas Bosnia and Herzegovina received $129 per capita. Aid as a share of recipient country GNI shows similar large divergence, ranging from 0.1 percent for India to 189 percent for Liberia. Some countries in Sub-Saharan Africa received net official development assistance flows in 2008 greater than their GNI (figure 5.12).

While aid allocation undoubtedly could be improved, defining an "equitable share" of aid is problematic. Compared with financing needs, most developing countries would likely claim to receive insufficient aid, and costing exercises for the achievement of the MDGs indicate large unmet financing needs for most developing countries. A recent World Bank study[18] identified several normative benchmarks for apportioning aid:

- An egalitarian approach, in which each country receives the same amount of aid per capita or as a share of GDP.
- An average donor behavior approach, based on the relative weights donors attach to each recipient country's needs and performance.

BOX 5.2   The allocation of aid from private sources

Aid from private sources has increased greatly in recent years. The 2009 Index of Global Philanthropy and Remittances estimates that aid to developing countries from private foundations, nongovernmental programs, and donations in OECD countries amounted to $49 billion in 2007, while official development assistance totaled $103 billion. Information on the allocation of private aid is limited, but recent studies suggest that allocations by nongovernmental organizations (NGOs) are driven by indicators of recipient need. One study finds that nongovernmental organizations exercise greater selectivity than official bilateral donors and provide, on average, more aid per capita to countries ranked by the United Nations as having the highest priority needs.

Some countries receive large amounts of aid from NGOs and others relatively little. The factors driving allocation include internal and external economies of scale and the tendency of NGOs to complement, not substitute for, bilateral aid. In that sense, NGOs may contribute to the problem of some countries receiving an inequitably small share of global aid.

A study in Sweden comparing aid allocation by NGOs with the country's official development assistance shows that the NGOs are more selective. Aid from both official and private sources declines as recipient country income rises, but the trend is more pronounced for aid from NGOs. A study of the impact of aid, measured per capita, finds a positive correlation between aid and the incidence of infant mortality and illiteracy for NGO aid but not for official aid.

Source: Hudson Institute 2009; Koch 2007; Dreher and others 2007; Masud and Yontcheva 2005.

- A poverty-efficient approach that maximizes global poverty reduction.
- A performance-based approach, using the mechanism that underpins the International Development Association (IDA) allocation formula.
- The OECD approach, which ranks aid receipts by ODA per capita and per capita income to identify relative underfunding.

Behind each approach are implicit or explicit value judgments on the relative importance of need and the ability to use aid effectively.

The countries considered to receive insufficient aid (aid receipts at least 1 percentage point of GDP below the benchmark allocation) vary according to the allocation benchmark selected. There are also wide disparities in the countries found to receive insufficient aid: extremely poor countries with low per capita incomes, where needs are greatest; poor performers, where aid may not be used effectively; strong performers that could productively use higher volumes of aid; and countries with a small population and high fixed costs

FIGURE 5.11   Net official development assistance from all sources, by income group, 2000–08

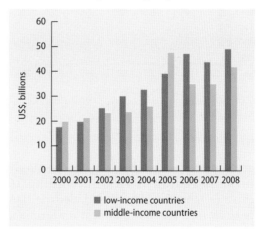

Source: OECD DAC.

for public service delivery. There is no evidence that fragile states have a greater or lesser propensity to receive insufficient aid than other low-income countries. Of the 61 low-income countries examined, 37 received insufficient aid according to at least one benchmark, 17

FIGURE 5.12   Net ODA varies widely as a share of GNI in Sub-Saharan Africa

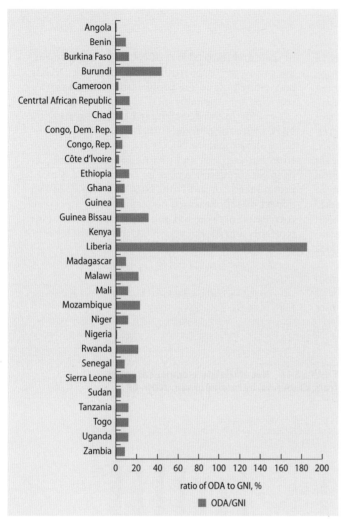

ratio of ODA to GNI, %

■ ODA/GNI

Source: OECD DAC.

demand and the relative merits or difficulties of investing in a given country. But donor agreement to clarify definitions and benchmarks would help set the stage for a best-effort commitment from all donors to raise ODA in some subset of countries faster than the average growth rate. Large-scale reallocation of current aid is neither feasible nor desirable, but donors should consider rebalancing future aid increases.

Debt relief: progress and challenges

Since the Monterrey Conference on Financing for Development in 2002, substantial progress has been made in implementing the Heavily Indebted Poor Countries (HIPC) Initiative and the Multilateral Debt Relief Initiative (MDRI). Of 40 eligible countries, 35 have passed the decision point and qualified for HIPC assistance. Of those, 28 countries have reached the completion point and qualify for debt relief as of January 2010. Several other countries are also well on their way to the completion point. As a result, the debt burdens of many poor countries have been markedly reduced. The overall assistance committed to the 35 post-decision-point countries represents an average of 40 percent of their 2008 GDP and, together with relief under traditional mechanisms and additional relief from Paris Club creditors, is expected to reduce their debt burden by more than 80 percent (figure 5.13). Poverty-reducing expenditures in these countries rose 2 percentage points of GDP between 2001 and 2008, while debt service obligations declined correspondingly.

Commercial creditors have also increased debt relief, largely through substantive debt relief to Côte d'Ivoire and Liberia. Debt relief for Côte d'Ivoire was provided through a rescheduling agreement in 1998. In April 2009 commercial creditors provided full debt relief to Liberia under a debt buyback operation supported by IDA's Debt Reduction Facility and contributions from bilateral donors.

Litigation by commercial creditors, an impediment to delivering full debt relief to heavily indebted poor countries, appears to have lessened although a small number of

according to two benchmarks, and 7—mostly in Sub-Saharan Africa—according to three or more benchmarks. Under the IDA performance-based aid allocation formula, the amount required to raise aid levels to the norm is estimated at $3.3 billion a year; under the poverty efficiency benchmark, the amount rises to $12.5 billion. These are large amounts representing roughly 7 percent and 25 percent, respectively, of programmable aid from bilateral donors to countries excluding Sub-Saharan Africa.

Variations in aid are not just supply driven. The decision to provide or withhold aid depends on many factors, including effective

new lawsuits were initiated in 2009. Support for countries facing litigation is available from the African Legal Support Facility, launched by the African Development Bank on June 29, 2009, and initiatives are under way in some donor countries to introduce legislation curtailing the scope of litigation against heavily indebted poor countries.

Important challenges remain. Some predecision-point countries are beset by severe political problems. Almost half the countries have been affected by war in recent years, and many are still at a high risk of conflict, political instability, or both. To reach the completion point, they will need to strengthen their policies and institutions and receive continuing support from the international community. For post-completion-point countries, debt relief has greatly reduced debt vulnerabilities (table 5.2). However, a few post-completion-point countries remain vulnerable to debt-related problems, and six are still at high risk of debt distress.[19] Although the risk of a major debt crisis in heavily indebted poor countries appears limited, the current global economic crisis has made debt sustainability more difficult and underscores the need to implement sound borrowing policies and to strengthen capacity to manage debt.

IFIs responded to the crisis quickly and decisively

The IFIs boosted lending and adopted innovative programs to confront the global crisis and the subsequent development emergency.[20]

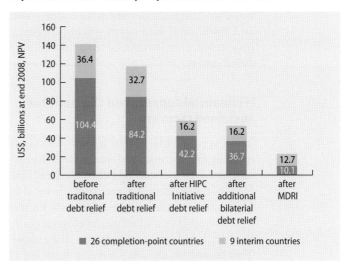

FIGURE 5.13   **Debt stock of heavily indebted poor countries is expected to come down by 80 percent in end-2009 NPV**

Source: HIPC Initiative country documents and IDA and IMF staff estimates.
Note: Estimates based on decision-point debt stock documents. NPV = net present value.

Total commitments (including concessional and nonconcessional loans plus grants) by the International Monetary Fund (IMF) and the multilateral development banks (MDBs) rose from $68 billion in 2007 to $234 billion in 2009. The goals of this assistance were to stabilize markets and avert the collapse of the banking and private sectors in developing countries, to limit the slide in economic growth and support the poor, and to minimize any interruption in development progress. The main instruments included balance of payments support for macroeconomic stabilization, budgetary support for government

TABLE 5.2   **Distribution of debt distress by country group, end-July 2009**
percent

Country group	Number of countries	Debt vulnerability			In debt distress (%)
		Low	Moderate	High	
All low income countries	67	29.9	35.8	22.4	11.9
Non-heavily indebted poor countries	28	32.1	39.3	25.0	3.6
Completion point, heavily indebted poor countries	28	39.3	39.3	21.4	0.0
Pre-completion point, heavily indebted poor countries	11	0.0	18.2	18.2	63.6
Interim countries	7	0.0	14.3	14.3	71.4
Pre-decision point countries	4	0.0	25.0	25.0	50.0

Source: Data are from individual countries' debt sustainability analysis in joint World Bank-IMF.
Note: Based on debt sustainability analyses as of end-July 2009. Low-income country group and non-heavily indebted poor countries exclude Azerbaijan, India, Kiribati, Maldives, Pakistan, Somalia, Timor Leste, and Uzbekistan. Pre-decision-point countries exclude Somalia. Countries that have passed the decision point qualify for full debt relief under the HIPC and MDRI Initiatives; interim countries are between the decision and completion points.

expenditures, guarantees to encourage investment in developing countries, technical assistance to strengthen development frameworks, and traditional lending to maintain critical investments in infrastructure and human development.

IFI financial support laid the basis for sustained recovery

The IMF quickly scaled up its assistance to help meet countries' increased financing needs. By the end of February 2010, the IMF had committed a record high total of $175 billion (including precautionary financing) to emerging and other developing countries with balance of payments difficulties. This financing included a sharp increase in concessional lending to the world's poorest countries—with new commitments amounting to almost $3.4 billion since the beginning of 2009, up from $1.4 billion for 2008. Fifty-five countries now have an arrangement with the IMF. The global financial safety net has also been strengthened with the general allocation of special drawing rights (totaling

$250 billion), with more than $32 billion to emerging market economies and $18 billion to low-income countries.

The global nature of the crisis led the IMF to take swift action to adapt its lending and conditionality frameworks to the new circumstances. Standard access to IMF financing have been doubled, and the provision of exceptionally large loans has become easier, while adequate safeguards have been preserved. The new flexible credit line, a facility without ex-post policy conditions for countries with very strong track records, has proven very effective. Colombia, Mexico, and Poland have received support under the facility, helping to stabilize their economies, mitigating contagion effects, and laying the basis for a recovery. Costa Rica, El Salvador, and Guatemala are receiving support under the High Access Precautionary Standby Arrangement, a regular lending window (box 5.3). The IMF's new conditionality framework encourages greater focus on the achievement of reform objectives in critical areas, while providing greater flexibility on the timing and content of policy measures.

BOX 5.3   The IMF's engagement with low-income countries

To make financial support more flexible and tailored to the diversity of low-income countries, the architecture of the IMF's concessional facilities has been substantially revamped. The new Poverty Reduction and Growth Trust, effective on January 7, 2010, provides support through three new lending windows:

- The Extended Credit Facility, which replaced the Poverty Reduction and Growth Facility, provides sustained engagement to address medium-term protracted balance of payments problems.
- The Standby Credit Facility is available to low-income countries that no longer face protracted balance of payments problems but may need occasional help. It provides support to address short-term financing needs caused by shocks or policy slippages. It can also be used on a precautionary

basis. In these respects it is similar to the non-concessional standby arrangement available to all member countries.
- The Rapid Credit Facility provides limited financial support in a single, up-front payout for low-income countries facing urgent financing needs; the facility replaces the Rapid Access Component under the Exogenous Shocks Facility and the subsidized Emergency Assistance for Natural Disasters and the subsidized Emergency Post-Conflict Assistance. Successive drawings can be made by countries in postconflict or other fragile situations.

Programs under all three facilities emphasize poverty alleviation and growth linked to country-owned poverty reduction policies and may include targets to safeguard social and other priority spending.

FIGURE 5.14   Multilateral development banks substantially increased their disbursements, 2000–09

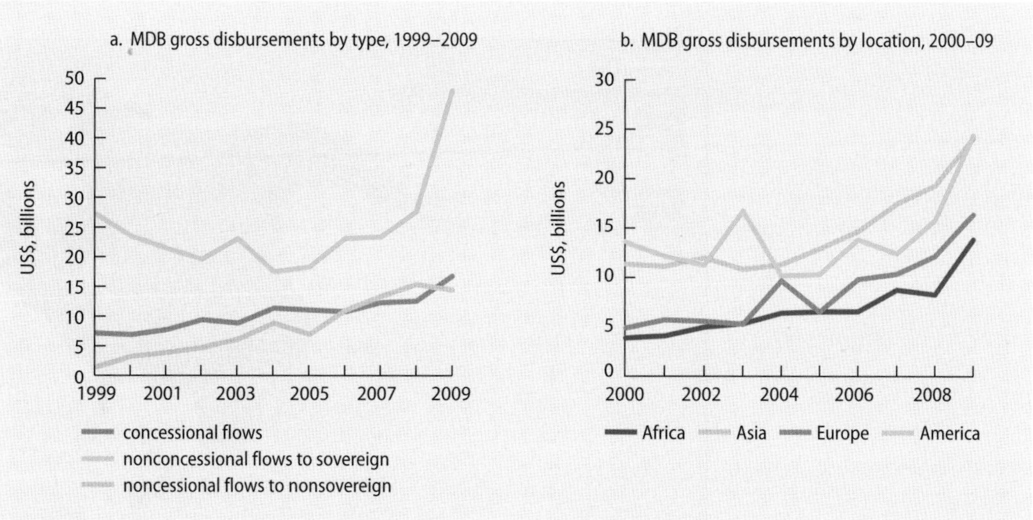

a. MDB gross disbursements by type, 1999–2009

b. MDB gross disbursements by location, 2000–09

concessional flows
nonconcessional flows to sovereign
nonconcessional flows to nonsovereign

Africa   Asia   Europe   America

Source: Staff of the big five multilateral development banks.

The multilateral development banks also substantially increased their lending. Total MDB commitments rose from $67 billion in 2007 to $115 billion in 2009. The heavy reliance on quick-disbursing support meant that increased commitments were translated into a sharp rise in disbursements, from under $50 billion in 2007 to about $79 billion in 2009 (figure 5.14). Nonconcessional loans totaled about $62 billion, and concessional flows more than $16 billion. Latin America and Asia remained the major recipients of funds (32 percent each). Latin America and Europe witnessed the largest increases from 2007, with jumps in lending of 54 percent and 35 percent, respectively.

All the multilateral development banks participated in the surge in lending.

The World Bank Group commitments totaled $87.6 billion from July 2008 to December 2009. Its disbursements during this period were $59.9 billion. The first half of fiscal 2010 shows the strongest IBRD (International Bank for Reconstruction and Development) commitments in history ($19.2 billion), and the surge in lending is set to continue: for fiscal 2010 IBRD lending is on track to exceed $40 billion (table 5.3). IDA commitments reached $14 billion in 2009, more than 20 percent above the previous year.

The Asian Development Bank (ADB) boosted its total commitments from $11.3 billion in 2008 to $16.1 billion in 2009. It also accelerated its disbursements by establishing the Countercyclical Support Facility in June 2009 as a time-bound budget support instrument with funding of $3 billion. Consistent with the facility's quick-disbursing nature, $2 billion was disbursed by the end of 2009, and another $500 million was disbursed in March 2010. The Asian Development Fund (AsDF) provided almost $1.2 billion over 2008–10 to help low-income Asian countries cope with the crisis, 85 percent in program loans and 15 percent in project loans. The high proportion of AsDF program lending exceeded the ceiling for 2007–09 based on a 3-year moving average. In June 2009 the ADB also approved the allocation of an additional $400 million in Asian Development Fund commitments to the most fiscally stretched countries with low access to nonconcessional resources.

Commitments by the Inter-American Development Bank (IDB) rose from $11.3 billion in 2008 to $15.6 billion in 2009. Disbursements rose to nearly $12 billion in 2009, up from $7.6 billion in 2008. The IDB also provided more incremental concessional financing than had originally been scheduled for the 2009–10 cycle, in the form of both

MAP 5.2   Emissions in high-income countries overwhelm those in developing countries

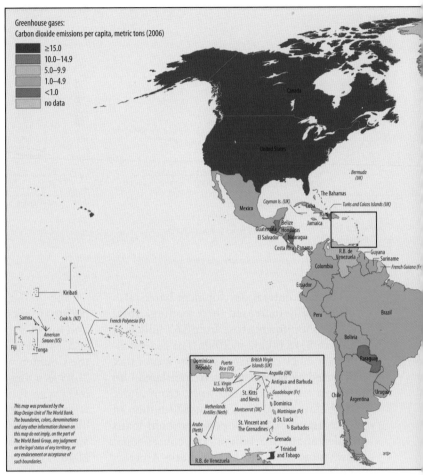

Source: World Development Indicators.

grants and blended financing. Its concessional resources, in the Fund for Special Operations, were severely constrained over the past several years because of debt relief. As a consequence, it stopped providing concessional lending purely from that fund in 2007 and implemented a blended loan structure with ordinary capital to maintain resources and concessionality.

The African Development Bank (AfDB) almost doubled its commitments in 2009, to $10.1 billion, while taking steps to front-load disbursements, improve response times, introduce new instruments to meet clients' evolving needs, and leverage its balance sheet. In response to the diminishing availability of

capital and the withdrawal of commercial partners from projects, it set up a $1.5 billion Emergency Liquidity Facility for bridging finance with fast-track approvals. The African Development Fund's (AfDF's) allocable resources increased by 1.4 percent in 2009, and nine fragile states received allocations that were on average, 11 percent larger than in 2008.

Commitments by the European Bank for Reconstruction and Development (EBRD) increased more than 50 percent in 2009, to $7.9 billion. Some 40 percent of the crisis response activity was provided to early and intermediate transition countries, which include the poorest members of the ERBD

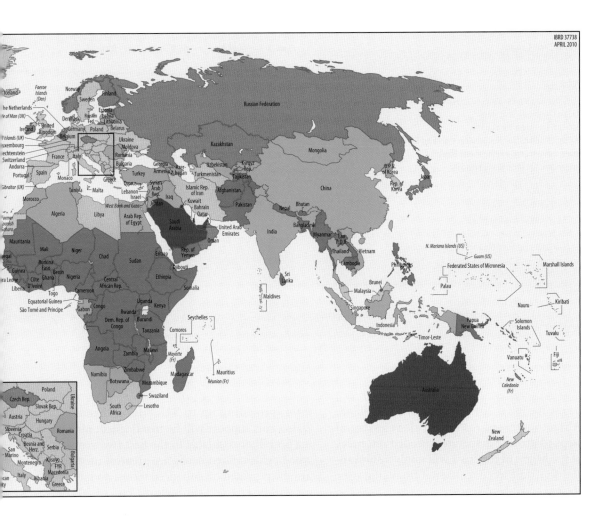

community. EBRD's operations are targeting the financial sector by strengthening bank balance sheets and ensuring bank capacity to continue lending for trade and the real economy, especially small and medium-sized enterprises, and by addressing firms' short-term refinancing needs through the enterprise response package and infrastructure projects left unfunded by the dwindling of commercial lending.

To accelerate their response to the crisis, the IFIs have boosted flows to the poorest countries by frontloading available resources. The standard IDA frontloading rule was relaxed in fiscal 2009, allowing countries to frontload up to half their annual allocation

(instead of 30 percent) for programs or projects that respond to the crisis. The Financial Crisis Response Fast-Track Facility was set up to fast-track up to $2 billion of IDA15 resources from existing country allocations and shorten the review period for eligible operations. By December 2009 more than $1.5 billion had been approved. AsDF-eligible borrowers were allowed to frontload up to 100 percent of their biennial allocation during 2009. AfDF assistance also has been heavily frontloaded. At the end of December 2009, two years into the AfDF-11 cycle, 86 percent of resources had been committed. The current AfDF balance available for operations commitment for 2010 is only $1 billion, well

TABLE 5.3   Gross commitments by IFIs, 2007–09

US$ billions (as of December 31, 2009)

Institution	2007	2008	2009	Jul. 2008–Dec. 2009
World Bank Group	**36.5**	**47.0**	**65.0**	**87.6**
International Bank for Reconstruction and Development	11.2	22.6	39.4	52.1
International Development Association	12.7	11.4	13.8	18.3
International Finance Corporation	10.3	11.5	10.5	15.3
Multilateral Investment Guarantee Agency[a]	2.3	1.5	1.3	1.9
Asian Development Bank[b]	**10.8**	**11.3**	**16.1**	**24.5**
African Development Bank	**4.9**	**5.4**	**10.1**	**—**
European Bank for Reconstruction and Development	**5.6**	**5.1**	**7.9**	**10.0**
Inter-American Development Bank	**8.8**	**11.3**	**15.6**	**23.4**
International Monetary Fund[c]	**1.3**	**48.7**	**119.0**	**169.8**
General Resources Account	1.1	47.7	116.4	166.6
Standby	1.1	47.6	35.9	86.1
Flexible credit line	0.0	0.0	80.4	80.5
Extended arrangement	0.0	0.0	0.0	0.0
Poverty Reduction and Growth Facility/Exogenous Shocks Facility				
Poverty Reduction and Growth Facility	0.3	1.1	1.9	2.0
Exogenous Shocks Facility	0.0	0.4	1.3	1.6
Memo: ENDA/EPCA	0.1	0.3	0.0	0.0

Source: Various IFIs.
Note: ENDA – Emergency Natural Disaster Assistance. EPCA – Emergency Postconflict Assistance. — = not available.
a. The amount of the guarantee is both the commitment and disbursement amount.
b. Data refer to approvals, net of cancellations, of sovereign and nonsovereign loans from ordinary capital resources, Asian Development Fund (ADF) loans, ADF grants, other grants, equities, guarantees, the Trade Finance Facilitation Program in 2009, and technical assistance.
c. The commitments were taken from the "IMF lending arrangements" report and include the total amount agreed only for those programs with "Date of arrangement" falling in the calendar year. Standard Drawing Rights were converted to U.S. dollars using the average conversion rate for the year. ENDA = Emergency Natural Disaster Assistance. EPCA = Emergency Post-Conflict Assistance.

below the fiscal 2010 pipeline of $2.3 billion. Absent increased resources, these essential steps to provide desperately needed resources at the height of the crisis will imply a substantial shortfall in concessional financing over the next couple of years.

The IFIs have also increased their lending to low-income countries by providing blends of concessional and nonconcessional loans. To tap the considerable potential for commercially viable and fiscally attractive foreign exchange–earning projects in many IDA countries, the IBRD is expanding the use of its resources for specific projects in IDA countries based on the IBRD Enclave framework for loans and partial risk guarantees for critical infrastructure and natural resource projects.

The IMF recently scaled up its concessional financial assistance, drawing on bilateral contributions and on resources linked to agreed gold sales, consistent with a new income model. The package doubles the Fund's concessional lending capacity over the medium

term, providing up to $17 billion through 2014. This support will be frontloaded, making $8 billion available in the first two years, when crisis-related needs are greatest. It will also be provided on enhanced terms: no interest will be charged through the end of 2011 on concessional loans, and thereafter a new mechanism for updating interest rates will ensure permanently higher concessionality. To meet these new financing commitments, $14 billion in additional loan resources are being mobilized from member countries, and $2.3 billion in new subsidy resources secured from the IMF's internal resources, including those from the agreed gold sales and bilateral contributions. In light of the increasing ability of some low-income countries to support nonconcessional debt, the IMF has moved from a single design for concessionality requirements toward a menu of options linked to country circumstances. At the same time, the Debt Sustainability Framework for low-income countries has been made more flexible through closer attention to the impact

---

BOX 5.4   Gender equality as smart economics: A World Bank Group action plan

The World Bank Group adopted an action plan in 2007 to intensify and scale up gender mainstreaming in economic sectors, such as agriculture, private sector development, finance, and infrastructure, where progress was lagging. The action plan aims to increase Bank Group lending and nonlending operations that promote women's economic participation and to build analytic evidence in support of gender equality as smart economics. The Gender Action Plan promotes the collection, quality, and use of sex-disaggregated statistics and supports rigorous impact evaluation of Bank operations in economic sectors. The four-year plan comes to a close in December 2010 and has to date financed 220 initiatives in 74 countries, with most operations taking place in low-income countries.

The plan has tested innovative mechanisms to increase gender mainstreaming in traditionally difficult sectors. For example, small amounts of seed funding have helped leverage the initiative across much larger Bank operations, and competitive calls for proposals have attracted proposals from large numbers of Bank staff outside of gender units, leading to learning by doing. One effect has been increased gender coverage in economic sector operations. With the close of the action plan, the successful mechanisms for raising gender coverage will be applied to an increasing share of mainstream Bank operations. A transition plan is being prepared to detail the modalities.

Some examples of initiatives funded by the Gender Action Plan include:

- **Labor markets.** Developing employment orientation tools and training for women and career ladders for domestic workers for a $350 million Heads of Household Transition Project, with some 400,000 low-income women expected to benefit.
- **Infrastructure.** Increasing women's access to infrastructure, particularly transport and energy. A rural electrification project helped increase the connection rate of poor female-headed households. Work has also addressed women's transport needs in a series of countries.
- **Agriculture.** Increasing women's agricultural productivity and access to markets through a range of interventions. A comprehensive sourcebook to support women in agriculture has been developed in collaboration with the Food and Agriculture Organization and the International Fund for Agricultural Development and is being used in five ongoing Bank operations.
- **Adolescent girls initiative.** Smoothing the transition from school to work and entrepreneurship—a key stumbling block on the road to earning a living—with a focus on low-income, postconflict countries.

---

of public investment on growth, the role of remittances, and the treatment of external debt of state-owned enterprises.

Sectoral focus of MDB support

Much of the increase in MDB financing over the past two years took the form of budget support to quickly disburse funds to protect the most vulnerable against the fallout of the crisis, maintain planned infrastructure investment, and sustain private sector–led economic growth and employment creation.

Protecting the most vulnerable. The MDBs expanded their activities to protect the most vulnerable, first by helping countries manage higher food and fuel prices. The World Bank Global Food Crisis Response Program committed about $1.2 billion to the purpose, with disbursements of $790 million in more than 30 countries, $380 million of it for safety nets and nutrition in 21 countries. The MDBs later strengthened social safety nets and helped mitigate the social impacts of the crisis, and they have supported economic and social policy reforms essential for achieving more pro-poor and gender-inclusive growth (box 5.4). World Bank lending to support social safety nets reached more than $3 billion in 27 countries in fiscal 2009, including support to middle-income countries and grant funding for small, targeted projects in 17 low-income IDA countries (totaling $95 million). Building on lessons from the safety net programs, the World Bank launched the Rapid Social Response Program to help countries finance services for maternal and infant health and nutrition and school feeding programs, build or scale up targeted safety net programs, and provide income support to the unemployed.

Maintaining planned infrastructure investment. Support to planned infrastructure investment provides a short-term stimulus and addresses long-term development needs. So far infrastructure spending accounts for about two-thirds of the stimulus programs in emerging economies. To address the funding gap for infrastructure projects in developing countries with fiscal constraints, the World Bank launched an Infrastructure Recovery and Assets Platform, an umbrella for mobilizing additional finance for energy, transport, water, and information and communications technology infrastructure in developing countries beyond targets envisaged before the crisis. Overall, the World Bank (IBRD-IDA) increased infrastructure lending by more than 50 percent, from $11.9 billion in fiscal 2008 to $18.3 billion in fiscal 2009; the International Finance Corporation contributed $3.1 billion; and the Multilateral Investment Guarantee Agency (MIGA), $0.1 billion. In addition, the IFC financed more than $800 million in general infrastructure and other projects.[21]

The ADB's countercyclical support fund also helped fill the gaps of critical public infrastructure investments, including labor-intensive infrastructure projects and projects in support of social protection and poverty reduction programs. For example, in Bangladesh $500 million in support sought to free up fiscal space for financing other parts of the government's countercyclical development program—particularly the planned scaling-up of infrastructure investment. The AfDB helped develop the Action Plan for Africa, a regional and continental strategy for 2010–15. Its rigorously ranked pipeline of operations requires $10.2 billion in resources, with $7.7 billion for infrastructure and $1.7 billion for agriculture and food security. EBRD's projects support

critical infrastructure left unfunded by the dwindling of commercial lending, with €1.3 billion worth of signed investments in 2009.

Sustaining private sector–led growth. The crisis has underlined the importance of quick and strong IFI support to private sector firms to help achieve growth, employment, and poverty reduction. The multilateral development banks' focus on access to finance for investment and trade, both expected to recover slowly, will be critical to preserve investments by small and medium-size enterprises. The IFC has launched a broad set of targeted initiatives, combining its funds with contributions mobilized from various sources (including governments and other IFIs) to help private enterprises cope with the global financial and economic crises (box 5.5). AsDB's crisis-related assistance to the private sector forcuses on rebuilding business confidence, providing incentives for private sector investments, and facilitating trade financing by expanding its Trade Finance Facilitation Program (TFFP).

Coordination with other development partners. To ensure speedy implementation, the IFIs have facilitated regional implementation programs to channel support by building a common platform for action among IFIs, regulators, and private groups in the banking sector. The IFIs have worked closely to assess and address the refinancing and recapitalization needs of banks, in collaboration with home and host country authorities.

Regional crisis initiatives include the joint IFI Action Plan for Africa, to leverage an additional $15 billion of financing to protect important ongoing programs and support investment-ready initiatives (box 5.6). The joint IFI Action Plan for Central and Eastern Europe, launched in March 2009, focuses on meeting the region's financial sector needs for capital and liquidity. The largest multilateral investors and lenders in the region agreed to provide up to $32.5 billion, with the World Bank Group providing up to $8 billion. This innovative arrangement has been augmented in 2010 by the Vienna Initiative, which brings together IFIs, European institutions,

---

BOX 5.5   Crisis-related initiatives of the International Finance Corporation

Over the past two years, the International Finance Corporation (IFC) board approved several initiatives that mobilized more than $10 billion in financing. While fund-raising continues, the initiatives are actively disbursing.

- The IFC Global Trade Finance Program, increased from $1 billion to $3 billion in response to the financial crisis, provides unfunded support in guarantees for trade transactions in emerging markets.
- The Global Trade Liquidity Program brings together governments, development finance institutions, and international banks to provide liquidity for trade-related transactions through banks in developing countries. Having begun operations in June 2009, it is expected to support more than $50 billion of trade finance assets through a network of more than 500 issuing banks.
- The Microfinance Enhancement Facility is a short- to medium-term facility expected to provide refinancing to more than 100 strong microfinance institutions in up to 40 countries.
- The Capitalization Fund aims to provide additional capital to ensure that banks in developing countries can continue to lend and support economic recovery and job creation during the crisis and after. The fund is making subordinated loans and equity or equity-linked investments in systemically important private banks or state-owned banks on a clear path to privatization, primarily in lower-income countries. The Japanese government, a founding partner, has invested $2 billion. IFC has invested $1 billion of its own in the fund.
- The Africa Capitalization Fund is a partnership among the African Development Bank, the European Investment Bank (EIB), the Organization of the Petroleum Exporting Countries' Fund for International Development, and Norway's Norfund. As a subfund of the IFC Capitalization Fund, it will focus on supporting the capital needs of strategically important banks in Africa.
- The Infrastructure Crisis Facility will provide short- to medium-term debt and equity funds to support private infrastructure projects affected by capital shortages caused by the global crisis. It will also include advisory services to help governments design or redesign public-private partnership projects. The IFC has committed to invest up to $300 million, and other parties, including KfW, Proparco, and the EIB, have already invested in debt and cofinancing.
- The Debt and Asset Recovery Program will make direct investments in strategically important private entities that have a good business model but require corporate debt restructuring and reprofiling. The program will also make direct IFC investments in nonperforming loan pools and equity investments in select distressed asset funds. With a target mobilization of $4 billion and the IFC contributions of $1.5 billion, the program will reduce the potential for financial crises while enhancing the market environment.
- IFC Asset Management Company, LLC, was established to manage some IFC-crisis response facilities. It is managing the IFC Capitalization Fund and an equity fund under the Sovereign Fund Initiative.
- The Global Food Fund seeks to shore up agribusiness and stabilize the global food supply chain with a short-term liquidity facility to provide working capital to agribusiness companies. A separate equity fund will support long-term growth in the sector. The IFC has approved $350 million for this initiative.

---

regulatory and fiscal authorities, and bank groups in an informal framework to discuss crisis management and resolution issues relating to systemically important cross-border bank groups. The Multilateral Crisis Initiative for Latin America and the Caribbean was organized to pool global financing from public and private sources and scale up crisis responses. Participating institutions are the IBRD, Andean Development Corporation, Caribbean Development Bank, and IDB. Together they pledge to provide up to $90 billion to support the private sector in Latin American and the Caribbean.

The IDB has also played a catalytic role in the flow of additional resources to Latin America through cofinancing agreements between the World Bank and major

BOX 5.6   Action Plan for Africa

The African financing partnership will pool resources and expertise to enable governments and institutions to more effectively reduce the humanitarian toll in the region. The participating institutions are the African Development Bank (AfDB) Group, the Agence Française de Développement (AFD) Group, the Development Bank of Southern Africa, the European Investment Bank (EIB), German Financial Cooperation, the International Islamic Trade Finance Corporation, and the World Bank Group. The plan envisages the following goals and actions.

- The AfDB will use an emergency liquidity facility of $1.5 billion to provide financial support to eligible countries and operations that are suffering from a lack of liquidity. It will introduce a new $500 million trade finance line of credit and consider committing $500 million to global trade finance liquidity programs to support commercial banks and other institutions that finance trade. It will contribute funds to support agribusiness and microfinance. And it will coordinate a platform for cofinancing projects in Africa through the African Financing Partnership.
- The AFD Group will contribute to investments and programs, totaling up to $3.1 billion, that focus on small and medium enterprises and infrastructure projects in Africa through Proparco, the Fonds d'Investissement et de Soutien aux Entreprises en Afrique, and loan guarantees. Launched with the AfDB, the International Fund for Agricultural Development, and Alliance for a Green Revolution in Africa, the African Agriculture Fund will raise €200 million during its first phase and €550 million subsequently to target private companies and cooperatives that increase and diversify agricultural production.
- The Development Bank of Southern Africa will boost its development financing for priority infrastructure projects by injecting more than $4 billion into these and other development sectors, an increase of more than 100 percent over the development finance disbursed in the past three years. The bank will also increase its technical and grant assistance for project development and training to more than $50 million.
- The EIB will step up its support for infrastructure and energy projects, notably through enhanced use of the European Union–Africa Infrastructure Trust Fund established at the initiative of the Euro-

pean Commission and managed by the EIB. It will also offer cofinancing in parallel with the IFC's infrastructure crisis facility. The EIB will further support Africa's financial sector through contributions to the Microfinance Enhancement Facility and other initiatives, lines of credit to banks with more flexible guidelines, and the provision of equity. And it will continue to work on private sector initiatives with partner institutions.
- Within the German Financial Cooperation with Africa, the Federal Ministry for Economic Development and Cooperation through the KfW Bankengruppe expects to contribute to initiatives and programs amounting to more than $1.4 billion in Sub-Saharan Africa to support the financial sector, the private sector, and infrastructure. The KfW Bankengruppe also expects to contribute to initiatives and programs amounting to more than $1.1 billion in Sub-Saharan Africa.
- The Islamic Development Bank Group, through the Islamic Corporation for the Development of the Private Sector, will contribute over the next five years to investments and programs totaling up to $250 million. Despite the current crisis, the Islamic Development Bank Group's Islamic Trade Finance Corporation, through its own resources, planned to maintain the same level of commitment of $150 million to support and facilitate financing for Africa in 2009. To scale up its intervention, it is intensifying its interaction with the IFC and AfDB to explore ways to leverage an additional $250 million by the end of 2009.
- As part of the World Bank Group's support, the IFC will contribute at least $1.0 billion to facilitate trade, strengthen the capital base of banks, improve infrastructure, increase microfinance lending, and promote agribusiness companies. The World Bank will frontload and fast-track its commitments and increase access to its funds to finance high-priority, high-return infrastructure investments that facilitate regional integration, asset preservation, and urban development. It will also assist partners in analyzing the impact of the crisis through knowledge products and outreach. The Multilateral Investment Guarantee Agency will provide up to $2 billion in investment guarantees to support investor demand for African infrastructure investment, small and medium investments, and support for the African financial sector, including banks and microfinance institutions.

international agencies. An agreement was signed with Japan's Bank for International Cooperation on building a framework to provide long-term financing for major infrastructure and critical social and economic investment projects. An agreement with Japan's International Cooperation Agency will offer concessional loans and technical assistance resources for projects in economic and social infrastructure, environment, and climate change. The Korean government, through Kexim Bank, signed an agreement to cofinance public and private sector projects in the region that could be worth as much as $2 billion. China and the IDB signed two partnerships at the Bank's annual meeting in March 2009.[22]

Other innovative ways to leverage the private sector. Beyond countercyclical financing, the multilateral development banks have moved forward with other programs to reduce risk in emerging markets. MIGA issued $1.4 billion in guarantees in fiscal 2009 and is increasing its support to systemically important financial institutions seeking political risk insurance for cross-border investments in their subsidiaries in emerging markets, about 90 percent of them in Eastern Europe. In fiscal 2010, $0.5 billion has already been signed, and MIGA is expected to issue an additional $2 billion to $3 billion in the context of the IFI Action Plan. The World Bank Group continues to explore new ways to use its balance sheet to create the conditions for reestablishing private capital flows. Recent efforts include formation of lender coalitions[23] and the expanded use of guarantees,[24] insurance instruments, and risk management products. The Bank is also continuing a dialogue with major underwriters of emerging market bond issuance and liability management experts to identify innovative cofinancing opportunities.

The AfDB has stepped up efforts to leverage private capital to maximize its impact through innovative financial products. In May 2009, in partnership with the Africa Commission (launched by the Danish Government in 2008), the AfDB agreed to set up an African Small and Medium Enterprises

Guarantee Fund to address the constraint to investment finance and capacity development for financial institutions and such enterprises. The fund is expected to have initial capital of $300 million to $500 million, to mobilize loans worth $1.8 billion to $3 billion. The AfDB recently started discussions with some middle-income countries to consider issuing bonds on international capital markets with an AfDB guarantee. A guarantee program is also being developed that would provide political risk mitigation and promote private investments in poor and high-risk countries. The AfDB continues to offer partial credit guarantees and partial risk guarantees for middle-income countries. The partial credit guarantees support the mobilization of private funds for project finance, financial intermediation, and policy-based finance. The partial risk guarantees cover a variety of government and government agency risks, including contractual payment obligations and the availability and convertibility of foreign exchange.

Meeting the challenges of the postcrisis world

Even as the recovery progresses, it is clear that the crisis has dramatically altered the development challenges facing low- and middle-income countries and hence, those facing the international community. Moreover, necessary short-term responses to the crisis have important implications for the ability of donors and the international financial institutions to support developing countries going forward. Without analyzing these issues in detail or providing a prescription for reform, this section raises some of the main issues facing the global economic community as a result of the crisis.

First, while dangers of competitive protectionist measures and a breakdown of the world trading system were avoided, ensuring an open trading system remains an important goal of international economic policy. Completing the Doha Round would substantially improve developing countries' market access and enhance their competitiveness through an agreement on trade facilitation. Beyond Doha, progress is needed in negotiating new rules and disciplines in trade-related climate change and in food and energy security. And increased support from donors and policy reform in developing countries will be required to ensure their institutions are capable of taking advantage of trade opportunities.

Second, the crisis has increased the importance of aid on addressing the rise in poverty. But the crisis has also led to substantial increases in government debt that will severely constrain fiscal resources in donor countries for the foreseeable future. It remains doubtful whether donors can sustain recent increases in aid, much less achieve the further increases required to meet donor commitments. In this context, it becomes more important than ever to make further progress in improving aid effectiveness through harmonizing donor activities, reducing the share of tied aid, increasing the predictability of aid disbursements, and improving aid allocations.

Third, in the absence of increased resources from donors, the crisis-induced frontloading of concessional resources by IDA and other multilateral agencies implies that concessional flows from these institutions must decline in the near future. It is unrealistic to expect that the IFIs can continue to achieve commitment and disbursement levels that exceed the resources set aside for concessional flows. However, the global recovery remains fragile, and a sharp decline in concessional assistance could seriously jeopardize development prospects in many low-income countries. Managing the availability and allocation of concessional resources will remain a major challenge for the IFIs as the recovery proceeds. Similarly, the sharp rise in IBRD commitments has highlighted the need for discussing a capital increase to avoid an eventual falloff in lending, while the need for nonconcessional resources is expected to remain high.

Fourth, the demand for technical support is likely to rise as countries seek to strengthen their financial sector regulation and supervisory frameworks; focus on improving the efficiency of public expenditures and the environment for private sector growth in light of increased budgetary stringency; and cope with increased debt burdens through adoption of sound borrowing policies and public debt management techniques.

These challenges are likely to require fundamental changes in the international financial institutions. Technical requirements for staff will shift (for example in favor of financial sector expertise). Bureaucratic structures may need to be redesigned (for example, there are discussions of decentralization at the World Bank). Coordination among the IFIs will need to be strengthened. And more resources will have to be mobilized. The international community has begun to respond to this agenda, as evidenced by the sharp increase in the IMF's lending resources and the discussions of the replenishment of concessional windows at the MDBs. The World Bank Group has initiated a postcrisis strategy or directions paper on development policy and is considering a proposed voting reform; measures to increase the World Bank's paid-in capital; and internal reforms to strengthen corporate governance, accountability, and operational effectiveness. But the urgency in establishing the appropriate policies for dealing with the postcrisis international economic environment leaves no room for complacency. The danger of a new Great Depression has been averted. But decisive leadership is still required to ensure a rapid and sustainable recovery.

Notes

1. World Bank 2010.
2. These included 88 major banks in 44 countries conducted in December 2008, March 2009, and August 2009 by the International Monetary Fund in cooperation with the Bankers Association for Finance and Trade (IMF-BAFT 2009); a World Bank survey of 425 firms and 78 banks and other financial institutions in 14 developing countries (Malouche 2009); and a survey by the International Chamber of Commerce of a sample of 122 banks in 59 countries from March 2009, updated in September 2009 (International Chamber of Commerce 2009).

3. Chauffour, Saborowski, and Soylemezoglu 2010.

4. Chauffour and Farole 2009.

5. International Chamber of Commerce 2009.

6. Gamberoni and Newfarmer 2009.

7. See the Global Anti-Dumping/Safeguard Database and the Global Trade Alert website http://www.globaltradealert.org/.

8. McKibbin, Warwick, and Stoeckel 2009.

9. www.globaltradealert.org

10. WTO, OECD, and UNCTAD 2009.

11. Hoekman, Martin, and Mattoo 2009.

12. WTO and OECD 2009.

13. If a country is not servicing its debt because of an unsustainable debt burden and is clearly unable to meet its obligations to external creditors, debt relief amounts to an accounting exercise for the recipient—it provides no additional financial resources.

14. It excludes aid that is unpredictable by nature such as humanitarian assistance, emergency relief, and debt relief; it includes no cross-border costs, such as administrative costs, student costs, and refugee costs in donor countries; and is not programmable by the donor, such as core funding of NGOs.

15. For information on the Accra Agenda for Action, see www.oecd.org/dac/effectiveness/parisdeclaration.

16. Hoeffler and Outram 2008.

17. Claessens, Cassimon, and van Camenhout 2007.

18. Utz 2009.

19. Burkina Faso, Burundi, The Gambia, Haiti, and São Tomé and Principe.

20. The IFIs covered in this section include the International Monetary Fund, the World Bank Group, and the four big regional development banks (African Development Bank, Asian Development Bank, European Bank for Reconstruction and Development, and Inter-American Development Bank).

21. Data for general infrastructure include funds and investments through financial intermediaries that have infrastructure objectives; data for "other projects" include chemicals and mining.

22. The first, with the China Exim Bank, signed at the annual meeting, will promote cofinancing and collaboration on infrastructure, trade finance, and other sectors hit in the crisis. The second, with the China Development Bank, aims to cofinance projects in infrastructure with or without a sovereign guarantee. In addition, the Bank of China has agreed to sign a cofinancing agreement with the IDB by the end of June.

23. An example of how the World Bank Group is leveraging its balance sheet in a non-traditional way can be seen in the design of the financial support to Indonesia to help access capital markets. The Bank extended the government a $2 billion Development Policy Loan–Deferred Drawdown Option, which formed the core of a larger $5 billion standby package, with additional commitments from the ADB, Japan, and Australia. The mechanism allowed Indonesia to raise private funds in subsequent issues under difficult market conditions at 5- and 10-year maturities.

24. The World Bank Group has programs that provide partial risk guarantees to mitigate risk for private lenders (and sponsors) to private participation in infrastructure projects and partial credit guarantees for debt issuance by sovereign (or subsovereign) entities.

References

Arvis, J-F., M. A. Mustra, L. Ojala, B. Shepherd, and D. Saslavsky. 2010. *Connecting to Compete 2010: Trade Logistics in the Global Economy.* Washington, DC: World Bank.

Chauffour, J.-P., and T. Farole. 2009. "Trade Finance in Crisis: Market Adjustment or Market Failure?" Policy Research Working Paper 5003. World Bank, Washington, DC.

Chauffour, J.-P., C. Saborowski, and A. Soylemezoglu. 2010. "Trade Finance in Crisis: Should Developing Countries Establish Export Credit Agencies." Policy Research Working Paper 5166. World Bank, Washington, DC.

Claessens, S., D. Cassimon, and B. van Camenhout. 2007. "Empirical Evidence on the New International Aid Architecture." World Bank, Economy and Finance Research Program, Washington (June 18).

Dreher, A., F. Moelders. and P. Nunnenkamp. 2007. "Are NGOs the Better Donors? A Case Study of Aid Allocation for Sweden." KOF Working Papers 180. KOF Swiss Economic Institute, Zurich (November).

Gamberoni E., and R. Newfarmer. 2009. "Trade Protection: Incipient but Worrisome Trends." Trade Note 37. World Bank, Washington, DC.

Hoeffler, A., and V. Outram. 2008. "Need, Merit or Self-Interest: What Determines the Allocation of Aid?" Working Paper Series 2008-19.

Centre for the Study of African Economics, Oxford, U.K. (July).

Hoekman, B., W. Martin, and A. Mattoo. 2009. *"Conclude Doha: It Matters."* Policy Research Working Paper 5135. World Bank, Washington, DC.

Hudson Institute.2009. *Index of Global Philanthropy and Remittances 2009*. Washington, DC.

IDA (International Development Association) and IMF (International Monetary Fund). 2009. "Heavily Indebted Poor Countries (HIPC) Initiative and Multilateral Debt Relief Initiative (MDRI): Status of Implementation." World Bank and the IMF, Washington DC. (September 15).

IMF-BAFT (International Monetary Fund–Bankers Association for Finance and Trade. 2009. "IMF-BAFT Trade Finance Survey: A Survey among Banks Assessing the Current Trade Finance Environment." (http://baft.org/content_folders/Issues/IMFBAFTSurveyResults20090331.ppt).

International Chamber of Commerce. 2009. "Trade Finance Survey: An Interim Report - Summer 2009." Document 470-1124 TS/WJ. Paris (September).

Koch, D-J. 2007. "Blind Spots on the Map of Aid Allocations: Concentration and Complementarity of International NGO Aid." UNU-WIDER Research Paper 2007/45. United Nations University–World Institute for Development Economics Research, Helsinki (August).

Malouche, M. 2009. "Trade and Trade Finance Developments in 14 Developing Countries post September 2008: A World Bank Survey." Policy Research Working Paper 5138. World Bank, Washington, DC.

Masud, N., and B. Yontcheva. 2005. "Does Foreign Aid Reduce Poverty? Empirical Evidence from Nongovernmental and Bilateral Aid." IMF Working Paper WP/05/100. International Monetary Fund, Washington (May).

McKibbin, W. J., and A. Stoeckel. 2009. "The Potential Impact of the Global Financial Crisis on World Trade." Policy Research Working Paper 5134. World Bank, Washington, DC.

Utz, R. 2009. "Will Countries that Receive Insufficient Aid Please Stand Up?" Paper for CFP research program on the International Aid Architecture, World Bank, Washington DC.

World Bank 2006. "Needs, Priorities and Costs Associated with Technical Assistance and Capacity Building for Implementation of a WTO Trade Facilitation Agreement: A Comparative Study Based on Six Developing Countries." Working Paper. World Bank, International Trade Department, Washington, DC.

———. 2010. *Global Economic Prospects, 2010*. Washington, DC: World Bank.

WTO (World Trade Organization). 2009. "Trade Policy Review." Geneva (November).

WTO and OECD (Organisation for Economic Co-operation and Development). 2009. *Aid for Trade at a Glance 2009: Maintaining Momentum*. Geneva.

WTO, OECD, and UNCTAD (United Nations Conference on Trade and Development). 2009. "G-20 Trade and Investment Measures." Joint Report. Geneva (September 14).

APPENDIX   Classification of economies by region and income, fiscal 2010

East Asia and Pacific		Latin America and the Caribbean		South Asia		High-income OECD economies
American Samoa	UMC			Afghanistan	LIC	
Cambodia	LIC	Argentina	UMC	Bangladesh	LIC	Australia
China	LMC	Belize	LMC	Bhutan	LMC	Austria
Fiji	UMC	Bolivia	LMC	India	LMC	Belgium
Indonesia	LMC	Brazil	UMC	Maldives	LMC	Canada
Kiribati	LMC	Chile	UMC	Nepal	LIC	Czech Republic
Korea, Dem. People's Rep.	LIC	Colombia	UMC	Pakistan	LMC	Denmark
Lao PDR	LIC	Costa Rica	UMC	Sri Lanka	LMC	Finland
Malaysia	UMC	Cuba	UMC			France
Marshall Islands	LMC	Dominica	UMC			Germany
Micronesia, Fed. Sts.	LMC	Dominican Republic	UMC	**Sub-Saharan Africa**		Greece
Mongolia	LMC	Ecuador	LMC			Hungary
Myanmar	LIC	El Salvador	LMC	Angola	LMC	Iceland
Palau	UMC	Grenada	UMC	Benin	LIC	Ireland
Papua New Guinea	LMC	Guatemala	LMC	Botswana	UMC	Italy
Philippines	LMC	Guyana	LMC	Burkina Faso	LIC	Japan
Samoa	LMC	Haiti	LIC	Burundi	LIC	Korea, Rep.
Solomon Islands	LMC	Honduras	LMC	Cameroon	LMC	Luxembourg
Thailand	LMC	Jamaica	UMC	Cape Verde	LMC	Netherlands
Timor-Leste	LMC	Mexico	UMC	Central African Republic	LIC	New Zealand
Tonga	LMC	Nicaragua	LMC	Chad	LIC	Norway
Vanuatu	LMC	Panama	UMC	Comoros	LIC	Portugal
Vietnam	LIC	Paraguay	LMC	Congo, Dem. Rep.	LIC	Slovak Republic
		Peru	UMC	Congo, Rep.	LMC	Spain
		St. Kitts and Nevis	UMC	Côte d'Ivoire	LMC	Sweden
Europe and Central Asia		St. Lucia	UMC	Eritrea	LIC	Switzerland
		St. Vincent and the Grenadines	UMC	Ethiopia	LIC	United Kingdom
Albania	LMC	Suriname	UMC	Gabon	UMC	United States
Armenia	LMC	Uruguay	UMC	Gambia, The	LIC	
Azerbaijan	LMC	Venezuela, R. B. de	UMC	Ghana	LIC	
Belarus	UMC			Guinea	LIC	**Other high-income economies**
Bosnia and Herzegovina	UMC			Guinea-Bissau	LIC	
Bulgaria	UMC	**Middle East and North Africa**		Kenya	LIC	
Georgia	LMC			Lesotho	LMC	Andorra
Kazakhstan	UMC	Algeria	UMC	Liberia	LIC	Antigua and Barbuda
Kosovo	LMC	Djibouti	LMC	Madagascar	LIC	Aruba
Kyrgyz Republic	LIC	Egypt, Arab Rep.	LMC	Malawi	LIC	Bahamas, The
Latvia	UMC	Iran, Islamic Rep.	LMC	Mali	LIC	Bahrain
Lithuania	UMC	Iraq	LMC	Mauritania	LIC	Barbados
Macedonia, FYR	UMC	Jordan	LMC	Mauritius	UMC	Bermuda
Moldova	LMC	Lebanon	UMC	Mayotte	UMC	Brunei Darussalam
Montenegro	UMC	Libya	UMC	Mozambique	LIC	Cayman Islands
Poland	UMC	Morocco	LMC	Namibia	UMC	Channel Islands
Romania	UMC	Syrian Arab Rep.	LMC	Niger	LIC	Croatia
Russian Federation	UMC	Tunisia	LMC	Nigeria	LMC	Cyprus
Serbia	UMC	West Bank and Gaza	LMC	Rwanda	LIC	Equatorial Guinea
Tajikistan	LIC	Yemen, Rep.	LIC	São Tomé and Principe	LMC	Estonia
Turkey	UMC			Senegal	LIC	Faeroe Islands
Turkmenistan	LMC			Seychelles	UMC	French Polynesia
Ukraine	LMC			Sierra Leone	LIC	Greenland
Uzbekistan	LIC			Somalia	LIC	Guam
				South Africa	UMC	Hong Kong, China
				Sudan	LMC	Isle of Man
				Swaziland	LMC	Israel
				Tanzania	LIC	Kuwait
				Togo	LIC	Liechtenstein
				Uganda	LIC	Macao, China
				Zambia	LIC	Malta
				Zimbabwe	LIC	Monaco
						Netherlands Antilles
						New Caledonia
						Northern Mariana Islands
						Oman
						Puerto Rico
						Qatar
						San Marino
						Saudi Arabia
						Singapore
						Slovenia
						Taiwan, China
						Trinidad and Tobago
						United Arab Emirates
						Virgin Islands (U.S.)

Source: World Bank data.

Note: This table classifies all World Bank member economies and all other economies with populations of more than 30,000. Economies are divided among income groups according to 2008 GNI per capita, calculated using the World Bank Atlas method. The groups are low income (LIC), $975 or less; lower middle income (LMC), $976–3,855; upper middle income (UMC), $3,856–11,905; and high income, $11,906 or more.